ANCIENT GREEK LYRICS

ΛΥΡΙΚΑΙ ΠΟΙΗΜΑΤΑΙ ΑΡΧΑΙΩΝ ΕΛΛΗΝΩΝ

ANCIENT GREEK LYRICS

Translated & Annotated by

Willis Barnstone

◇

Introduction by William E. McCulloh

◇

Drawings by Elli Tzalopoulou Barnstone

INDIANA UNIVERSITY PRESS

Bloomington & Indianapolis

This book is a publication of

Indiana University Press
601 North Morton Street
Bloomington, IN 47404-3797 USA

www.iupress.indiana.edu

Telephone orders   800-842-6796
Fax orders   812-855-7931
Orders by e-mail   iuporder@indiana.edu

Library of Congress Cataloging-in-Publication Data

Ancient Greek lyrics / translated and annotated by Willis Barnstone ; introduction
by William E. McCulloh ; drawings by Elli Tzalopoulou Barnstone. — 4th ed.
    p. cm.
  Rev. ed. of: Sappho and the Greek lyric poets. New York : Schocken Books, c1988.
  Includes bibliographical references.
  ISBN 978-0-253-22121-6 (pbk : alk. paper) 1. Greek poetry—Translations
into English. 2. Sappho—Translations into English. I. Barnstone, Willis,
1927– II. McCulloh, William E. III. Sappho and the Greek lyric poets.
  PA3622.B3A53 2009
  881.008—dc22

                              2009015795

1   2   3   4   5   15   14   13   12   11   10

To Helle Phaedra Barnstone

who led me to Greece and to Greek

Song and the lyric poem came first. Prose was invented centuries later. In Israel, Greece, and China came the primal, model lyrics for two and a half millennia. Read the biblical Song of Songs in Hebrew, Sappho in Greek, and Wang Wei in Chinese and be deeply civilized. You will know the passions, tragedy, spirit, politic, philosophy, and beauty that have commanded our solitary rooms and public spaces. I emphasize *solitary*, because the lyric, unlike theater and sport, is an intimate dialogue between maker and reader. From the Jews we have their two bibles of wisdom poetry, from the Chinese we have thousands of ancient nightingales whose song is calm ecstasy, and from the Greeks we have major and minor names and wondrous poems. However, because of bigotry, most of Greek poetry, especially Sappho, was by religious decree destroyed from the fall of the Roman Empire to the Renaissance. So apart from one complete ode, we read Sappho in fragments. Yet there survive fragrant hills for lovers and dark and luminous mountains for metaphysicians. Most of ancient Greek lyric poetry is contained in this volume. Do not despair about loss. You are lucky if you can spend your life reading and rereading the individual poets. They shine. If technology or return to legal digs in Egypt and Syria are to reveal a library of buried papyri of Greek lyrics equivalent to the *Dead Sea Scrolls* or the Gnostic *Nag Hammadi Library,* we should be able to keep singing and dancing for ten moons straight. For now, we have the song, human comedy, political outrage, and personal cry for centuries of good reading.

PIERRE GRANGE, *Strolling with Eternity*

ΠΕΡΙΕΧΟΜΕΝΟΙ

Contents

ΕΙΣΑΓΩΓΗ ΠΕΡΙ ΑΟΙΔΩΝ ΑΛΗΤΩΝ

Preface on Vagabond Songsters

Ancient Greek Lyrics combines three earlier volumes: *Sappho and the Greek Lyric Poets* (1988), *Sappho* (1965), and *Greek Lyric Poetry* (1962). Like three Spanish *pícaros,* whom Cervantes or Quevedo might have invented, each volume has gone separately from master to master publisher, acquiring new guises, tricks, and innovations. With each reformation and reprinting, the volume hopes to survive by picking pockets of new readers to possess them. Books always have three masters—author, publisher, and reader—who are also beggars asking for eyes to love and esteem them. Without love and esteem, a work drifts away to nowhere. Somehow, these Greek poems, which I helped into English nearly half a century ago, remain alive and cheerful. I had a hand in forming them, but their survival is due to their own intrinsic beauty, song, and message. They are our earliest songs in European antiquity. They were imitated by Rome, and later by all, but that ancient song has not been surpassed. Sappho, though often distraught, tells us prophetically,

> Someone, I tell you,
> will remember us.

What a complex memory for these itinerant survivors.

The first masters at Bantam Classics and Doubleday Anchor dressed *Greek Lyric Poetry* and a bilingual *Sappho* only in paper. A bold step. But in those years no respectable reviewer would glance at paperbacks, and libraries were loath to buy and shelve any book in English unless it came to them in cloth. Libraries did, however, catalog books in foreign tongues, which had contrary dress codes. Anglo-American publishers sent new books out in cloth before marketing them as small paperbacks or "pocketbooks," as these innovations were called. By contrast, an elegant French volume with Miro color lithos and Paul Eluard poems would appear in both expensive numbered and in popular mass editions, all in tasteful paper covers. Bound copies were original paperbacks a local binder glued into expensive leather coats for a home library. That delightful format wouldn't do in America. So, my vagabonds were "backsold" to New York University Press and Indiana University Press, who attired them in hardboards and jackets. Came good reviews, decades of survival on their wits, and then bare lonely years, prompting two beggar books to marry. The Random House imprints of Schocken and Pantheon combined the volumes under one title: *Sappho and the Greek Lyric Poets.*

Marriage caused loss of some pleasures of the single life. Sappho lost her Greek voice. (The original *Sappho* volume contained facing Greek texts.) More, she gave up the ample *Testimonia* containing all the extant ancient biographical accounts of her life. A selection of these has been restored to this edition.

Fortunes rise and fall. The publishing masters Schocken and Pantheon split, and those perky performers, the largest gang in English of Greek nightingales, joined the homeless, with memories of better days. But not for long. First, Sun and Moon Books and Green Integer gave Sappho a paper home. Then Shambhala Books found Sappho a mansion, permitting her song in both English and Greek, along with abundant source material.

Finally, Indiana University Press has again recognized Sappho's earlier marriage to her extraordinary Greek companions, from outrageous Archilochos and Olympian Pindar to Hellenistic love and satire poets composing all over the Greco-Roman empire up to the ultimate vital survivors in gold Byzantium. The new Indiana edition includes some additional poems not in their previous edition. A long one by Archilochos (7th c. BCE), Greece's earliest iambic poet, was discovered in a Swiss archive. I translated it, lost it, and retranslated it with William McCullough, my former Wesleyan colleague. And Sappho gained more poems, including the recent third-century BCE papyrus (frag. 58) found in the Cologne University archives. I deciphered some twenty fragmentary lyrics from the almost indecipherable, moving them from incoherence to minimalist modernity. In addition to the restoration of the testimonia, the introduction to Sappho's life and poems, sources and notes, glossary, and bibliography are all revised. Bill McCulloh has lightly edited his fine introduction.

I invite you to receive this crowd of homeless street singers, their Greek cosmos newly restored under one concise name: *Ancient Greek Lyrics.*

Willis Barnstone
Oakland/Bloomington, 2008

ACKNOWLEDGMENTS

Certain of these poems first appeared in the *Antioch Review, Arizona Quarterly, Chelsea Review, Chicago Review, Evergreen Review, Wesleyan Cardinal,* and *The World's Love Poetry.*

ΕΙΣΑΓΩΓΗ

INTRODUCTION

Suppose, in our time, the War actually comes. With no current refinements wasted, the elephantine blasts, fire storms, and fallout finish their appointed tasks. Several decades later the literary archaeologists from Tierra del Fuego and the Samoyedes rake loose from London's heaps part of a volume of literary criticism in which stand, entire, Yeats' lines "My fiftieth year had come and gone"—and the "Second Coming," with a few single lines quoted amid the unknown critic's comments. Then a gutted Pittsburgh mansion yields two charred anonymous sheets of a poem whose style—what can be seen of it—resembles Yeats. A fragmentary dictionary cites, as a rare alternate pronunciation of fanatic: "Fá-na-tic. Thus in W. B. Yeats' 'Remorse for Intemperate Speech.'" There are similar further recoveries, equally scanty. So much for the poet whom T. S. Eliot has called the greatest of the twentieth century.

But this has happened already, in time's glacial cataclysm, to the greatest lyric poet (so men say) of the West before the thirteenth century—to Sappho. And to Archilochos, whom some ancients paired with Homer. And to many others, the Herricks, Donnes, and Herberts of Greece's first lyric flowering. For however much one may take it as unmerited grace that one has at least Homer, at least the iceberg tip of the fifth century and its epigones, one must still question the providence which allowed from the vastly different age between—the Lyric Age of the seventh and sixth centuries[1]—only Pindar and the scraps for one other small book. That uniquely organic outgrowth of successive literary styles and forms in Greece—forms which are the ineluctable basis for most Western literature[2]—is thus desperately mutilated for us in what seems to have been its most explosively diverse and luxuriant phase.

Homer is the culmination of a long and now invisible tradition of heroic poetry which was the literary voice of a monarchical society. His heroes are the archetypal ancestors of the royalty in whose courts the epic lays flourished and whose values the bard celebrated. But, like Bach, he seems to have written in times which

---

1. Thus the title given it by A. R. Burn in *The Lyric Age of Greece* (London, 1960).
2. See for example Gilbert Highet, *The Classical Tradition* (New York, 1957).

had already moved past his own poetic world. The city-state was beginning to displace the tribal monarchy. The conflict between monarchy and aristocracy had begun, and perhaps also that conflict between aristocracy and commons which led to the great tyrannies (somewhat like the dictatorships of our century) and—at least in some cities—to democracy. But most important for poetry, the poet had begun to emerge as an individual speaking for himself, not an impersonal celebrant of ancestral glory and doom.

While the elder Bach composed his *Art of Fugue "ad maiorem Dei gloriam,"* his sons were breaking the homophonic trail toward the secular divinity of the Beethoven symphony. And within the lifetime of "Homer" (though dates are of course uncertain), Archilochos, the first Western man whom we know as a personality, and the first European lyric poet of whom fragments remain, was fusing and transforming popular and anonymous song and dance into the personal poem. So it is with Archilochos that we must begin, the first historical Western personality, and for us, the impoverished heirs, the inceptor of European lyric.

THE FORMS OF GREEK LYRIC

But here an academic detour is required. What we shall call Greek "lyric" poetry is in fact a cluster of several quite distinct types, each with its own tradition and development. "Lyric" means literally "accompanied by the lyre," and implies poetry that is sung, not spoken. Now it is likely that all forms of Greek poetry originated in ritual performances which blended word, music, and dance. But in historical times only one branch of that poetry retained all three elements: the choral ode. *Choros,* for the Greeks, meant a performing group which both danced and sang. (Compare "choreography.") *Ôide* meant song. Chorodic poetry, then, remained closer to its ritual origins than did any of the other forms. It was associated with a variety of public ceremonies. Already in Homer one finds most of these mentioned or described.[3] There is the *Thrênos,* or dirge for the dead (the lament for Hektor, *Iliad* XXIV, 746ff.). There is the *Paian,* or hymn to Apollo (*Iliad* I, 472–74), of which some hymns of Hölderlin and Shelley are modern mutations. Of the *Hymenaios* or wedding song (*Iliad* XVIII, 493), Spenser's "Epithalamion," "O Promise Me," and the charivari are schizoid remnants. And compare the *Hyporchêma* or mimetic-narrative dance (*Odyssey* VIII, 261ff.) with *The Seven Deadly Sins* of Weil-Brecht-Balanchine. The

---

3. The classification given here is taken from C. M. Bowra's full discussion in the introduction to his *Greek Lyric Poetry* (Oxford, 1936. 2nd ed., 1962).

Prosôdion, or processional song (still surviving in some religious services), is not found in Homer. Nor is the dithyramb, originally an intoxicated improvisation in honor of the god of ecstasy, Dionysos. According to Aristotle, though his claim is much disputed,[4] it was the dithyramb which took on dramatic form and became tragedy. If so, this is the most portentous of all chorodic forms: the bulk of European drama is its grandchild.

In the sixth century, choral odes came to be written in celebration of human, rather than divine, excellence. The *Enkômion* praised great men. Victors in the great athletic contests of Greece were honored in the *Epinîkion.* For those to whom the decathlon is not a revelation of one of the cardinal excellences of man, it seems curious that such should have been the occasion for the poetry of Pindar, who has been called "one of the four spiritual reasons for setting ourselves to the toil of mastering the Greek language."[5]

Throughout this apparent wilderness of chorodic types there are three nearly universal common features. First, the language is usually ornate and complex, with some features of the Doric dialect. Second, the typical choral ode (apart from drama) is composed of a series of paired and metrically identical stanzas, with each pair separated from the next by a stanza of similar but not identical metrical character. The pair consists of a strophe and antistrophe, or "turn" and "counter-turn." (These terms are thought to refer to the fact that the dance movements in the second stanza of each pair were exactly reversed from those of the first.) The third, dividing stanza is the epode. The metrical patterns in chorodic poetry are more complex than those of any other Greek poetry—in fact, more complex than any other European poetry. And the patterns of no two odes are identical. Diversity and regularity, freedom and balance, have never been more perfectly fused.

The third feature common to nearly all choral odes is the material of which the odes consist.[6] There are moral maxims. (In Pindar these can become abrupt revelations.) Individuals involved in the festival or celebration are mentioned. And—most important for literature—a myth is retold, often, as in Pindar, from a striking viewpoint, with daring ellipses and compressions in the narrative—the antipode to Homer's way. Alkman's *Partheneion,* the earliest choral ode to survive *in extenso,* exhibits all three of these elements.

There have been modern attempts at close imitation of the Greek choral ode. Among these are the choruses of Swinburne's

4. As, for example, in A. W. Pickard-Cambridge's *Dithyramb, Tragedy, and Comedy* (Oxford, 1927).

5. Lewis Richard Farnell, *The Works of Pindar* (London, 1930), I, vii.

6. Bowra, *Greek Lyric Poetry,* introduction.

Erectheus and Arnold's *Merope,* Gray's Pindaric odes, and some of the choruses in the Helena section of Goethe's *Faust II.*

With the elimination of the dancing chorus one reaches the second of the two forms of poetry which are, in the Greek sense, genuinely lyric: the solo song, or monody. Monody is much closer to the usual modern lyric in its relative simplicity and its preoccupation with the poet's personal concerns. But ancient monody ranged more widely—into politics and satire, for example—than one would expect of "lyric" poetry. And unlike much modern lyric, the poem is never an utterly private communing of the poet with himself; it is always conceived of as addressed to an audience. The audience here, however, is usually not that of an official public occasion, but a private gathering—of friends (Sappho), or of companions at a drinking party or *symposion* (Alkaios, Anakreon).

Monodies were composed of a single line or short stanza-pattern repeated throughout the poem. Unlike the choral lyric, the same stanza-pattern could be re-used in many poems, and the types of stanzas were limited. Two of the finest types are the Sapphic (employed by its eponym, for example, in the poems translated by Willis Barnstone under the titles "Prayer to Aphrodite" and "Seizure") and the Alcaic (in which Alkaios's "Winter Evening" and "A Nation at Sea" were written).[7] Some idea of their character may perhaps be grasped in Tennyson's imitations:

> SAPPHIC: Faded every violet, all the roses;
> Gone the promise glorious, and the victim,
> Broken in this anger of Aphrodite,
> Yields to the victor.

> ALCAEIC: O mighty-mouthed inventor of harmonies,
> O skill'd to sing of Time and Eternity,
> God-gifted organ voice of England,
> Milton, a name to resound for ages.

Among modern imitations, one of Ezra Pound's earlier poems, "Apparuit," is in Sapphics, and a number of Swinburne's imitate monodic meters. But the one modern who consistently transcended imitation in his use of Greek monodic forms, who has earned a place with Horace for having snatched the lyric club from the Greek Hercules, is Hölderlin.

In addition to poetry accompanied by music there are two further kinds of Greek verse which one today might roughly class

---

7. All titles used in this introduction are those given by the translator. The originals are usually untitled.

as lyric. Both may originally have been sung, but early lost their music. Iambic poetry, allegedly the invention of Archilochos, was composed of lines predominantly in iambic or trochaic (the reverse of iambic) rhythms. It was at first chiefly employed, as one can see in Archilochos, Semonides of Amorgos, and Hipponax, for personal abuse, satire, and polemic. But even in Archilochos its range was wider (see for example the fragment "Moderation"). Solon used iambics to defend his political and economic policies at Athens.

The greatest offspring in Greek of iambic poetry was the dialog in Athenian drama. The drama is thus a hybrid of the chorodic and iambic traditions. But it has been further maintained that even Shakespeare's blank verse originally came, by way of Italian Renaissance imitations, from ancient drama and thus originally from the iambic poets.[8]

Finally, there is the elegiac poetry. Coleridge's adaptation of Schiller gives some idea of its basic unit, the elegiac couplet:

> In the hexameter rises the fountain's silvery column;
> In the pentameter aye falling in melody back.

The first line, the hexameter, has six feet of dactyls, often replaced in various feet by spondees (two long syllables). The second line, misnamed the "pentameter," is simply a hexameter with the second half of the third and sixth feet silent.

Of all forms of "lyric" verse, the elegiac has had the most nearly continuous existence, from the late eighth century or earlier into modern times. From the beginning it was used for highly diverse purposes.[9] 1) Like monody, it served to embellish the symposium. There it could speak of love and current political and military affairs, as it does in Kallinos, Mimnermos, and the collection attributed to Theognis. 2) It was used for long military and political harangues, such as those of Tyrtaios and Solon, and for historical narrative. 3) It was used in dedications inscribed on statues and other gifts to the gods. 4) It appeared on epitaphs, the short inscriptions on gravemarkers. Simonides's epitaph for the Spartan dead at Thermopylae is the most famous (it was quoted in the 1960 presidential campaign) of a noble company. 5) The form of the lament, especially in its later hybrid, the pastoral elegy, is the one best known in modern times. (Milton's "Lycidas" and *"Epitaphium Damonis,"* Gray's "Elegy," Shelley's "Adonais," Arnold's "Thyrsis.")

---

8. Highet, *Classical Tradition,* p. 131.
9. The categories here are approximately those of Bowra in his article "Elegiac Poetry, Greek," *Oxford Classical Dictionary* (Oxford, 1949).

The elegiac form was transplanted into Latin and grew nobly in the Augustan period under the care of such men as Propertius and Ovid. It struggled bravely through the Middle Ages until the Renaissance gave it new life, and it survived into the nineteenth century for its finest harvest (apart from its mutation into the English heroic couplet) since the Augustans, in Goethe's *Roman Elegies,* and those of Hölderlin. Since then the couplet form itself has languished. But the spirit passed from Hölderlin into those poems supreme among all which bear the name elegy, the *Duino Elegies* of Rilke.

DEVELOPMENT OF GREEK LYRIC

So much for the forms of Greek lyric and their afterlife. It is time now to return to Archilochos and treat of the temporal phases of lyric. The subject is by nature erratic and fragmentary, and the following brash survey of the principal remains will suffer even more heavily from these defects. For full and proper treatment, the reader should consult the bibliography.

We have seen that the social changes in the late eighth century contributed to the development of the poem as individual expression. But much is owing to the innovating personality of Archilochos himself. Born a bastard, of a Greek father and a Thracian mother, he was an outsider from the start. His life as a freelance soldier, moreover, intensified his alienation from group traditions. Thus thrown upon himself, he rejected the values of the aristocracy, particularly that supreme aristocratic value, Honor (which at the time was roughly chivalric in character). Honor, to the conventional aristocrat of his age, was something worth dying for, since death was in any case inevitable, and an "honorable" death gave one at least the secular immortality of renown. Says Sarpedon to Glaukos in the *Iliad* (XII, 322ff.), "Man, could we survive this war and live forever, deathless and strong, I would not be fighting out in front, nor would I urge you to this fray which gives us glory. But death in myriad forms is closing in—no mortal can slip past it. Come with me; no matter if another will boast over us, or we over him."

Archilochos, as his fragment "On His Shield" makes clear, chose another way. To throw away one's shield in a hasty retreat was not worse than death. It was simple common sense. What counted was not the deathless fame, but the tangible delights of the present, precious moment. Together with future glory Archilochos discarded the equally impalpable worth of present reputation; it was better to make enemies than to appease. Some would hold that the short fragment here titled "Proverb for a Great Scoundrel" refers in fact to the poet himself. If so, the image of the self-reliant, self-enclosed hedgehog is an apt one for this first on Europe's honor-able roll of prickly, renegade poets.

Archilochos' revolution did not of course transform the whole of subsequent poetry. It seems to have been the regions of the Eastern Greeks, the Aiolians and Ionians of Asia Minor and the islands, which proved most receptive to the new spirit. Meanwhile at Sparta, the heart of the younger Western, or Dorian branch of Greek culture, Tyrtaios was composing martial elegies in which an older communal ethos still lived. The Spartans were the nearest approximation among the Greeks to the collectivist mentality. It is therefore fitting that their gift to the Lyric Age should have been the most collective of forms, the choral ode.

To be sure, as earlier mentioned, the choral ode had existed, in a sense, from the beginning of cult, and thus perhaps ever since the tribal organization of man. But the wealthy patronage of the Spartan state during its years of peaceful abundance, in the later seventh century, attracted talented poets and gave them the means to produce their choruses for the public festivals. Significantly, most of the earlier of these commissioned poets were from the East, the older and subtler culture. The Eastern influence and the years of peace are perhaps the explanation for the un-Spartan playfulness and charm of the first surviving choral poet, Alkman.

Even in the choral form—a clear mark of the Lyric Age—one hears the voice of Alkman the individual. One of the most impres-sive aspects of that voice is its vivid perception of nature. Alkman was apparently the first to distinguish four seasons (rather than three). And, as in the poem "Rest," he shows a sense for the life of the inanimate world. "Rest" has suggested to some a parallel with Goethe's "Über allen Gipfeln."

Until Simonides, choral poetry after Alkman is attested only in a bitterly small collection of scraps. Stesichoros, a native Dorian (this time from the far West, from Sicily), is credited with the intro-duction of greatly extended mythical narratives into the choral ode. The loss of his *Oresteia* or *Helen* was perhaps as irreparable as we should judge the perishing of Keats's "Eve of St. Agnes." Ibykos (he too from the far West) has at least left us with enough to establish that we have certainly lost much fine poetry.

With Ibykos we must touch on a matter which needs less be-laboring today than it might have in the past. Much of Greek love poetry is about homosexual love. Greek society in general, and par-ticularly in Dorian lands, was so arranged that women could not readily become full emotional companions of men. Marriage was often a purely practical affair entered upon by a man in his middle thirties for the purpose of raising a family. The wife was essentially a housekeeper. Consequently the deepest erotic experiences were frequently—and for the poetry of the Lyric Age, predominantly—homosexual, between older and younger men, and between older and younger women. Often, of course, the affairs were mere adventures in the flesh. At other times they were as luminous and mature as any of the heterosexual passions of later ages. Poets such as Kavafis and George have shown in their poetry, as nearly as is possible in a different society, what pederasty could mean to the Greeks.

Ibykos brings choral poetry down to somewhere in the middle of the sixth century BCE. We must return to the end of the seventh for the commencement and, at the same time, the climax of monody.

Here Eastern Greece (Asia Minor and the islands)—the Aiolic island of Lesbos in particular—is the focus of creation. Alkaios and Sappho, both aristocrats of Lesbos, were contemporaries, and both in their own way reveal at its most intense the subjective individualism of Archilochos, now winged with lyric meters and those melodies which for us must be unheard.

The times were bad for aristocrats—both Alkaios and Sappho were exiled by a middle-class tyranny—and much of Alkaios' poetry is that of a militant reactionary. Other poems, archetypes of their kind, are devoted to the delights of the drinking party, whether as refuge from the outer political darkness or as a brief forgetting of the darkness of death.

In the poems of Sappho hardly a whiff of politics appears. Her persistent subjects are family, private friends and foes, and love. One view holds that she was head of a cult which was at the same time a finishing school for girls of the aristocracy—a cult devoted to poetry and Aphrodite—no mere symbol of beauty and love, but the genuine goddess. From within the group of her friends she found her favorites. With these perhaps she shared that epiphany of her goddess of which she sings in her only wholly surviving poem, "Prayer to Aphrodite."

Simplicity and directness are the manner of all monody, in contrast to choral poetry. In Sappho these qualities are at their highest. For many, therefore, Sappho in her precious rags will stand above Pindar in his full effulgent robes at the thin-aired pinnacle of ancient lyric.

More than a full generation after Sappho comes the next and last personality in ancient monody. Anakreon, again from the East, but this time Ionia, became in popular legend a sort of poetic Silenus: a lovable, drunken, old infatuate. But, somewhat incongruously, this Silenus displays a deft, ironic wit which later imitators (the many anonymous authors of the *Anakreonteia*), playful and delightful as they often are, could not fully reproduce. It is, from our retrospective vantage, hard to believe that readers for centuries could have accepted the *Anakreonteia* as Anakreon's own.

The monodic strand in the Lyric Age comes to an end in a series of anonymous *Skolia* or drinking songs. These *Skolia* are the only native Athenian contribution, apart from Solon, to the poetry of the Lyric Age. Some of them are quite strong and vivid, but one could not guess from them that the fifth century in literature was to belong to Athens.

Three figures close the great period of Greek lyric. All three were choral poets chiefly, and were closely associated through family ties or rivalry. Simonides was uncle of Bakchylides. Pindar strove with both.

Simonides, eldest of the three, seems in many ways more modern, more a man of the fifth century, than the other two. Such things as his poem in criticism of Kleoboulos and his lecture-poem to Skopas on the limits of mortal virtue reflect a critical, intellectualist strain in Simonides, a readiness to modify received standards not, as with Archilochos, by mere subjective vehemence, but by rational judgment. His short fragment on "Arete" (virtue or excellence) is one of several poems which show a tendency toward dealing with abstract entities rather than traditional mythological divinities.

Like Pindar and Bakchylides, Simonides frequented the mansions of the great where his skills were welcomed and rewarded. But he seems to have given his ultimate sympathies to Athenian democracy, the fifth century's wave of the future. In his style he was celebrated for the controlled, vivid sobriety which can be seen in the long fragment on Danaë and Perseus.

Bakchylides survived in an even more fragmentary state than his uncle until 1896, when Egyptian sands surrendered a papyrus containing a tolerable proportion of his works. The odes of Bakchylides, as we can now see, are fluent, attractive, and often of great power.

Pindar, who deserves—even in translation—a volume of his own (and has received it in Richmond Lattimore's fine versions), must here be dealt with even more inadequately than all who have gone before. Unlike Simonides, he was not at home in the new currents of the fifth century. Like Homer and Bach, he is the culmination of a tradition—the chorodic—which the times were leaving behind. He was most in his element not at democratic Athens, but in Aigina and Thebes (the chief city of his native Boiotia)—the cultural dinosaurs of the age. Proud, aloof, assured of his genius, and wonderstruck by the brief, god-sent radiance of mortal excellence, he is deservedly the "Theban eagle." For some of those who cleave the knotted oak and swirling ocean of his Greek, there is no greater lyric in the world.

After Pindar there is much that is brilliant, touching, and entertaining in the lyric forms, but the highest energies in Greek literature are now found in drama, history, oratory, and philosophy. There were of course still practitioners of chorody and monody; even Aristotle tried his hand at the former and wrought yeomanly. But a new musical style increasingly subdued the text to mere libretto. The predominant form for pure poetry was henceforth the elegiac epigram.

Elegiac poetry and iambic poetry after Archilochos have been left to one side in our review thus far. Most of the significant poets in both genres have been mentioned above in the initial discussion of the forms of Greek lyric. It should be noted that a fraction of the poetry of Archilochos and Anakreon is in elegiacs, and that a few iambic lines of Anakreon survive. The elegiac epigrams of Simonides are, next to the work of Theognis, the largest body of elegiac poetry by one man to survive before the third century. Judging from the remains, the epigram, apart from anonymous inscriptions, did not greatly flourish in the latter part of the fifth and in the fourth centuries. The epigrams some think to be Plato's, if in fact they do belong to this period, are the one bright patch in these years.

But in the third century, at the hands of Asklepiades, Kallimachos, and their successors, epigram acquired new range and freshness. The short, pointed poem, usually in elegiacs—whether erotic, epitaph (real or simulated), satirical, or gnomic—became a popular lyric form.

And so it remained for all the succeeding centuries of Greek as an ancient language. Scholars and litterateurs, while Rome was refocusing the world, continued to refine a form which had lost touch with any vital, transforming, outside forces. But frozen as it was, the epigram could still gleam, most brightly in such men as Meleagros, Philodemos, Marcus Argentarius, grim Palladas—and even in the sixth-century CE Byzantine, Paulus Silentiarius. Gathered four times or more in successive collections, the harvest of epigram which is the *Greek Anthology* was stored in roughly its present form by Constantine Cephalas in the tenth century.

The death which came thus slowly to the Greek lyric can come to no other poetry with such apt grace. For in no other poetry does the conviction of the bitter, lesser glory of mortal works dwell so near the center.

Greek lyric lives, of course, in another way—as part of the enriching stream from which each new age of poetry draws. "Death by Water" in *The Waste Land* is a form taken from the *Anthology*. Pound writes poems after Ibykos and Sappho. Salvatore Quasimodo translates the Greek lyricists. And those researchers of atomic rubble, with whom we began, could find a fit Hellenic epitaph for all our troublesome days in Yeats' lines for his own tomb:

Cast a cold eye
On life, on death.
Horseman, pass by!

William E. McCulloh

Ο ΑΠΟΛΟΓΙΣΜΟΣ ΠΕΡΙ ΤΩΝ ΕΠΙΛΕΞΩΝ ΚΑΙ ΤΩΝ ΚΕΙΜΕΝΩΝ ΚΑΙ ΤΗΣ ΜΕΤΑΦΡΑΣΕΩΣ

A Note on Selections, Texts, and Translation

Fire, religion, and time have treated the lyric poetry of ancient Greece very poorly. Texts have disappeared by intention and through neglect. Today there is little hope of finding original papyrus manuscripts in Greece, for papyrus cannot easily survive in even the relatively dry climate of Greece.[1]

Only in waterless parts of Egypt, in the rubbish heaps of antiquity, may ancient documents still be preserved, buried in tombs or with ancient cities under the sand. Indeed, there is always hope that the sands of some provincial city of Egypt will yield a new poem or fragment, such as the odes and dithyrambs of Bakchylides or Alkman's choral ode found in 1896 at Oxyrhynchos.

In what has survived—a small percent of the important lyric poetry—we still have enough to comprise one of our great achievements in the arts. For we have poems by Sappho, Pindar, Bakchylides, Meleagros, Archilochos, Simonides, Alkaios, Anakreon, and many others. The largest single collections are the victory odes of Pindar and the more than four thousand poems in the *Greek* or *Palatine Anthology*. A very large proportion of Greek lyric poetry survives as exempla quoted in studies of Greek and Latin scholars.

A single line in Greek by Sappho or an elegiac couplet ascribed to Plato may be precious to us in its own right:

World

I could not hope
to touch the sky
with my two arms.   (Sappho)

or

I am a sailor's tomb. Beside me lies a farmer.
    Hell is the same, under the land and sea.   (Plato)

But lines from Greek lyric poetry may also be precious when they are all we have left from which to form an image of an ancient poet.

---

1. In 1961, for the first time, original papyrus was found in continental Greece, at Dervani (Lagada). See Herbert Hunger, "Papyrusfund in Griechenland," *Chronique d'Egypte* 37, no. 74 (July 1962).

Because, therefore, the number of poems from shorter lyric poetry is so limited, I have translated virtually all the true lyric poems and intelligible fragments—monodic and choral—from the poets of the sixth and seventh centuries BCE, with the exception of Pindar and Bakchylides, who are represented only in part. By considering fragments and epigrams one may perhaps read enough lines from poets like Archilochos, Anakreon, Alkaios, Ibykos, Alkman, to see them in at least clear profile. Of the later poets, found in the *Greek* or *Palatine Anthology,* I have tried to make a generous selection of the better poems.

But the very fact that ancient papyri and later copies of Greek lyrics have been so maltreated makes one all the more mindful of omissions, and these too should be stated. From Pindar I have translated only a selection of the odes and fragments. Pindar's victory odes, a book in themselves, may be read in the luminous translations in Richmond Lattimore's *The Odes of Pindar.* There is also the serious omission of some longer elegiac and iambic poems. Thus while Tyrtaios, Semonides, Solon, and Xenophanes are well represented, they have been denied inclusion of one or more of their significant extant compositions.[2] It is a tangible omission, however, which a later edition may hopefully correct. Another edition might also include a larger selection of sepulchral inscriptions.

More painful is the omission of many longer poems by Bakchylides. While he is represented here, the entire opus—thirteen epinikia, six dithyrambs, and various short pieces—appears in lively translation in Robert Fagles' book *Bacchylides: Complete Poems,* which both fills the gap and conveys the narrative eloquence and pristine imagery of this neglected poet. Bakchylides, like Thomas Traherne, is a relatively recent discovery; though there is as yet no piggyback tradition of praise—indeed, he has not been considered on his own but has been consistently and foolishly downgraded as a secondary Pindar—he is assured of his ancient place in the canon of the nine lyric poets.

The most formidable problem in translating from Greek has been to find a just approximation of Greek stanza forms and meter. It is at least consoling that there can never be a single solution

2. In this anthology the *lyric* poem is emphasized. For this reason excerpts are not given from epic poetry or from the plays. In using the word *lyric* no rigid definition is intended, e.g., the early Greek concept of lyric poems for the lyre as opposed to elegiac poems for the flute. Rather, lyric here simply means a short poem that sings. In this sense, and this alone, I have given preference to the more purely lyrical pieces from the Greek poets. The longer poems in elegiac couplets tend at times, like heroic couplets in English, to become essays in verse. This is true of longer poems of Tyrtaios, Semonides, Solon, and Xenophanes.

for the transfer of prosodic techniques from one language to another. Poems in ancient Greek were composed primarily to be sung, chanted, or recited, to be heard not read. In the original papyrus scripts the words were all run together as in Sanscrit. There were no indentations of shorter lines as in later manuscripts, for the poetic lines were also run together. Only capital letters were used. Thus even the question of whether English lines should begin with upper- or lower-case letters has no real precedence in the original scripts, and the most faithful translations would use upper-case letters exclusively. So, the first stanza of Sappho's poem to Anaktoria might read,

SOMESAYCAVALRYANDOTHERSCLAIM
INFANTRYORAFLEETOFLONGOARSIS
THESUPREMESIGHTONTHEBLACKEAR
TH.ISAYITIS

Even the stanzaic appearance of a Sapphic hymn or a Simonidean epigram as printed traditionally in Greek texts was determined by later scholars on the basis of metrical pauses.

I have tried to give order to these translations in several ways. To approximate the easy conversational flow of many of the Greek poems, I have more often given a syllabic rather than an accentual regularity to the lines. An exception is the longer elegiac poem where the forceful dactyls seemed to call for a regular (though free-falling) beat in alternating lines of equal feet. In the matter of diction, it is important to remember that the Greeks, as most poets in the past—a Spenser or Kavafis excepted—wrote in a language which seemed natural and contemporary to their readers.[3] My intention has been to use a contemporary idiom, generally chaste, but colloquial as the occasion suggests.

Until very recently, it has been a uniform practice to impose rhyme on poems translated from ancient Greek. But the Greeks did not use end rhyme as a common poetic device. Rhyme was used only in rare instances, usually for humor or satire (see Palladas, 561), and so rhyme is not used in these translations. In most of the poems I have tried to retain the stanzaic patterns suggested by the metrical stops in the Greek texts. In others I have been more original, or perhaps perverse, in seeking an equivalent of the Greek. I am especially guilty of license where I seek to convey the humor of *Greek Anthology* epigrams.

3. Many writers did use archaic Homeric words and phrases, but this too was at least natural in common poetic usage.

In most cases the Greek rather than Latinized spelling has been followed, thus Alkaios and Theokritos, not Alcaeus and Theocritus. In recent years the English transliteration of Greek words has become common and it is, I believe, essentially more pleasant and satisfying to read. It is a new practice, however, with rules unfixed, used differently by different hands; I am aware of instances where I have not been entirely consistent where the sin of inconsistency is in the end less gauche than the virtue of absolute order. So, while making the reader aware that Pindar and Plato are really Pindaros and Platon, I have persisted in referring to them as Plato and Pindar. Perhaps in a few years when original places and texts are more familiar to us than English maps and translations, we shall speak of Livorno, not Leghorn, Thessaloniki not Salonika, and even Pindaros not Pindar.

I have used standard texts: Lobel and Page, Diehl, Bowra (Pindar), Gow (Theokritos) and Loeb Library editions. I have also gone to Italian, French, and modern Greek editions where they have been helpful. For some of the earlier poets, especially Sappho, I have in some cases followed the conjectural reconstructions of Treu (*Sappho Lieder*), Edmonds (Loeb Library), and Page (*Sappho and Alcaeus*)—when the only alternative to the reconstructed text is no poem at all. But I have misgivings about this. However, where a mutilated text can be used, it often offers, quite accidentally, very striking effects; in such poems as Sappho's "Age and Light," "Dream," and "The Laurel Tree," the very poverty of the lacuna-ridden text contributes a poignancy and quality of modernity which the reconstructed text lacks.

In innumerable cases there are variant readings in the Greek texts. I have usually followed the more recent editions.

A word about titles. All the poems included here have titles, yet few of these are traditional in the Greek. Why use titles then in English translations? Most of the poems and fragments are quotations found in other ancient writings. Though sometimes merely grammatical in nature, the context in which the poem appears usually gives additional information about the complete poem. The titles here are primarily informational, based on contextual information or on common ancient allusions with which a modern reader may be unfamiliar. Hopefully, titles will serve to replace lengthy footnotes and make the poems more complete.

Ideally, poetry in translation should one day lead a reader to a reading of the poem in the original tongue. The poem in its native phonemes, we often forget, was primarily a poem, and a good one, presumably, if chosen for translation. A poem in translation should be faithful, if to anything, to this primary quality of the original—that of its being an effective poem.

With this in mind we may say something about the general possibilities of poetry in translation. Many banal ideas are commonly held about the disadvantages of poetry in translation—this despite the modern additions to our language of verse translations by Lattimore, Fitts, Fitzgerald, Wilbur, Lowell, or Auden. Poems may be poorly translated, as they may have been poorly written originally, but they are not necessarily poorer or better than the original—though the translator must secretly and vainly aim for the latter. The quality of the poem in translation will depend on the translator's skill in writing poetry in his own language in the act of translating. If he is T. S. Eliot translating Saint-Jean Perse or Mallarmé translating Poe or the scholars of the King James Version translating the psalms, the result may indeed be superior—or at the very least equal. Only one thing is certain: the poem in translation will be different. The translator's task, then, is to produce a faithful forgery. The quality and resemblance of the new product to the old lie somewhere between such fidelity and fraud.

But it is said that certain memorable lines or phrases cannot be expressed in any other language. Yet it should also be said that while at times we must lose, at others we gain, and the good translator will take advantage of the text, improving upon the weaker lines of the original, while doing his best with the best. More important, it is forgotten that translation provides an opportunity for languages to interact upon each other, for one tongue to alter and enrich the possibilities of expression in another. In the past some translated works have changed both literary language and tradition: notably the Petrarchan sonnet, Luther's Bible, Judith Gautier's haiku. Milton went as naturally to the King James Version for vocabulary as Shakespeare turned to Holinshed for plots; when Rimbaud's *Illuminations* were translated into English, the tradition of our literature was expanded to the extent that diction and subject never before found in English were presented to us.

In a word, the quality of a work in translation is dependent on the translator's skills. His forgery is not necessarily better or worse than the original or than other works in his own language; it is only necessarily different—and here the difference, if new and striking, may extend the verbal and thematic borders of his own literature. And as a corollary to his work the new poem may also be seen as an essay into literary criticism, a reading, a creative *explication de texte.*

Discussion of translations of poetry usually confuses *kind* with *value.* One type of translation is thought to be intrinsically superior to others, be it free translation, close translation, poetry *after,* imitation, metaphrase, paraphrase, etc. In the critic's mind the quality of a translation often depends on how closely it conforms to his own preferred method. This error of descriptive rather than evaluative criticism—where kind determines value—probably occurs more often in regard to poetry translation than in any other form of literary criticism. But in the end, method is secondary, and determines neither the virtues nor sins of a poem. The translator need only clearly and honestly indicate his method—whatever it is—and then be judged, not on this choice, but on the quality of the new poem. If the new poem is good, the translator as artist will be performing his ancient function of retelling, in his own form, a given content he has overheard from the immediate or the distant past.

Willis Barnstone
Indiana University

THE GREEK PERIOD

ARCHILOCHOS

According to the most probable view, Archilochos lived during the latter half of the eighth century BCE. (The event referred to in "An Eclipse of the Sun" may have occurred either in 711 BCE or 647 BCE.) He was the son of Telesikles, a nobleman of the island of Paros, and a slave-woman: hence, a bastard. He took part in the Paran colonization of the island of Thasos and seems to have spent most of his life as a soldier in the pay of his country. The only striking event in his life which has been preserved in the tradition is the "Lykambes affair." Lykambes, a nobleman, promised his daughter Neoboule to Archilochos and then went back on the promise. Archilochos took revenge in the poetic invective which has ever since been regarded (too narrowly) as his special gift. The legend that the potency of his satire produced the suicide of Neoboule, or Lykambes, or the whole family, is probably only legend. In later years, according to some interpreters of the fragments, Neoboule became a prostitute and even made advances to Archilochos, who rejected her with bitter comments on his former love. Archilochos died in battle. A cult in his honor was later established on Paros, and, by the third century BCE, his shrine had become a center for scholars.

Chief works: 1) elegies dealing with warfare, consolation ("On Friends Lost at Sea"), personal expression, conviviality; 2) epodes (stanzas composed of several distinct meters) of personal or satirical content, often employing illustrative narratives—especially fable ("An Animal Appeals to Zeus"); 3) poems in iambic or trochaic meters, of satirical, personal, hortatory or narrative content. (The trochaic tetrameter was the popular equivalent of the more aristocratic narrative meter, the dactylic hexameter.)

Archilochos' language is chiefly the Ionic of his day, but in the elegies it is strongly influenced by Homeric diction.

As suggested in the Introduction, the ambiguous social position of Archilochos probably helped to make him the spokesman par excellence of the new spirit of the Lyric Age. This spirit included a preoccupation with the "now," "here," and "I" (as Adrados has said),* rather than with an archetypical past. It further manifested

---

* Francisco R. Adrados, Líricos griegos: elegiacos y yambógraphos arcaicos (Barcelona, 1956), I, 15.

a greatly increased sense for man's helpless subjection to circumstance ("Providence," "Moderation").

Archilochos exercised considerable influence in various ways over Kallimachos (iambics), Catullus (satire), and Horace (epode).

The iambus was invented by Archilochos of Faros.

CLEMENT OF ALEXANDRIA, *Miscellanies**

Of the three iambic writers in Aristarchos' canon, the one who achieves the greatest mastery is Archilochos. We find in him the most developed sense of expression, with terse and vigorous phrasing, and abundance of blood and muscle.

QUINTILIAN, *Guide to Oratory*

I would shun the poisonous tooth of slander. Though removed in time, I have seen the cantankerous Archilochos in poverty because he fattened on the abuse of enemies.

PINDAR, *Pythian Odes*, 2

In this grave lies Archilochos whom the Muses guided to the writing of furious iambics to preserve the supremacy of Homer's dactyls.

ADRIANOS, *Palatine Anthology*

Fields of Desire

But my friend I am crippled
   by desire.

If it is urgent and your hot desire
   can't wait, there is one in
   our house who longs for a man.

She is a beautiful thin virgin.
   I think her body perfect.
   Why not make her a friend?

---

* Clement is in error here.

So she said, and I replied,
  Daughter of Amfimedo,
  a noble woman

whom dark earth now lies upon,
  Afroditi's pleasures are
  many for young men

apart from holy copulation.
  One will do with ease.
  When it grows dark

you and I with the god's help
  will talk of this. I'll do
  what you say. You burn me.

Below the arch and through the gate
  don't hold back, darling.
  I'll float to the grassy

garden. As for Neobouli,
  let another man have her.
  She's ripe and twice your age.

Her girlish flower is barren
  like her earlier enchantment when
  she could never have enough.

That crazy woman showed her stuff.
  Give her to the crows.
  I won't touch it. No way

I'll be hanged with such a wife
  and give neighbors a laugh.
  The one I crave is you.

You are not loose or two-faced.
  She's quick and on the make,
  picking up hordes of men.

I fear if I rush in, I'll come out
  stuck with blind loused up
  kids from the bitch.

So I said. And I took the virgin
   amid the flowers and laid
   her down, and covered her with

my soft cloak, holding her neck
   in my arm. She froze
   like a fawn. She didn't run.

Gently I touched her breasts. Her fresh
   flesh at the edge of her dress
   showed in a burst of youth.

Caressing all her body, I shot
   my white sperm into her,
   feeling her dark blond hair.

Translated by Willis Barnstone and William McCulloh

Thasos and Sicily

This wheatless island stands like a donkey's back.
It bristles with a tangle of wild woodland.
Oh,
there is no country so beautiful,
no sensual earth that keys my passion
as these plains around the river Siris.*

An Island in the North Aigaian

All, O all the calamities of all the Hellenes
are set loose on this battleground in Thasos.

The Doublecross†

Let brawling waves beat his ship
against the shore, and have the mop-haired Thracians
take him naked at Salmydessos,
and he will suffer a thousand calamities

---

* These two separate fragments are found together.
† This poem is also ascribed to Hipponax.

as he chews the bread of slaves.
His body will stiffen in freezing surf
as he wrestles with slimy seaweed,
and his teeth will rattle like a helpless dog,
flopped on his belly in the surge,
puking out the brine. Let me watch him grovel
in mud—for the wrong he did me:
as a traitor he trampled on our good faith,
he who was once my comrade.

Paros Figs

Say goodbye to the island Paros,
farewell to its figs and the seafaring life.

Threat

Let the stone of Tantalos
no longer overhang this island.

War

Look, Glaukos, how heavy seawaves leap skyward!
Over the Gyrai rocks hangs a black cloud,
a signal of winter storm.
From the unforeseen comes fear.

A Vessel of Wine

Go take your cup and walk along the timber deck
of our roaming ship; drain the hollow casks
of all their red wine. How can we stay sober
on the watch when all the rest are drunk?

A Drowning

They laid down their lives
in the arms of waves.

Shipwreck

The vessel wavered on the cutting edge
between the stormwinds and the waves.

Prayer at Sea

Often, when their vessel was threatened by the gray salty
    sea,
they prayed to Athene of the lovely braids for sweet return.

On Friends Lost at Sea

If you irritate the wound, Perikles, no man
in our city will enjoy the festivities.
These men were washed under by the thudding seawaves,
and the hearts in our chest are swollen with pain.
Yet against this incurable misery, the gods
give us the harsh medicine of endurance.
Sorrows come and go, friend, and now they strike us
and we look with horror on the bleeding sores,
yet tomorrow others will mourn the dead. I tell you,
hold back your feminine tears and endure.

*On the lack. Of Proper Burning and Burial for
His Brother-in-Law Who Was Shipwrecked*

If only his head and handsome limbs
had been wrapped in white burial cloth
and touched by Hephaistos' hand of fire.

An Eclipse of the Sun

Nothing in the world can surprise me now. Nothing
is impossible or too wonderful, for Zeus, father
of the Olympians, has turned midday into black night
by shielding light from the blossoming sun,
and now dark terror hangs over mankind.
Anything may happen, so do not be amazed if beasts
on dry land seek pasture with dolphins in

the ocean, and those beasts who loved sunny hills
love crashing seawaves more than the warm mainland.

Dawn

Dawn was rising full white.

Her Beautiful Rose

Her sprig of myrtle clothed her beautiful rose
That her hands were happily playing with,
And her hair fell
As darkness on her back and shoulders.
Someone
Right in the middle of the myrtle.

On Pasiphile, a Friend of All

As the figtree on its rock feeds many crows,
so this simple girl sleeps with strangers.

Sudden Love

And to fall upon her heaving belly,
and thrust your groin into her groin,
your thighs between her thighs.

On the Male Organ

Feeble now are the muscles in my mushroom.

Like a Donkey

His penis is swollen
like a donkey from Priene
taking his fill of barley.

Qualities of a Girlfriend

She is a common woman for rent,
but what sensuality and fat ankles.
O fat whore for hire!

Riches

Enormous was the gold he amassed
from many years of work,
but all he owned
fell into the luscious arms
of a common whore.

Providence

Let the gods take care of everything. Many times
they resurrect a man whom disaster left lying
face down on the black earth. Many times they topple
a man and pin him, back to the soil, though he
was solid on his feet. A multitude of evils
batters him as he wanders hungry and mad.

On Dead Animals

Many of them, I hope, will be dried up
by the sharp rays of the sun in its zenith,
by the sun in the time of the Dog Star.

Proverb for a Great Scoundrel

The fox knows many tricks,
the hedgehog only one. A good one.

His Two Virtues

I am a servant of the kingly wargod Enyalios
and am also skilled in the lovely arts.

Wine of Naxos Is like Nectar but His Javelin Is Much More

My javelin is good white bread and Ismarian wine.
When I find rest on my javelin I drink wine.

On the Short-Haired Warriors in the Lelantine
War between Chalkis and Eretria Who
Agreed Not to Use Missile Weapons

Perhaps fewer bows will be stretched and slings hurled
when Ares begins battle on the noisy plain,
but then the mournful labor of the sword is worse.

This is warfare in which the spear-famed islanders
from Euboia are godlike and easily masterful.

Aphrodite Is Censured

Passionate love relentlessly twists a cord
under my heart and spreads deep mist on my eyes,
stealing the unguarded brains from my head.

On His Shield

Well, what if some barbaric Thracian glories
in the perfect shield I left under a bush?
I was sorry to leave it—but I saved my skin.
Does it matter? O hell, I'll buy a better one.

My Kind of General

I don't like a general
who towers over the troops,
lordly with elegant locks
and trim mustachios.
Give me a stumpy soldier
glaringly bowlegged,
yet rockfirm on his feet,
and in his heart a giant.

Charon the Carpenter

The gold booty of Gyges means nothing to me.
I don't envy that Lydian king, nor am I jealous
of what gods can do, nor of the tyrants' great
powers. All these are realms beyond my vision.

Mercenary Friendship

Glaukos, soldier of fortune, will be your friend
until he begins to fight.

Wedding Dedication

When Alkibia became a married woman, she gave
the holy veil of her hair to Queen Hera.

On the Daughter of Lykambes

I pray for one gift: that I might merely touch
Neoboule's hand.

Love

I live here miserable and broken with desire,
pierced through to the bones by the bitterness
of this god-given painful love.

O comrade, this passion makes my limbs limp
and tramples over me.

Thirst

I want to fight you
just as when I am thirsty I want to drink.

On a Hanging

They hung their heads to one side, choking,
and disgorged their remaining arrogance.

Quality in Love

How can I like the way she makes love?
Give me sweet figs before sour wild pears.

Old Age

A life of doing nothing is good for old men,
especially if they are simple in their ways,
or stupid, or inane in their endless blabber
as old men tend to be.

Perikles the Guest

Like the Mykonians, Perikles,
you drink our unmixed wine
and pay for nothing.
You broke into this party, uninvited,
and act as if among old friends.
Your stomach has tricked the brains in your skull
and now you are shameless.

On the People's Censure

No man, Aisimides, who bows to the mud-slinging
mob has ever been capable of profound pleasures.

On Wrongdoers

One big thing I understand:
I know how to spit back with black venom
against the man who wrongs me.

The Robe

Your telltale robe is bulging, you poor tramp,
and the men you love sit beside you.
The ditchdigger is in on your fancy story
and so is your husband Ariphantos.
Lucky Ariphantos didn't catch the fumes
of that stinking billygoat thief.
While he was staving off the potter Aischylides,
the digger dug out your cherry,
and now your swollen belly tells the tale.

After the Drowning of His Sister's Husband

Now, I have no desire for poetry or joy,
yet I will make nothing better by crying,
nor worse by seeking good foods and pleasure.

Moderation

O my soul, my soul—you are mutilated helplessly
by this blade of sorrow. Yet rise and bare your chest,
face those who would attack you, be strong, give no ground.
If you defeat them, do not brag like a loudmouth,
If they beat you, don't run home and lie down to cry.
Keep some measure in your joy—or in your sadness during
crisis—that you may understand man's up-and-down life.

On the Death of Two Friends*

Broad earth, now you entomb Megatimos and Aristophon
who were the two tall columns of this island Naxos.

On a Lewd Servant

And wandering about the household
was that hateful chattering eunuch.

Perikles to Elpinike

Lady, you are much too old
to rub yourself with perfume.

An Animal Appeals to Zeus†

O father Zeus, you who control the cosmos,
and oversee the actions of man,
his criminal and lawful acts,
you also judge the arrogance and trial of wild beasts.

---

* Ascription to Archilochos is uncertain.
† Probably a fox.

Justice

My lord Apollo, single out the guilty ones,
and in your customary way, destroy them all.

Perfume

Her breasts and her dark hair were perfume
and even an old man would desire her.

Discretion

They lay down in the shadow of the wall.

Generosity

You have taken in many blind eels.

To a Girlfriend's Father

Father Lykambes, what is this new silliness?
Are your natural brains wholly rotted?
The neighbors laugh openly at your absurd life
and you persist in chattering like a cricket.

On Drowned Bodies

Let us hide the dreadful
gifts of lord Poseidon.

Death

When dead no man finds respect or glory from men
of his town. Rather, we hope while alive for some
favor from the living. The dead are always scorned.

Kallinos

The content of the fragments indicates that Kallinos was active roughly in the middle of the seventh century BCE. The Cimmerians were barbarians from the Crimea and Southern Russia who for a time threatened to overwhelm parts of Asia Minor, including the Greek cities of the coast. Kallinos lived in Ephesos, one of these cities. The surviving fragments—like those of Tyrtaios—show essentially an adaptation of Homeric style and language to the demands of the present (as if one were to create war propaganda from the King James Version of the Old Testament prophets). The only major change from Homer is the exclusive focus on courage as sacrificial patriotism rather than a means chiefly for the acquisition of individual glory. All the fragments are elegiac.

> (On Elegy) Among the best writers in this meter Proklos includes Kallinos of Ephesos, Mimnermos of Kolophon, and also Philetas the son of Telephos, from Kos, and Kallimachos the son of Battos.
>
> PHOTIOS, *Library*

A Call to Arms against the Cimmerian Invaders

When will you show some courage, young comrades?
How long will you lie back and do nothing?
Lazing in shabby peace on our land bled by war,
have you no shame before the neighboring townsmen?

Let each man hurl his spear once more before he dies,
for glory dazzles on our helmets when we battle
the enemy for farmland and children and true wife.
Death will come only when the web of destiny is spun.
So move out, charge into the barbarous ranks
with spear held high and shield gripping a brave heart.
From death there is no escape; all men face the dark,
even those with blood of gods in their veins.

Often a man flees from the clash and thud of spears
and comes home to fall into sudden doom,
but he is neither loved nor missed by his townsmen.

Yet when a hero dies the great and small shed tears;
by a whole people a brave warrior is mourned.
In life he seems a demigod before the crowd;
as a marble pillar they look upon his strength,
for all alone he does the great deeds of an army.

To Zeus

Pity the people of Smyrna,
and now recall
if they ever burned for you
the choice thighs of oxen.

Tyrtaios

Tyrtaios was active at Sparta during the Second Messenian War, that is, some time in the seventh century BCE. The legend that he came originally from Athens seems to be false. His works included marching songs (row lost) and elegies. In the remains of the latter, martial exhortations predominate, as with Kallinos. And like Kallinos, Tyrtaios modifies the Homeric tradition in the direction of a more corporate and collective ethos. He came at the time of Sparta's transition from an ordinary Greek to a severely disciplined military commune.

> The Spartans swore that they would take Messene or die themselves. When the oracle told them to take an Athenian general, they chose Tyrtaios, the lame poet, who rekindled their courage, and he took Messene in the twentieth year of the war.
>
> *Suda Lexicon*

> And Philochoros says that when the Spartans overpowered the Messenians through the generalship of Tyrtaios, they made it a custom of their military expeditions that after the evening meal when the paean had been sung each man would sing a poem by Tyrtaios, and the leader would judge the singing and give the winner a prize of meat.
>
> ATHENAIOS, *Scholars at Dinner*

Spartan Soldier

It is beautiful when a brave man of the front ranks
falls and dies, battling for his homeland,
and ghastly when a man flees planted fields and city
and wanders begging with his dear mother,
aging father, little children and true wife.

He will be scorned in every new village,
reduced to want and loathsome poverty, and shame
will brand his family line, his noble figure.
Derision and disaster will hound him.
A turncoat gets no respect or pity;
so let us battle for our country and freely give
our lives to save our darling children.
Young men, fight shield to shield and never succumb
to panic or miserable flight,
but steel the heart in your chests with magnificence
and courage. Forget your own life
when you grapple with the enemy. Never run
and let an old soldier collapse
whose legs have lost their power. It is shocking when
an old man lies on the front line
before a youth: an old warrior whose head is white
and beard gray, exhaling his strong soul
into the dust, clutching his bloody genitals
in his hands: an abominable vision,
foul to see: his flesh naked. But in a young man
all is beautiful when he still
possesses the shining flower of lovely youth.
Alive he is adored by men,
desired by women, and finest to look upon
when he falls dead in the forward clash.
Let each man spread his legs, rooting them in the ground,
bite his teeth into his lips, and hold.

Frontiers

You should reach the limits of virtue
before you cross the border of death.

SEMONIDES

Born on Samos, Semonides may have become associated with the island of Amorgos as leader of a colony there. He probably was active in the second half of the seventh century BCE. His works included iambic poems (a bather long satire on women is extant) and two books of elegies. In the iambics his language is Ionic.

In his response to the experience of human subjection to the gods (a topic particularly characteristic of the Lyric Age) Semonides differs from Archilochos. The earlier poet had concluded upon a fusion of activism and resignation. But Semonides deduced instead a code of passivity and hedonism.

> Amorgos is one of the Sporades islands and was the home of the iambic poet Semonides.
>
> STRABON, *Geography*

> Semonides, son of Krines, from Amorgos, writer of iambic verse. Originally he was from Samos but during the colonization of Amorgos he was sent by the Samians as a leader. He built three cities in Amorgos: Minoa, Aigialos and Arkesime. He lived 390 years after the Trojan War. According to some, he was the first to write iambic verse, and he wrote the History of the Samians in two books of elegiac verse, and other diverse poetry.
>
> *Suda Lexicon*

> I know that you have lived a thousand things worthy of iambic satire, and so bad that even Archilochos himself could not stand to write about even one of your outrageous acts, even if he called in as collaborators Hipponax and Semonides.
>
> LOUKIANOS, *The Liar*

The Darkness of Human Life

My child, deep-thundering Zeus controls the end
of all that is, disposing as he wills.
We who are mortals have no mind; we live like cattle,
day to day, knowing nothing of god's plans
to end each one of us. Yet we are fed
by hope and faith to dream impossible plans.
Some wait for a day to come, others watch
the turning of years. No one among the mortals
feels so broken as not to hope in coming time
to fly home rich to splendid goods and lands.
Yet before he makes his goal, odious old age
lays hold of him first. Appalling disease
consumes another. Some are killed in war
where death carries them under the dark earth.
Some drown and die under the myriad waves
when a hurricane slams across the blue salt water
cracking their cargo ship. Others rope a noose
around their wretched necks and choose to die,
abandoning the sun of day. A thousand black spirits
waylay man with unending grief and suffering.
If you listen to my counsel, you won't want
the good things of life; nor batter your heart
by torturing your skull with cold remorse.

Life and Death

Later we will have a long time to lie dead
yet the few years we have now we live badly.

Remembrance of the Dead

If we were sensible we would not spend
more than a day of sorrow for the dead.

On Matrimony

Man gets nothing brighter than a kind wife
and nothing more chilling than a bad hag.

Brevity of Life[*]

One verse by the blind poet of Chios is indelible:
"The life of man is like a summer's leaf."
Yet few who hear these words take them into their heart,
for hope is rooted in every youthful soul,
the lovely flower of youth grows tall with color,
life will have no end,
or there is no place for growing old, for death;
and while in health, no fear of foul disease.
Poor fools! in islands of illusion,
for men have but a day of youth and life.
You few who understand, know when death is near
the food you give your soul must be supreme.

---

[*] Ascribed by Edmonds to Semonides. The "blind poet" is Homer.

Terpandros

Traditionally regarded as the first to make the choral lyric a developed art form, Terpandros was a fellow countryman of Alkaios and Sappho. But he was earlier by about a generation (his period of activity was the middle of the seventh century BCE) and seems to have worked chiefly at Sparta, where he only briefly preceded Alkman. He is credited with increasing the strings of the lyre from four to seven. No fragments survive whose authenticity is uncontested.

Furthermore, Pindar claims that Terpandros was the inventor of skolia (drinking) songs.

Music was first established in Sparta by Terpandros.

PLUTARCH, *On Music*

The Spartans were fighting among themselves and sent to Lesbos for the musician Terpandros; he came and made their minds tranquil and stopped the quarrel. After that whenever the Spartans listened to a musician, they would say, "He is not the equal of the poet of Lesbos."

Suda Lexicon

Hymn to Zeus

Zeus, inceptor of all,
of all things the commander,
Zeus, I bring you this gift:
the beginning of song.

To Apollo and the Muses

Let us pour a libation
to the Muses, daughters
of Memory, and to Leto's
son, their lord Apollo.

Sparta

The Muse sings brilliantly and
spears of young men flower.
Justice, defender of brave works,
goes down the street of light.

ALKMAN

The first fully visible representative of the choral ode lived at Sparta, and was active probably during the middle of the seventh century BCE. It is possible that he was (like several other poets of his time) brought in from the East—in Alkman's case, from Sardis in Lydia (Asia Minor).

His works were arranged in six books. They included *partheneia*, hymns and *prooimia* (hexameter preludes to recitations of epic poetry). His language is strongly Doric, with Aiolic and Homeric influences.

Alkman in his fragments seems a poet of wayward and playful sensitivity. The long and difficult fragment of a *partheneion* ("Song for a Choir of Virgins") illustrates this sensitivity in the vivid, glancing personal references, while "Rest" and "Lakonian Wine" may serve to show its range in nature and conviviality.

> Do not judge the man by the gravestone. The tomb you
> see is small but it holds the bones of a great man. For
> know that this is Alkman, supreme artist of the Lakonian
> lyre, who commanded the nine Muses. And twin conti-
> nents dispute whether he is of Lydia or Lakonia, for the
> mothers of a singer are many.
>
> ANTIPATROS OF THESSALONIKE

Ars Poetica

I know the tunes
of every bird,

but I, Alkman, found my words and song
in the tongue
of the strident partridge.

Rest

Now chasms and mountain summits are asleep,
and sierra slopes and ravines;

creeping things nourished by the dark earth,
hillside beasts and generations of bees,
monsters in the depths of the purple brine,
all lie asleep,
and also tribes   of flying birds.

On the Feats of a Young Girl

Often at night along the mountain tops,
when gods are reveling by torch light,
you came carrying a great jar
like one shepherds use but of heavy gold.
You filled the jar with milk
drawn from a lioness, and made a great cheese
unbroken and gleaming white.

On the Worm

The dappled worm is the murderer
within the eye of blooming vines.

In Mythology

Dew, a child of moon and air,
causes the deergrass to grow.

Song for a Choir of Virgins*

THE WHOLE CHOIR
There is a vengeance from the gods,
but happy is the man who weaves
the fabric of his days with peace,
and without tears.

AGIDO'S HALF-CHOIR
But I sing
of Agido's light. I see her

---

* The choir consists of ten virgins. The half-choirs speak in the first person
singular, in friendly rivalry, each praising its own half-choir leaders.

like the sun who shines on us
by order of Agido.

HAGESICHORA'S HALF-CHOIR
Our splendid
leader will not have us praise
or abuse her, for her brilliance
is as if among a herd of cattle
one had set a champion racehorse,
sinewy, strong, with thunder-ringing hooves,
a creature from a dream with wings.
Do you see? The horse is Venetian,
and the mane of our cousin
Hagesichora is a blossom
of the purest gold,
and below is her silver face.
Can I tell you this; more clearly?
There you have Hagesichora.
In beauty she may be second to Agido
but she will run like a
Skythian horse against a Lydian racer.
For as we carry Orthria's plow
so the Pleiades of dawn will rise
and strive against us
like the burning star of Sirios
through the ambrosial night.

AGIDO'S HALF-CHOIR
All our wealth of purple dye
or the dappled snake of full gold
about our wrist or our Lydian
wimple that is the sweet glory
of all these tender-eyed women,
no, nothing will keep them off.
Not Nanno's soft braids,
nor Areta's godlike beauty,
neither Thylakis nor Kleësisera.

HAGESICHORA'S HALF-CHOIR

You need not go to Ainesimbrota
and say: let Astaphis be mine,
have Philylla look my way,
and Damareta and darling Ianthemis.
For Hagesichora is our saviour.
Is Hagesichora of the lovely
ankles not right here with us?

AGIDO'S HALF-CHOIR

Yes, she waits by our Agido,
and commends our ceremonies.
O gods, receive our prayers,
for you determine everything
accomplished. My choir leader,
I tell you I a girl shrieked
in vain like an owl
from the roof tops.

HAGESICHORA'S HALF-CHOIR

But my great wish
is to please the Lady of the Dawn
who has healed our sore wounds.
Only Hagesichora could give
her women the peace they desired.

THE WHOLE CHOIR

A great chariot simply follows
the course of its trace-horse;
in a vessel all must swiftly
heed the shouting of the helmsman,
so our combined choir may not
sing more sweetly than the Sirens—
for they are gods—but how we sang,
we ten women with even one away!
And her song is like a swan
by the Xanthos river, and she
with the splendor of her blond hair.

Supplication

The girls fell to their knees, helpless—
like small birds under a hovering hawk.

Home of the North Wind

The Rhipé mountain flowering with forests
is the breast of black-flowing night.

To the Dioskouroi

Kastor and noble Polydeukes, you trainers
of swift stallions, are extraordinary horsemen.

To Hera

I pray to you, Hera,
and bring you as my offering
a delicate garland of marigold
and galingale.

On the Poet Alkman

He is no boorish farmer or
a clumsy pigkeeper or even
a sheep-chaser. He was not born
in Thessaly or Erysiche
but in Sardis on the high hills.

On a Poet

Aphrodite commands and love rains
upon my body and melts my heart

for Megalostrata to whom the sweet
Muse gave the gift of poetry.
O happy woman of the goldenrod hair!

Alkman's Supper

Get him that enormous caldron on the tripod
so he can bloat his stomach with every food.

It is cool but soon will boil with good soup
which gobbler Alkman likes sparkling hot,
especially in the cold season of the solstice.
The glutton Alkman abstains from fancy dishes
but like the demos eats a plain massive meal.

Wedding Feast

Seven couches and as many tables
spread with poppy cakes and linseed and
sesame, and among the wooden flagons
were honey cakes for the young.

The Four Seasons

Three seasons were created: summer
and winter and a third in autumn,
and even a fourth—the spring—
when the fields are heavy with crops
and a glutton still goes hungry.

Lakonian Wine

I know the wine from the Five Hills,
wine from Oinos or Denthiades
or Karystos or wine of Onogla
or Stathmi—unboiled, unfired wines
of fine aroma.

On the Kalcha Flower

She wears a gold chain
made from slender petals
of purple kalcha flowers.

The Journey

Narrow is our way of life
and necessity is pitiless.

On Tantalos

The guilty man sat
among pleasant things under a hanging rock,
and from his chair he looked
and then the vision faded.

Aphrodite

You are from the beautiful island Kypros
and from the sea-surrounded city Paphos.

Wandering Love

It is not Aphrodite but riotous Eros who is
playing like a child,
scuttling down across the tips of meadow ferns.
Please, do not crush them.

To the Moon Goddess

I am your servant, Artemis.

You draw your long bow at night,
clothed in the skins of wild beasts.

Now hear our beautiful singing.

I Am Old

Women of honey-sweet voices, my limbs are weak.
They will not bear me. I wish, ah, I wish I were
a carefree kingfisher flying over flowering foam
with the halcyons—sea-blue holy birds of spring.

Man's Lessons

Experience and suffering
are the mother of wisdom.

On His Poetry

Muse of the round sky, daughter of Zeus,
I sing my poems loud and clear to you.

Windflower

Bright-shining.

Calm Sea

The calm sea falls dumbly
on the shore
among a tangle of seaweed.

ALKAIOS

Alkaios' poetry is deeply involved in his political vicissitudes. The greater part of his life was spent in fighting reform movements which shook the established aristocracy of his native island Lesbos. He was born around 630 BCE. Some twenty years later the reigning tyrant, Melanchros, was overthrown by Pittakos and the brothers of Alkaios. Alkaios was for a time involved in the alliance with Pittakos, and even fought with him against the Athenians at Sigeion (near Troy). But a break came, and Pittakos allied himself with Myrsilos to govern Mytilene while Alkaios went into exile at Pyrrha (another town on Lesbos). At the death of Myrsilos, Alkaios returned home but was soon in exile again, this time apparently traveling widely, as far as Egypt. (His brother served in the army of Babylon under Nebuchadnezzar, in campaigns which led to the capture of Jerusalem, 597 BCE.) Some time after 590 BCE Pittakos forgave Alkaios, and the latter probably returned home.

Alkaios' works consisted of at least ten books, chiefly monodic. Hymns, political, erotic and sympotic poems predominate. He wrote in the Aiolic dialect, in a direct and emphatic style.

In his political poems Alkaios shows considerable similarity to Theognis. Both were hard-core aristocrats, convinced of the superiority of their class and cause, identifying private values with public right. (Alkaios seems to have gone so far as to support revolution against the established government.)

The influence of Alkaios is probably most seen in three places: the appropriations of Alkaios' forms and subjects by Horace; the recurrent metaphor (in poetry and elsewhere) of the "ship of state"; and the convivial poem (compare "Winter Evening" with Horace, *Odes 1.9,* and Milton, Sonnet XX).

> Alkaios is rightly awarded the golden quill in that part of his work where he assails tyrants; his ethical value is also great; his style is concise, magnificent, exact, very much like Homer's; but he stoops to humor and love when better suited for higher themes.
>
> QUINTILIAN

Instant

I already hear the flowering spring.

Prayer to the Constellation Dioskouroi,
Patron Deities of Mariners

Come with me now and leave the land of
Pelops, mighty sons of Zeus and Leda,
and in kindness spread your light on us,
Kastor and Polydeukes.

You who wander above the long earth
and over all the seas on swift horses,
easily delivering mariners
from pitiful death,

fly to the masthead of our swift ship,
and gazing over foremast and forestays,
light a clear path through the midnight gloom
for our black vessel.

Winter Evening

Zeus rumbles and a mammoth winter of snow
pours from the sky; agile rivers are ice.

Damn the winter cold! Pile up the burning logs
and water the great flagons of red wine;
place feather pillows by your head, and drink.

Let us not brood about hard times. Bakchos,
our solace is in you and your red wines:
our medicine of grape. Drink deeply, drink.

Summer Star

Wash your gullet with wine for the Dog Star returns
with the heat of summer searing a thirsting earth.
Cicadas cry softly under high leaves, and pour down
shrill song incessantly from under their wings.
The artichoke blooms, and women are warm and wanton—

but men turn lean and limp for the burning Dog Star
parches their brains and knees.

Why Wait for the Lighting of the Lamps?

Let us drink. Why wait for the lighting of the lamps?
Night is a hair's breadth away. Take down the great goblets
from the shelf, dear friend, for the son of Semele and Zeus
gave us wine to forget our pains. Mix two parts water, one
    wine,
and let us empty the dripping cups—urgently.

Drink, Song and Ships

Why water more wine in the great bowl?
Why do you drown your gullet in grape?
I cannot let you spill out your life
on song and drink. Let us go to sea,

and not let the wintry calm of morning
slip by as a drunken sleep. Had we
boarded at dawn, seized rudder and spun
the flapping crossjack into the wind,

we would be happy now, happy as swimming
in grape. But you draped a lazy arm
on my shoulder, saying: "Sir, a pillow,
your singing does not lead me to ships."

Costume

But let them hang braided garlands
of yellow dill around our necks,
and drape strands of redolent myrrh
across our breasts.

On His Brother's Homecoming

You have come home from the ends of the earth,
Antimenidas, my dear brother; come
with a gold and ivory handle to your sword.

You fought alongside the Babylonians
and your prowess saved them from annihilation
when you battled and cut down a warrior giant
who was almost eight feet tall.

The Lyre

Daughter of the rock and the gray sea,
you fill all hearts
with triumph, tortoise shell of the sea.

Birds

What birds are these
wildgeese—flying from precincts where the earth
and oceans end—
with their enormous wings and speckled throats?

On Money

Aristodemos wasn't lying
when he said one day in Sparta,
"Money is the man; and a poor man
can be neither good nor honorable."

To the River Hebros

Hebros, most beautiful river near Ainos,
you carry a shining bath of Thracian foam
out into the purple sea. And many women
stand near you,

and with soft hands rub oil on the smooth flesh
of their beautiful thighs. And they pour
your water over themselves like a sooth-
ing unguent.

Helen and Thetis

Helen, your sinful deeds brought a bitter end
to Priam and his lovely children. They say

because of you holy Ilium was destroyed
by climbing fire.

But the son of Aiakos did not find such a wife
when he summoned the blessed gods to his wedding
and took the delicate sea nymph Thetis from
the watery palace

of Nereus, bringing her to the mountain cave
of the centaur Cheiron. There, the love of Peleus
for his sea-nymph led him to lie naked with
the untouched virgin,

and within the year she bore a son, Achilles;
bravest demigod and splendid driver of
tawny stallions. But for Helen, Ilium and
her people were destroyed.

*Hymn to Apollo**

Our king Apollo, O child of mighty Zeus,
when you were born your father gave you
a gold headband and a lyre of tortoise shell,
and more: a chariot drawn by swans. You were
to go to Delphi and the Kastalian springs
whose waters are the gift of broad Kephissos,
and there deliver justice to the Hellenes
through the oracles. But when you seized the reins,

you made the swans sail north to the distant land
of the Hyperboreans, and though the Delphians
begged you to return—with paeans of flutes
and circles of women dancing about the tripod—

Apollo, you remained to rule that people
through the long year. Came the season when the tripod
rings loud and clear in Delphi, you turned the swans
to Parnassos. It was high noon of summer

---

* Text is derived from a paraphrase of Alkaios' poem.

when you glided back from the far northlands;
swallows and nightingales were singing; cicadas
also sang about you; silver brooks poured down
from Kastalia, and the great river Kephissos

threw blue-foaming waves into the bright wind, yes,
even the waters knew a god was coming home.

The People's Sickness

Poverty, our painful and uncontrolled disease,
you maim great peoples with your sister Helplessness.

A Woman*

Bad,
every misery and disaster I've known, a woman

with a home
of shameful death,

incurable decrepitude coming on
and madness in the terrorized heart of the stag,

out of his mind
and ruined.

Things of War

The great house glitters with bronze. War has patterned
the roof with shining helmets,
their horsehair plumes waving in wind, headdress
of fighting men. And pegs
are concealed under bright greaves of brass
that block the iron-tipped arrows. Many
fresh-linen corslets are hanging and hollow shields
are heaped about the floor,
and standing in rows are swords of Chalkidian steel,
belt-knives and warriors' kilts.

* Very fragmentary text but not reconstructed.

We cannot forget our arms and armor when soon
our dreadful duties begin.

Walls and the City

Not homes with beautiful roofs,
nor walls of permanent stone,
nor canals and piers for ships

make the city—but men of strength.

Not stone and timber, nor skill
of carpenter—but men brave
who will handle sword and spear.

With these you have city and walls.

Hypocrisy

Father Zeus, in our worst moment of hardship,
the Lydians selflessly gave us two thousand
staters, and gave us hope that we might re-enter
our sacred city
of Mytilene. There we were only strangers,
but in our own homeland the cunning fox
made honeyed speeches for the blackmail gold,
and then betrayed us.

On Premature Political Activity

It is late, for the harvest is in.
Before, we hoped that the full vines
would bring a plenitude of fine grapes,
but the clusters are slow
to ripen and the landlords
picked unripe bunches from the branch.
We have many grapes now—green and sour.

On the Tyrant Pittakos

One and all,
you have proclaimed Pittakos, the lowborn,
to be tyrant of your lifeless and doomed
land. Moreover, you deafen him with praise.

A Nation at Sea

I can't tell you which way the gale has turned
for waves crash in from west and east, and we
are tossed and driven between, our black ship
laboring under the giant storm.

The sea washes across the decks and maststep
and dark daylight already shows through long rents
in the sails. Even the halyards slacken as
windward waves coil above the hull.

What sore labor to bale the water we've shipped!
Let us raise bulwarks and ride out the storm,
heeding my words: "Let each man now be famous."
Yet base cowards betray the state.

To the Mytilenians

The local tyrant
rants and blusters and you are silenced
like a school of frightened neophytes
confronting the dead in holy rituals.

But I tell you, O citizens of Lesbos,
rise up and quench the smoldering logs
before their flames climb and consume you all
in total fire!

Earthquake

The tyrant's craze for absolute power will soon
demolish his country. Already the earth trembles.

To the Baseborn Tyrant

I say this to him too: he is a strident
lute who would like to be heard at a party
of the well-born people of Lesbos. Better
had he chosen to drink with the filthy herd.
He married a daughter from the ancient
race of Atreus. Now let him offend our people
as he did the former tyrant Myrsilos
until the Wargod makes us revolt. We must
forget our anger and cease these pitiful
clashes between brothers. Only a god
could have maddened our people into war
and so give Pittakos his bit of glory.

To His Friend Melanippos

Drink and be drunk with me, Melanippos.
Do you think when you have crossed the great fuming river,
you will ever return from Hell to see the clean
bright light of the sun? Do not strive for wild hopes.

Even the son of Aiolos, King Sisyphos, wisest of men,
thought he had eluded death. But for all his brains
Fate made him recross Acheron, and the son of Kronos
assigned him a terrible trial below the dark earth.

Come, I beg you not to brood about these hopeless
matters while we are young. We will suffer what must
be suffered. When the wind is waiting in the north,
a good captain will not swing into the open sea.

Sappho*

Sappho was the compatriot and approximate contemporary of Al-
kaios. Her home on Lesbos was at Mytilene. She came of a noble
family. The names of some of her family have been preserved:
Skamandronymos was her father, Kleïs her mother. Her husband
was Kerkylas of Andros, and she named her daughter Kleïs for her
mother. One of her brothers was Charaxos. Political changes led to·
her exile (with other members of the aristocracy) around 600 BCE.
She spent some time in Sicily before she was allowed to return home.

Her chief concerns, apparently, were with personal relation-
ships, and these above all among a circle of young women of the up-
per class. Among those whom she loved were Atthis and Anaktoria.
We hear also the names of several rivals: Andromeda and Gorgo.
Fittingly, the goddess who she affectionately worshiped was Afroditi
(Aphrodite). Indeed the connection between life and religion was so
close for Sappho that she might have repeated the words of Eranna
in Rilke's poem:

> . . . denn die schöne Göttin in der Mitte
> ihrer Mythen glüht und lebt mein Leben.
> [For the fair goddess amid her myths glows
>   and lives my life]

The story that Sappho loved a certain Phaon and died by leap-
ing from the Leukadian rock for love of him resulted probably from
a misunderstanding of a ritual dirge for the vegetation god Phaon.

In appearance she is said to have been small and dark.

The works of Sappho were arranged in seven books, the seventh
comprising wedding songs. They survived into Byzantine times, but
were then probably destroyed by Christian intolerance.

There seems to be a slight difference in style between some
works of Sappho which may have been written for a more pub-
lic audience (e.g., the "Wedding of Andromache and Hektor") and
the poems which are more private and personal in character. The

---

* A more complete introduction to Sappho and her poetry, with
  notes and sources, can be found below, beginning on p. 249.

former show an inclination to admit Homeric forms and prosody; the latter are purely in the Aiolic dialect. The intense power of her simple and euphonious style has been remarked upon from the ancient critics until now.

In her outlook Sappho is notable, among other things, for her interpretation of love: unlike many of the poets of the Lyric Age, she regarded love not as a dangerous obsession, but as fulfillment. And she elevated love into the criterion of value ("Supreme Sight on the Black Earth").

Her influence on later literature, whether in style or subject, has been considerable. One could start with the following: Catullus Ll, Ovid's Saphho Phanoni in the Heroides, plays by Grillparzer and Durrell, Rilke's Saphho poems in Neue Gedichte, and the poems of H.D.

> Some say nine Muses—but count again.
> Behold the tenth: Sappho of Lesbos.
>
> PLATO

> A contemporary of Pittakos and Alkaios was Sappho—a marvel. In all the centuries since history began we know of no women who in any true sense can be said to rival her as a poet.
>
> STRABON, *Geography*

> O violet-haired, holy,
> honeysmiling Sappho
>
> ALKAIOS (b. 620 BCE)

Prayer to Afroditi

On your dappled throne eternal Afroditi,
cunning daughter of Zeus,
I beg you, do not crush my heart
 with pain, O lady,

but come here now if ever before
you heard my voice from far away,
and yielding left your father's house
 of gold and came,

yoking birds to your chariot. Beautiful
quick sparrows whirring on beating wings
took you from heaven down to mid sky
    over the dark earth

and soon arrived. O blessed one,
on your deathless face a smile,
you asked me what I am suffering
    and why I call you,

what I want most to happen in
my crazy heart. "Whom shall I persuade
again to take you into her love? Who,
    O Psapfo, wrongs you?

If she runs away, soon she will pursue.
If she scorns gifts, now she will bribe.
If she doesn't love, soon she will love
    even unwillingly."

Come to me now and loosen me
from blunt agony. Labor
and fill my heart with fire. Stand by me
    and be my ally.

    *1**

Afroditi of the Flowers at Knossos

Leave Kriti and come here to this holy
temple with your graceful grove
of apple trees and altars smoking
    with frankincense.

Icy water babbles through apple branches
and roses leave shadow on the ground
and bright shaking leaves pour down
    profound sleep.

---

* The numbers indicate the source of the poem. See
  "Sappho: An Introduction," below.

Here is a meadow where horses graze
amid wild blossoms of the spring and soft winds
   blow aroma

of honey. Afroditi, take the nectar
and delicately pour it into gold
wine cups and mingle joy with
   our celebration.

   2. [2a]

Moon and Women

The moon appeared in her fullness
and women took their place around the altar

   154

Dancers at a Kritan Altar

Kritan women once danced supplely
around a beautiful altar with light feet,

crushing the soft flowers of grass.

   16 Incert

In Time of Storm

Brightness

and with good luck
we will reach the harbor
and black earth

We sailors have no will
in big blasts of wind,
hoping for dry land

and to sail
our cargo
flowing about

Many
labors
until dry land

20

To Lady Hera

Be near me Lady Hera while I pray
for your graceful form to appear,
to which the sons of Atreus prayed,
those dazzling kings

who did bountiful deeds,
first at Troy, then on the sea,
but sailing the road to this island,
they could not reach it

till they called on you and Zeus god of suppliants,
and Dionysos lovely son of Thyoni.
Now be gentle and help me too
as in old days,

holy and beautiful
virgin
in circles

to sail safely
to the shrine

17

Invitation

An invitation for one
not all
to come to a feast

for Hera accomplishing
as long
as
I am alive

9

Sacrifice

To you I will pour wine

over flesh of a white goat

40, Incert 13

Death of Adonis

Afroditi, delicate Adonis is dying.
What should we do?
Virgins, beat your breasts
and tear your garments.

140

Adonis Gone

O for Adonis!

168

To Afroditi

O gold-crowned Afroditi,
if only I could win this lot!

33

Afroditi

Queen
to you
a horse

87e,f Voigt

Afroditi to Psapfo

Both you and my servant Eros

159

Days of Harshness

Quiet
Zeus
of the goatskin shield

and Kythereia
I pray

holding a good heart,
and if ever

like other days when you left Kypros,
hear my prayer

and come
to my
severities

86

Artemis on Solitary Mountains

Gold-haired Phoebus borne by Koios's daughter
after she joined with Kronos's son Zeus god of high clouds
    and high name.
Artemis swore the great oath of the gods to Zeus:
"By your head, I shall always be a virgin
untamed hunting on peaks of solitary mountains.
Come, grant me this grace!"
So she spoke. Then the father of the blessed gods
nodded consent. Now gods and mortals
call her by her thrilling eponym, *The Virgin Deer Hunter.*
Eros, loosener of limbs, never comes near her

44a

Artemis

blame
delicate
Artemis

84 *Voigt*

Evening Star

Hesperos, you bring home all the bright dawn
scattered,
bring home the sheep,
bring home the goat, bring the child home
to her mother.

    104a

Hesperos

Of all stars the most beautiful

    104b

Moon

Stars around the beautiful moon
conceal their luminous form
when in her fullness she shines
   on the earth

in silver

    34

Earth

Earth is embroidered
with rainbow-colored garlands

    168C

Nightingale

Nightingale with your lovely voice
you are the herald of spring

    136

Cicada

Flaming summer
charms the earth with its own fluting,

and under leaves
the cicada scrapes its tiny wings together
and incessantly
pours out full shrill song

101a

Doves Playing Dead

When their souls grew cold they dropped
their wings to their sides

42

Of Gello Who Died Young, Whose Ghost Haunts Little Children

She was even fonder
of children than Gello

178

World

I could not hope
to touch the sky
with my two arms

52

Eos

Lady Dawn

157

Dawn

Suddenly
Dawn in gold sandals

123

Hair Yellower than Torch Flame

My mother used to say

in her youth
it was a great ornament to wear
a purple ribbon

looped in her hair. But a girl
with hair yellower than torch flame
need wear just

a wreath of blooming
flowers, but lately maybe
a colorful headband

from Sardis
or some Ionian city

    98a

   Time of Youth

You will
remember
we did these things
in our youth,

many and beautiful things.

In the city
for us the harsh

We live
opposite

a daring
person

stone foundation
thin-voiced

     24a,b,c

   Of a Young Lover

When I was young I wove garlands

    125

My Daughter

I have a beautiful child like gold flowers
in form. I would not trade
my darling Kleis for all Lydia or lovely . . .

132

Wildflowers

A very tender girl picking wildflowers

122

The Virgin

Like a sweet apple reddening on a high branch,
on the tip of the topmost branch and forgotten
by the apple pickers—no, beyond their reach.

Like a hyacinth in the mountains that shepherd men
trample down with their feet, and on the earth
the purple flower

105a,c

Girl

A sweet-voiced girl

153

Remorse

Do I still long for my virginity?

107

Words with Virginity

Virginity, virginity, where have you gone, leaving me
abandoned?
No longer will I come to you. No longer will I come.

114

The Lyre Speaks

Tell of the bride with beautiful feet
let Artemis

the violet-robed daughter of Zeus
let the violet-robed put aside her anger.

Come holy Graces and Pierian Muses
when songs are in the heart
listening to a clear song

the bridegroom   annoying   companions

her hair   placing the lyre

Dawn in gold sandals

103

Wedding of Andromache and Hektor

From Kypros
a herald came
Idaos the swift-running Trojan messenger

telling of the wedding's imperishable fame in all Asia:
"Hektor and his companions are bringing dancing-eyed
delicate Andromache on ships over the salt sea
from holy Thibai and Plakia's flowing water
along with many gold bracelets and purple
fragrant clothes, exquisite adornments
and countless silver cups and ivory."

He spoke, and Hektor's dear father sprang to his feet
and news spread to friends throughout the spacious city.
Instantly the sons of Ilos, founder of Troy;
yoked mules to carriages with smooth-running wheels,
and a whole crowd of women and slender-ankled virgins
    climbed aboard.
The daughters of Priamos came in their own carts,
and young unmarried men yoked stallions to chariots
in great spirit,

charioteers
    moved like gods
    holy all together
and set out   for Ilion
in a confusion of sweet-voiced flutes and kithara
and small crashing castanets,
and young virgins sang a loud heavenly song
whose amazing echo pierced the ether of the sky.
Everywhere in the streets
were bowls and cups.
Myrrh and cassia and frankincense rode on the wind.
Old women shouted in happiness
and all the men sang out with thrilling force,
calling on far-shooting Paean Apollo nimble on the lyre
and sang a hymn to godlike Hektor and Andromache.

    44

Walking to a Wedding

Yes you who were a tender child
come sing these things
talk to us and give us
   your grace

We are walking to a wedding, and surely
you know too, but quickly as you can
send the young virgins away. May gods
   have

Yet for men road to
   great Olympos

    27

Song to the Groom

What are you like, lovely bridegroom?
You are most like a slender sapling.

    115

Song for the Bride

O bridegroom, there is no other woman now
 like her

   113

Lesbian Bride

O beautiful, O graceful girl

   108 Voigt

Guarding the Bride

Take care of her
O bridegrooms
O kings of cities!

   161

Chamber

Room
the bride with her beautiful feet
now
for me

   103B Voigt

Hermis at a Wedding

There a bowl of ambrosia
was mixed, and Hermis
took the jug and poured wine for the gods
and then they all
held out cups and poured
libations and prayed for all blessings
for the groom.

   141a,b

Fragments

Carry

Arheanassa

once

in lovely

heard

virgins

of the springs

Voigt 103Ca,b

To Hymen, Wedding God

High! Raise the roof!
O Hymen.
Lift it up, carpenters!
O Hymen.
The bridegroom is coming, the equal of Aris,
O Hymen.
taller than a giant!
O Hymen!

111

Song to Groom and Bride

Happy groom, your marriage you prayed for
has happened. You have the virgin bride
of your prayer.

You the bride are a form of grace,
your eyes honey.
Desire rains on your exquisite face.

Afroditi has honored you exceedingly

112

Night Song

Night

Virgins
will all night long sing
of the love between you and your bride
in her violet robe.

Wake and call out young men
of your age,
and tonight we shall sleep less than
the bright-voiced nightingale

30

*A Guard Outside the Bridal Chamber Who
Keeps the Bride's Friends from Rescuing Her*

The doorkeeper's feet are seven fathoms long.
It took five oxhides for his sandals
and ten shoemakers to cobble them together.

110

End of a Party

Beautiful
he throws peace into frenzy
and exhaustion and dumbs the mind.
Sitting

But come, my friends.
Soon daybreak.

43

Seizure

To me he seems equal to gods,
that man who sits facing you
and hears you near as you speak
    softly and laugh

in a sweet echo that jolts
the heart in my ribs. Now
when I look at you a moment
    my voice is empty

and can say nothing as my tongue
cracks and slender fire races
under my skin. My eyes are dead
    to light, my ears

pound, sweat pours from me.
I convulse greener than grass
and feel my mind slip as I go
    close to death,

yet I must suffer all, even poor

31

Alone

The moon has set and
and the Pleiades. Middle
of the night, time spins
away and I lie alone.

168b

Emptiness

Never have I found you more repulsive,
    O Irana.

91

Eros

Love shook my heart like wind
on a mountain punishing oak trees.

47

Love

Eros came out of heaven,
dressed in a purple cape

54

Supreme Sight on the Black Earth

Some say cavalry and others claim
infantry or a fleet of long oars
is the supreme sight on the black earth.
   I say it is

the one you love. And easily proved.
Didn't Helen, who far surpassed
all in beauty, desert the best of men
   her husband and king

and sail off to Troy and forget
her children and dear parents? Merely
love's gaze made her bend
   and led her

from her path.
These tales
remind me now of Anaktoria
   who is gone.

I would rather see her supple step
and motion of light on her face
than chariots of the Lydians or ranks
   of foot soldiers in bronze.

Now this is impossible
yet among the living I pray for a share

and unexpectedly

16

To Eros

You burn us

38

Absence

I long and yearn for

36

Goatherd

Goatherd

a rose

longing

sweat

74a,b,c Voigt

Shall I?

I don't know what to do.
Two thoughts in me.

51

Pleasure

On a soft pillow
I will lay down my limbs

46

Encounter

Finding something
desires
Carry out a plan
suddenly
I call out from my heart.
for all you want to win
fight for me
persuaded by a voluptuous woman
as you know very well

60

Homecoming

You came and I went mad about you.
You cooled my mind burning with longing.

48

Desire

Nor
desire
but together
a flower
desire
I was happy

78

A God

And this

disastrous
god

I swear did not love
but now because

and the cause neither
nothing much

67a

Absent

Away
from her

yet she became
like gods

sinful Andromeda
a blessed one

did not hold back
her insolence

sons of Tyndareus
gracious

no longer innocent
Megara

68a

Of Those Unwilling to Take the Bitter with the Sweet

I care for neither honey
nor the honey bee

146

Endure

Bring about?

I want
to hang on
she said

76

I Shall

As long as you want to

45

To a Friend Gone, Remember

Honestly I wish I were dead.
When she left me she wept

profusely and told me,
"Oh how we've suffered in all this.
Psapfo, I swear I go unwillingly."

And I answered her,
"Be happy, go and remember me,
you know how we worshiped you.

But if not, I want
to remind you
of beautiful days we shared,

how you put on wreaths of violets,
roses and crocuses,
at my side

and tied garlands
made of flowers
round your tender throat,

and with sweet myrrh oil
worthy of a queen
you anointed your limbs

and on soft beds
delicate you would satisfy
your longing

and how there was no
holy shrine
where we were absent,

no grove
no dance
no sound"

94

Beauty in a Man

A man who is beautiful is beautiful to see
but a good man at once takes on beauty.

50

Atthis

I loved you Atthis once long ago.

To me you seemed a little child and graceless.

49

Her Friends

For you the beautiful ones my thought
   is unchangeable

    41

Sweetbitter

Eros loosener of limbs once again trembles me,
a sweetbitter beast irrepressibly creeping in.

    130

Return, Gongyla

A deed
your lovely face

if not, winter
and no pain

I bid you, Abanthis,
take up the lyre
and sing of Gongyla as again desire
floats around you

the beautiful. When you saw her dress
it excited you. I'm happy.
The Kypros-born once
blamed me

for praying
this word:
I want

    22

You Can Free Me

I hoped for love

When I look at you face to face
not even Hermioni

seems to be your equal.
I compare you to blond Helen

among mortal women.
Know that you can free me
from every care,

and stay awake all night long
on dewy riverbanks

23

Kydro

I'm waiting
to offer you a good thing
in sacrifices

but going there
we know
is labor

later toward
Kydro say
I am coming

19

You in Sardis

In Sardis
her thoughts turn constantly to us here,

to you like a goddess. She was happiest
in your song.

Now she shines among Lydian women
as after sunset
the rosy-fingered moon

surpasses all the stars, and her light reaches
equally across the salt sea
and over meadows steeped in flowers.

Lucent dew pours out profusely
on roses blooming,
on frail starflowers and florid honey clover.

But wandering back and forth she remembers
gentle Atthis and in pain
a heavy yearning consumes her

but to go there
the mind
endlessly is singing

96

Afroditi and Desire

It is not easy for us to equal
the goddesses
in beauty of form of Adonis

desire
and
Afroditi

poured nectar from
a gold cup
With hands Persuasion

to the Geraistion shrine
lovers
of no one

I shall enter desire

96b

A Handsome Man

Stand and face me, my love,
and scatter the grace in your eyes.

138

Myths

All would
say
that my tongue
tells tales

and for a greater
man

18

Paralysis

Sweet mother, now I cannot work the loom.
Sleek Afroditi broke me with longing for a boy.

102

Behind a Laurel Tree

You lay in wait
behind a laurel tree

and everything
was sweeter

women
wandering

I barely heard
darling soul

such as I now am
you came

beautiful
in your garments

62

Companions

For my companions,
now of these things I shall sing beautifully

160

Lito and Niobi

Lito and Niobi were deep friends

142

As Long as There Is Breath

You might wish
a little
to be carried off

Someone
sweeter
you also know

forgot

and someone would say
yes
I shall love as long as there is breath in me
and care
I say I have been a strong lover

hurt
bitter
and know this

no matter
I shall love

88, columns b,a

Return

I have flown to you like a child to her mother.

25 Incert

Fury

When anger is spreading through your chest
best to quiet your reckless barking tongue.

158

Abuse

Often
those
I treat well are just the ones
who most harm me
vainly

You I want
to suffer
In me
I know it

    26 (lines 1–5, 9–12)

Gorgo

By now they have had enough of Gorgo

    144

Andromeda

Andromeda has a beautiful exchange,

"Psapfo, why ignore Afroditi rich in blessings?"

    133a,b

Atthis Disappearing

At this, now the mere thought of me
is hateful and you fly off to Andromeda.

    131

Where Am I?

But you have forgotten me

or you love some man more than me

    129a,b

A Ring

Crazy woman
why are you bragging to me about a ring?

5a Incert

Madden

Don't madden
my mind

5b Incert

Delicate Girl

Delicate girl
once again
I wandered

5c Incert

Andromeda, What Now?

What farm girl dolled up in a farm dress
captivates your wits
not knowing how to pull her rags down to her ankles?

57

Hello and Goodbye

A hearty good day to the daughter of the house
of Polyanax

155

Mika

You have done wrong, Mika,
I won't allow you to

faithless you chose love in the house
of Penthilos

A sweet song
in honey voice
sings
clear nightingales
over dew fields

    71 Diehl

Alkaikos Speaks and Sapfo Responds

"I want to say something to you but shame
  prevents me."

"If you longed for the good or beautiful
  and your tongue were not concocting evil,
  shame would not cover your eyes.
  Rather you would speak about the just."

    137

In My Pain

My pain drips

May winds and sorrows carry off him
who blames me

    37

From Her Exile

For you Kleis I have no embroidered
headband and no idea
where to find one while the Mytilinian rules

These colorfully embroidered
headbands

these things of the children of Kleanax
In exile
memories terribly wasted away

    98b

Protect My Brother Haraxos

O Kypris and Nereids, I pray you
to sail my brother home unharmed
and let him accomplish all
   that is in his heart

and be released from former error
and carry joy to his friends
and bane to enemies and let no one
   bring us more grief.

Let him honor me his sister.
But black torment
   suffering for early days,

citizens accused.
Was it over millet seed?

Holy Kypris, put aside
old anger and free him from
   evil sorrow

    5

To My Brother Haraxos

By giving

good fame
beauty and nobility
to such friends
you sicken me with pain

Blame you? Swollen
Have your fill of them
For my thinking it is poorly done
and all night I understand baseness

Other
minds
the blessed

    3

To Afroditi about Her Brother's Lover

Blessed one

May he be released from his past wrongs
with luck
now in harbor

Kypris, may she feel your sharp needles
and may she Doriha not go on crowing
how he came back a second time
to his desired love.

15

Doriha

Doriha
commands them
not to come

she is arrogant
like young men
who are loved

7 Cam

Holy Tortoise Shell

Come holy lyre speak to me
and become a voice!

118 Cam

Some Honored Me

Some honored me by giving me
the secret of their works

32

Graces

Holy Graces with arms of roses,
come to me, daughters of Zeus

53

Singer

Towering is the Lesbian singer
compared to those in other lands

106

Graces and Muses

Come to me now tender Graces
and Muses with beautiful hair

128

The Muses

Muses come here again to me
leaving the gold house

127

Happiness

Wealth without virtue is no harmless neighbor
but by mixing both you are on the peak of joy.

148

Light

I cannot imagine in the future
any girl who looks on the light of the sun
will have your skill and wisdom.

56

A Swan's Egg Containing Kastor and Polydeukis

They say that Lida once found an egg
hidden and the color of hyacinth

166 Cam

Comparisons

Far sweeter in sound than a lyre
more golden than gold

far whiter than an egg

   f156, 167

A Swallow

O Irana, why is king Pandion's daughter
now a swallow waking me?

   135

Jason's Cloak

A mingling of all kinds of colors

   152

Robe

robe
colored with saffron

purple robe
cloak

garland crowns
beauty

Phrygian purple
rugs

   92

Chickpeas

And gold chickpeas grew on riverbanks

   143

Purple Handcloth

These purple handcloths
perfumed
she sent you from Phokaia
expensive gifts

101

Beauty of Her Friends

Mnasidika is more beautifully
shaped than soft Gyrinno

82a

On Going Bareheaded

Rebuff other ways
as quickly as you can

and you, Dika, with your soft hands take stems
of lovely anise and loop them in your locks.

The blessed Graces love to gaze at one in flowers
but turn their backs on one whose hair is bare.

81

Sandal

Colorful straps covered
her feet
in beautiful Lydian work

39

Garment

She was wrapped all around with a delicate
woven cloth

100

Dawn with Gold Arms

Go
so we can see
Lady Dawn
with gold arms.
Doom

> 6

Sleep

May you sleep
on your tender girlfriend's breasts

> 126

Black Sleep

When all night long
    sleep closes down

and on the eyes black sleep of night

> 149 and 151

In a Dream

In a dream I talked with you born in Kypros

> 134

Dream

O dream on black wings
you stray here when sleep

sweet god, I am in agony
to split all its power

for I expect not to share.
Nothing of the blessed gods

I would rather not be like this,
with trinkets

but may
I have them all

63

Innocence

I am not of a wounding spirit
rather I have a gentle heart

120

Clear Voiced

I will go
hear
harmony
beautiful dance choir
clear voiced
to all

70

Dew

Afroditi
soft-worded desires
hurl
holding
a seat

flourishing
lovely
dew

73*a*

A Face

Now in my
heart I
see clearly

a beautiful
face
shining back on me,

stained
with love

4

Old Man

Rich
like listening to
an old man

85 column b Voigt

Gods

Among gods
right off
the one
who sheds
no tears

139

Angry with Her Daughter when She Psapfo Was Dying

It is not right in a house serving the Muses
to have mourning. For us it is unbecoming.

150

Old Age

In pity
and
trembling

old age now
covers my flesh.
Yet there is chasing and floating

after a young woman.
Pick up your lyre
and sing to us

of one with violets
on her robe, especially
wandering

21

No Oblivion

Someone, I tell you, in another time,
will remember us.

147

To Hermis Who Guides the Dead

Gongyla

surely a sign
especially for children
who came here

I said, O master by the blessed
Afroditi I swear I take no pleasure
in being on the earth

but a longing seizes me to die
and see the dewy
lotus banks of the Aheron

95

To a Woman of No Education

When you lie dead no one will remember
or long for you later. You do not share the roses
of Pieria. Unseen here and in the house of Hades,
flown away, you will flitter among dim corpses.

55

Menelaos

They lie received in the black earth,
sons of Atreus,
released now from their agony.

27 Incert

Wish

Both distress and good health

My children, let me fly back
youth

18b,c Incert

Age and the Bed

Really, if you are my friend,
    choose a younger bed.
I can't bear to live with you
    when I am the older one

121

Afroditi to Psapfo

Andromeda
forgot

but Psapfo
I love you

In Kypros I am queen
for you a power

to all on whom sun blazes
glory everywhere;

even by the Aheron I am with you

65

Growing Old

Those lovely gifts of the fragrant-breasted Muses,
girls, seek them eagerly in thrilling song of the lyre.

My earlier delicate skin old age has grasped
and my black hair has become white,

my spirit turned heavy, my knees no longer
carry me nimble for dancing like a fawn.

About these things I groan. What can I do?
For a human not to grow old is impossible.

They say Dawn, dazzled by love, took Tithonos
in her rose arms to the utter end of the earth.

Once beautiful and young, time shoved him
into gray old age, husband of a deathless wife.

> *Cam 58b (lines 11–22)*
> *Martin West (TLS 6.24.05)*
> *A Cologne Papyrus translated by Willis Barnstone*
> *and William E. McCulloh*

Desire and Sun

Yet I love refinement and Eros got me
brightness and the beauty of the sun.

> *58c*

Death Is Evil

Death is evil. So the gods decided.
Otherwise they would die.

> *201 Aristotle,* Rhetoric *1398b*

Gold

Gold is indestructible.

> *204*
> *Scholiast on Pindar's* Pythian Odes *4.410c (2 153 Drachmann)*

ELEGIAC POEMS FROM THE GREEK ANTHOLOGY WRONGLY ATTRIBUTED TO SAPPHO

On Pelagon

Pelegon the fisherman. His father Meniskos left here
    his basket and oar, relics of a wretched life.

    D 159

On Timas

Here is the dust of Timas who unmarried
    was led into Persefoni's dark bedroom,
and when she died her girlfriends took sharp
    iron knives and cut off their soft hair.

    D 158

Solon

A member of the Athenian aristocracy, Solon had begun his poetic activity earlier than ca. 600 BCE. For it was at this time that he wrote an elegy to his fellow citizens urging them to the reconquest of Salamis. But the most notable part of his life, and the subject of a good deal of his surviving poetry, was his involvement in the Athenian Social Question. In the conflict between the landed grandees and the dispossessed peasants (many of whom had been enslaved through debt) Solon took a middle position. In 594–593 BCE he was elected as an Archon with extraordinary powers to carry out social and constitutional reforms in an effort to avoid civil war and revolution. Among other things, he abolished existing debts, established a council of four hundred as a counterweight to the aristocratic council of the Areiopagos and gave each class of the citizenry a certain voice in the political affairs of the country. After making his laws (and his name of course has since become a synonym for legislator), he bound the people to retain them unchanged for ten years, and went abroad for the duration. As one would expect, Solon displeased both sides by his moderation, and in fact the detente he had effected came to nothing in the end: Athens spent a good part of the sixth century under a tyranny based on the support of the commoners. However, even under the tyranny much of the substance of his reforms was retained, and the Solonian spirit, with its insight and discretion, prepared the way for the later brilliant and precarious forms of Athenian democracy.

The poetry of Solon, which constitutes the first Athenian literature, includes elegiac and iambic verse. The subject matter is political and moral, but also sometimes convivial and erotic.

> It seems that the three most democratic aspects of Solon's rule were: first and greatest, the prohibition of loans on the person; second, the right of redress for those who were wronged; third, the right of appeal to courts of law, which more than all else strengthened the people. Once master of the vote, the people became master of the constitution.

> ARISTOTLE, *Constitution of Athens*

He died in Kypros at the age of eighty. He left orders with
his family to have his bones taken to Salamis and there
burn them to ashes and scatter them over the soil.

DIOGENES LAERTIOS, *Life of Solon*

And when Kroisos (Croesus) stood on the pyre, in such
an evil moment, it is said that he remembered how truly
inspired was Solon's saying that no mortal is happy.

HERODOTOS, *Histories*

Apologia of His Rule

Where did I fail? When did I give up goals
for which I gathered my torn people together?
When the judgment of time descends on me,
call on my prime witness, Black Earth, supreme
excellent mother of the Olympian gods,
whose expanse was once pocked with mortgage stones,
which I dug out to free a soil in bondage.

Into our home, Athens, founded by the gods,
I brought back many sold unlawfully as slaves,
and throngs of debtors harried into exile,
drifting about so long in foreign lands
they could no longer use our Attic tongue;
here at home men who wore the shameful brand
of slavery and suffered the hideous moods
of brutal masters—all these I freed. Fusing
justice and power into an iron weapon,
I forced through every measure I had pledged.
I wrote the laws For good and bad alike,
and gave an upright posture to our courts.
Had someone else controlled the whip of power,
a bungler, a man of greed, he would not
have held the people in. Had I agreed
to do what satisfied opponents, or else
what their enemies planned in turn for them,
our dear city would be widowed of her men.
But I put myself on guard at every side,
spinning like a wolf among a pack of dogs.

Civil War in Attica

I know it, and sorrow lives in my heart
that the oldest land of Ionia is burning.

The Signs of Dictatorship

The power of hail and snow springs from a cloud,
and thunder from the fire of lightning.
Strong men destroy a city, and a tyrant
enslaves a people through their ignorance.
A ship once out of port is hard to capture:
know this now before it is too late.

To Phokos

(On his refusal to assume dictatorial
powers from which there is no retreat.)
If I have spared my country
by not descending into tyranny and unrelenting violence;
if I have not piled odious dung on my good name,
I am unashamed.
No, I contend that my policy
won far greater victories for the common person.

Indifference to Wealth

Vast silver, gold, wheatlands, horses, mules
are only equal to the wealth
of him whose belly, ribs and feet are warm,
who may be poor but enters love
with men or women when he comes upon
the proper season in his youth.
This is plenitude for a man. No one goes down
to Hades with fabulous belongings.
Even ransom will not spare him from repugnant
disease, evil old age and death.

Virtue among the Poor

Many malicious men are rich. Many good people
suffer through poverty. Yet who would trade
virtue for gold? While the name of virtue endures,
money drops from hand to hand, lasting little.

Solon before the Crowds in Athens

I am a herald from lovely Salamis. In place
of talk I bring a song, an ornament of words.

A City of Ten Thousand in Tears

May I meet death without tears. But let my death
bring sorrow and mourning to my friends.

Lesson in Citizenship

You must obey the law of the land,
whether you think it right or wrong.

The Erotic Man

In the tender flower of youth he loves a boy,
desiring his thighs and delicious mouth.

The Gods

The mind of the eternal gods
can not be seen by man.

Mortal Man

No mortal is happy, and all men on earth
who look upon the sun are wretched.

Ten Ages in the Life of Man

A boy who is still a child grows baby teeth
and loses them all in seven years.
When God makes him fourteen, the signs

of maturity begin to shine on his body.
In the third seven, limbs growing, chin bearded,
his skin acquires the color of manhood.
In the fourth age a man is at a peak in
strength—a sign in man of excellence.
The time is ripe in the fifth for a young man
to think of marriage and of offspring.
In the sixth the mind of man is trained in all
things; he doesn't try the impossible.
In the seventh and eighth, that is, fourteen years,
he speaks most eloquently in his life.
He can still do much in the ninth but his speech
and thought are discernibly less keen,
and if he makes the full measure of ten sevens,
when death comes, it will not come too soon.

MIMNERMOS

Mimnermoś was active around 600 BCE or some ten years later. He was a citizen of either Kolophon or Smyrna. The milieu of his poetry is that of the Anatolian Greek city, fighting against Oriental domination, but already under various sorts of Oriental influence, including that of intermarriage. Mimnermos' name is apparently itself Oriental. He is symptom and spokesman of the decadence of Ionia, enervated by despair and by pleasure.

His works included a Smyrneid (long poem on the history of Smyrna) and a collection of elegies probably addressed to Nanno (a flute-girl who accompanied the performance of his poems) and dealing in part with his love. In his erotic elegies Mimnermos is one of the ancestors of the later love-elegists of Alexandria and Rome.

> Mimnermos discovered the sweet sound and soft breath of iambic pentameter, after much suffering. He loved Nanno . . . reveled with Examyes and irritated the oppressive Hermobios and hostile Pherekles because he hated their verse.
>
> HERMESIANAX IN PHOTIOS, *Library*

> If as Mimnermos says, there is not joy without love and play, then you should live with love and play.
>
> HORACE, *Epistles*

Censure of Age

What good is life when golden love is gone?
Frankly, I would rather be dead than ignore
a girl's warm surrender, her soft arms in bed
at night, the lovely flower of youth that all women
and men desire!
When old age comes
a man feels feeble and ugly and crawls under
a crushing sorrow.

He loses the simple joy
of looking at the sun.
Children despise him.
He is repulsive to young women—in this sad
blind alley which God has made of old age.

Time

When a man's good hour is past
though he once shone among mortals
he is neither honored nor loved.
Not even his own children favor him.

Now

Be young, dear soul. Soon others will be men
and I being dead will be black earth.

A Pledge

Between us, dear friend,
let there always be truth,
most just of all things.

For the Golden Fleece

Jason went to the city of King Aietes
where the sun's swift rays are stored
in a gold chamber by the ocean's lips.

Refuge against Talk

Be happy in your own soul. Among pitiless townsmen
one will always abuse you, another speak praise.

A Warrior of the Lydian Wars

No man could match his strength or heroic heart,
so the elders told me who had seen him
cutting through the phalanx of massed Lydian cavalry,
swinging his ashwood spear on the plain

of Hermos. Pallas Athene could find no fault
with the stinging courage in his heart
when he plunged first-line into the bloody clash,
rushing through the rain of bitter shafts.
No man ever battled more bravely than he
when he darted forward like a ray of sun.

Helios at Night

The sun works every day and there's no rest
for him or for his horses once
the rose-fingered dawn leaves the ocean waters
and begins to scale the firmament.
For with night the sun is swept across the waves
in a hollow cup of gleaming gold,
a wondrous bed with wings, forged by Hephaistos.
It speeds him sleeping over salt foam
from the Hesperides to the Ethiopian desert.
There his fleet chariot and horses wait
till Dawn comes, early child of morning.

Expectation

Like fragile shoots in the polyflowered spring
growing quickly in amazing sun,
we love the blossom of youth for a brief season
knowing from the gods nothing of evil
or good. Yet near us loom black Keres, and
painful old age, or worse, death.
The fruit tree of our life ripens swiftly
like a morning sun. But our brilliance gone,
we are soon better dead than alive. Our heart
is torn, our home is dark with poverty.
One man longs for a son and goes down childless
into Hell; another shrivels in murderous
disease. No man on earth eludes the net
of unending sorrows sent by Zeus.

Expedition

We left the craggy city of Neleian Pylos
and came on ship to handsome Asia
and lovely Kolophon our base.
There we brashly mustered our immense army
in dreadful pride,
and set out along the river flowing inside
the forest.
Aided by the gods
we captured the Aiolian city of Smyrna.

Phokylides

Perhaps a contemporary of Solon and Mimnermos (ca. 600 BCE), Phokylides was a citizen of Miletos. He wrote a series of maxims, each with the "seal" of the author (i.e., each beginning with a formula which included the author's name). Some have seen in this pride of authorship a sign of the new consciousness of the individual. Phokylides wrote in dactylic hexameters instead of elegiacs. (The verses known as the *Carmen Phokylideum* are an interesting 230-line succession of maxims written by either a Jew or a Christian ca. 100 CE.)

> To prove this we might consider the poetry of Hesiod, Theognis and Phokylides, who are declared to be the best counselors ever known in matters of human life.
>
> ISOKRATES, *To Nikokles*

> Archilochos may be reproached for his subject matter, Parmenides for his prosody and Phokylides for his poverty of expression. . . . Yet each deserves praise for his special innate ability to stir and lead his audience.
>
> PLUTARCH, *On Listening*

Appearance of Wisdom

Many empty-headed clods pass by like sages
when they walk with chin erect and stern eyes.

On the Problem of Choosing a Wife

In the words of Phokylides, the tribes of women
come in four breeds: bee, bitch and grimy sow,
and sinewy mare with draping mane. The mare
is healthy, swift, roundly built and on the loose.
The monster-looking sow is neither good nor rotten,
and the bristling bitch lies snapping at the leash.

Yes, the bee is best: a whizz at cleaning, trim and good in cooking. My poor friend, I tell you, for a bright, balmy marriage, pray for a bee.

ASIOS

Of Samos. Sixth century BCE. Wrote genealogies, satirical hexameters, elegiacs, etc.

> In the epic poems of Asios, son of Amphiptolemos of Samos, Phoinix had two daughters by Perimede, daughter of Oineos. These were Astypalaia and Europa.
>
> PAUSANIAS, *Description of Greece*

> You are blind to history, Sir Potbelly. You are an ass-licker, and to recall the old Samian poet Asios, an ass-kisser.
>
> ATHENAIOS, *Scholars at Dinner*

An Old Parasite

Clubfoot, branded like a runaway slave,
the old ass-kisser came like a beggar,
crashing the wedding party of Meles.
He asked for soup and stood among us
like a phantom risen from the mud.

STESICHOROS

A poet who was ranked with Homer by some of the ancients, Stesichoros was born in Sicily around 630 BCE and died around 555 BCE. He was active both at Akragas (where he seems to have come into conflict with the tyrant Phalaris) and Himera. He may have made a visit to mainland Greece, and Sparta in particular.

His works were abundant: they were arranged in twenty-six books by the Alexandrian scholars. They seem to have involved a confluence of the Doric choral traditions and the Ionian epic, with an admixture of local Sicilian legend. Stesichoros introduced full-fledged narrative into choral poetry, and told his stories more directly than, e.g., Pindar. Among the subjects of his narratives were Herakles, Europa, Helen, the Sack of Troy and the Orestes legend. Tradition further ascribes to Stesichoros the innovation of the triadic structure of the choral ode (strophe, antistrophe and epode). His language was Doric, with strong Homeric influence.

The influence of Stesichoros on the subjects of sixth-century painting was apparently very great. Thanks to Stesichoros, Athena was shown fully armed at birth, Herakles acquired his club, lionskin and bow, and Geryon his wings. If more of him had survived, the effect on the literature of modern Europe would probably have been greater than if Alkman, Ibykos or even Simonides had been preserved entire.

> There is a story that while Sokrates was in prison, awaiting his death, he heard a man sing skillfully a song by the lyric poet Stesichoros, and begged him to teach it to him before it was too late, and when the musician asked why, Sokrates replied, "I want to die knowing one thing more."
>
> AMMIANUS MARCELLINUS

On the Iliad

The white-horsed myth.

*Recantation to Helen**

I spoke nonsense and I begin again:

The story is not true.
You never sailed on a benched ship.
You never entered the city of Troy.

On Klytaimnestra

    Foreseeing the end of
    the Aigisthos line.
She dreamed that a serpent appeared
with blood-dripping scales,
and from his belly stepped a king
from the ancient dynasty
of Pleisthenes and Agamemnon.

On the Marriage of Helen and Menelaos

Many quince apples were cast upon the chariot
of the king,
many leaves of myrtle,
hundreds of roses and thousands of braided violets.

On the Marriage of Admetos and Alkestis

Bring your virgin's dowry
cakes of every kind—sesame, groats, sweet oil—
and bring yellow honey too.

Birthplace of Eurytion

Eurytion was born in famous Erytheia
in the hollow of a rock,
near the inexhaustible silver-rooted springs
of the river in Tartessos.

---

* According to Plato in the Phaedros, when Stesichoros was blinded for
having slandered Helen, he, unlike Homer who was blinded for the same
sin, wrote a Palinode, a recantation, and immediately recovered his sight.

Herakles' Quest of the Cattle of Geryon

Then the sungod Helios, child of Hyperion,
soared in his gold-flashing bowl above the ocean
and entered the depths of black holy night,
seeking his mother, young wife and darling children.

But crossing the and on foot was Herakles, son of Zeus,
on his mission through the shadowy laurel grove.

A King's Punishment

On the day of sacrifice,
Tyndareos remembered all the gods but one:
the gift-giving Kyprian,
and in her rage the queen of love
made his daughters marry two times
and three times,
made them walk out on their husbands.

On Song and Lament

Apollo loves happy play and cadenced singing
but he leaves groans and mourning to Hades.
Yet how futile even to weep for the dead.
When dead, a man's glory dies among men.

Season of Song

Forget the wars.
It is time to sing.
Take out the flute from Phrygia
and recall the songs of our blond Graces.

With the clamor of babbling swallows,
it is spring.

IBYKOS

Born of a noble family at Rhegium in the toe of Italy in the first half of the sixth century BCE, Ibykos went to the island of Samos after he had begun his poetic career. It is said that he went to Samos as an alternative to assuming the tyranny which was offered him in his native town. In any case, he went probably at the invitation of the famous Tyrant of Samos, Polykrates), who made his court a center of culture and sophistication—Anakreon was another of Polykrates' guests. Ibykos was said to have been murdered by robbers and avenged by birds who were present at the murder. (See Schiller's ballad "The Cranes of Ibykos.")

In his work, Ibykos brought about a fusion of the West Greek choral lyric as developed by Stesichoros and the East Greek personalism as seen, e.g., in Alkaios and Sappho. In his early work Ibykos seems clearly to have followed Stesichoros' tradition of lyric narrative ("On Herakles" is probably a fragment from this period). But on moving to Samos, he appropriated erotic themes to the choral form, giving them a more ornate and elaborate expression than they had received at the hands of the monodists. Both subject and style, it may be imagined, suited the tastes of the Polykratean court. His language is the composite language of most choral poetry, with Doric traces.

> Caught by robbers in a deserted spot, he was killed exclaiming that the very cranes which flew over at the moment would be his avengers. Some time afterward one of the robbers saw some cranes in the city and cried, "Look! the avengers of Ibykos." Whereupon one of the bystanders enquired into the matter of this speech of his. The crime was admitted, and the robbers brought to justice. Hence the proverb: "The cranes of Ibykos."
>
> *Suda Lexicon*
>
> As foolish as Ibykos.
>
> PROVERB BY DIOGENES

What extravagant things Alkaios writes on the love of youths! And as for Anakreon, his poetry is erotic from beginning to end. Yet to judge from his works they all were surpassed in this matter by Ibykos of Rhegium. And the love of all these poets was sensual love.

CICERO

Love's Season

In spring the quince trees
ripen in the girls' holy orchard
with river waters;
and grapes turn violet
under the shade of luxuriant leafage
and newborn shoots.

But for me, Eros
knows no winter sleep, and as north winds
burn down from Thrace
with searing lightning,
Kypris mutilates my heart with black
and baleful love.

Morning

Dawn that ends our sleep
also wakes
the loud nightingale.

Like an Old Champion

Even now Eros looks at me with tenderness
from under dark eyelids, and casts me spellbound
into Aphrodite's nets where I lie caught
inextricably,

for I swear his mere approach makes me tremble
like an old champion chariot horse, as he
draws a swift cart unwillingly to the race.

Resembling the Birds

In the high branches perch the mottled ducks
and purple cormorants with their sleek throats
and kingfishers of the long wings.

O let my heart always be like the birds
of the purple crest and long wings!

On Flowers

Myrtles and violets and yellow cassidonies,
apple flowers and roses and glossy laurel.

On Euryalos

Euryalos, child of the exquisite Graces
and darling of the lovely-haired Muses,
you were reared by Kypris and soft-eyed Peitho
among the blossoms of the rose.

On Feminine Nature and Public Decency

Spartan girls
are naked-thighed and man-crazy.

Constellation

Burning across the endless night
like brilliant Dog Stars.

On Herakles

I killed the boys on the white horse,
the sons of Molione.

Their bodies were alike,
their age and faces were identical,
being twins and born together
in a silver egg.

The Impossible

When a man is dead one can find
no medicine to bring him life.

On a Man-Made Peninsula in Syracuse

With mortal hands they joined the island
of Ortygia to the stony mainland,
where once there was a hunting zone
for seasnails and carnivorous fish.

HIPPONAX

Hipponax was banished from Ephesos ca. 545 BCE. He spent much time as a wandering beggar in the neighboring city of Klazomenai. He seems to have had quarrels with two sculptors named Boupalos and Athenis. There are indications of a liaison with the former's girlfriend Arete.

In style and subject matter Hipponax is set off from the other major poets of the Lyric Age by his total preoccupation with private topics and his adoption of the demotic manner. He is for Adrados an instance of the increasing dissolution of Hellenism in the Greek cities of Asia Minor.*

Hipponax wrote choliambs ("lame" iambics, also known as "scazons," with a dragging final foot in each line), other iambic and trochaic verse, hexameters and epodes—not the epodes of a choral triad, but, as with Archilochos, a quasi-stanzaic form usually composed of two different kinds of metrical lines.

Hipponax influenced Greek comedy, and was the fountainhead of several different types of choliambic poetry: Kallimachos' iambics, Herondas, Kerkidas, etc.

> O stranger, stay clear of the horrible tomb of
> Hipponax, which hurls abuse as thick as hail and
> whose very ashes compose iambics in hatred
> of Boupalos. You might wake the sleeping wasp
> whose bile would not rest even in Hades, but
> launches straight shafts of song in lame measure.†
>
> PHILIPPOS, *Palatine Anthology*

On the Scoundrel Boupalos

Hold my coat while I belt Boupalos in the eye.
I am ambidextrous and never miss a punch.

---

* Adrados, Liricos griegos, 2: 13.
† Hipponax invented the choliamb, or lame iambic.

*Keep Going, Monster**

Keep going, monster, all the long way to Smyrna.
Pass through Lydia and past the tomb of Attales,
the grave of King Gyges and the stele of Megastrys,
the funereal monument of Atys, and king of Attalyda,
and turn your belly toward the sinking sun.

Midwife

What navel-snipper wiped you, god-blasted one,
and washed you as you kicked about the floor?

On a Serpent Painted at the Wrong End of a Ship

Mimnes, you degenerate artist! Don't paint
a snake running up the rear end
of our trireme.†
Unbearable disgrace and evil luck
will tag us, slave of slaves. You leave the helmsman
open to being bitten on the shins.

Prayer to Hermes

Hermes, dear Hermes, Maia's son from Kyllene,
I pray to you, for I'm frozen and I shiver.
Give Hipponax a woolen overcoat, a Persian
cape, some sandals and felt slippers,
and sixty gold staters for his inner wall.

Give Hipponax a woolen overcoat. I tell you,
his teeth are rattling in his head!

But from you never even a shabby coat against the very cold
or slippers to keep my toes from freezing.

---

* Attales: brother of Alyattes, King of Persia, whose tomb still exists. Megastrys:
  lover of Gyges. Atys: mythical lover of Kybeles. Attalyda: founder of city of
  same name. Text is corrupt and with many variations and interpretations.
† A galley having three banks of oars.

Ways of Providence

Never yet has the blind god, Wealth,
come to my house and said: "Hipponax,
I'm giving you thirty silver minas
and much more." No, he's far too tight.

A New Charybdis

O Muse, sing to me of that sea-monster, Eurymedon's son,*
whose stomach, like a knife, fattens on all it finds.
Tell of his dreadful end, and how by public order
the town will stone him to death beside the sterile sea.

Medication for Sadness

I will abandon my agonized soul to vice
if instantly you don't send a medimnos
of barley. From the flour I'll make a brew
to drink as medicine against my sorrows.

Miseries

In a Lydian voice she said, "Come quick,
I will plug up your tight asshole."
And she beat my balls with a branch
as though I were a scapegoat. I tripped,
and stuck on the gallows I suffered
a double torture: a branch lashed
my chest; someone wet me with cowshit
and my ass stank. Beetles came, drawn
by the stinking gook like summer flies.
They fell on me, shoved, filing their teeth
on my bones. The invasion complete,
I ached more than from a Pygelian plague.

* Parody of Homer.

Injustice

It is outrageous. Now they rail at Kritias,
the upright islander from Chios,
and condemn him for adultery,
merely because they saw him
wandering in the rooms of a cathouse.

Anakreon

The only great Ionian monodist was born in Teos in Asia Minor around 572 BCE. Soon after the capture of Sardis by the Persians in 541 BCE Anakreon fled with his fellow townsmen to Abdera in Thrace, and established a colony there. "On a Virgin" may date from this period. The Tyrant of Samos, Polykrates, invited him to come and teach his son music and poetry. Anakreon and Ibykos thus both were poetic luminaries of the court of Samos. Anakreon in particular seems temperamentally suited to the sophisticated conviviality and eroticism which was the Polykratean style. In 522 BCE Polykrates was killed by Persian treachery, and Anakreon went to Athens—in a boat, it is said, sent especially for him by Hipparchos, brother of the reigning Athenian tyrant Hippias. Hipparchos, who was a sort of cultural commissar under his brother, seems to have fostered a style of life much like that at Samos under Polykrates. Upon the assassination of Hipparchos in 514 BCE Anakreon moved to Thessaly for a time, but was then received back in Athens (now a democracy) with apparently no hard feelings over his earlier friendship with the tyrants. During this period he was a friend of Xanthippos, the father of Perikles. Anakreon died at the age of eighty-five, probably soon after 490 BCE. The legend was that he choked, appropriately, on a grape pip.

The works of Anakreon, in six books, consisted of lyrics (mainly monodic), iambics and elegiacs. The bulk of the surviving fragments are lyric. The language of Anakreon is almost entirely the Ionian of his day.

The most remarkable feature of the poetry of Anakreon, the one most commented on, is its varying tone of playfulness, sophistication, detachment or irony (as seen, for instance, in "The Vision of Love," "On an Old Lover" and "Preparations for Love").

His influence in later poetry has probably been greater than that of either Alkaios or Sappho. The numerous two-dimensional projections in the *Anakreonteia* are often delightful, but sweet, not savory. Horace adapted some themes. But the poetry of Renaissance France and England is the locus of the most flourishing Anakreonism. Even though filtered in large part through the *Anakreonteia*, the poet's manner is still perceptible in Ronsard, Herrick, Ben Jonson and others.

> Anakreon's poetic works are entirely erotic.
>
> CICERO, *Tusculan Disputations*

> The grammarian Didymos wrote four thousand books . . .
> in which he discusses whether Anakreon was more of
> a rake than a sot, whether Sappho was a prostitute, and
> other questions the answers to which you should forget if
> you knew them.
>
> SENECA, *Letters to Lucilius*

> Stranger, passing near the tomb of Anakreon,
> pour me a libation as you approach,
> for in life I was a drunkard.
>
> ANONYMOUS

Artemis

On my knees I speak to you,
Artemis, hunter of deer,
blond child of Zeus and queen
of roaming beasts. From pools
of the river Lethaios you gaze
across a city of brave men.
Serenity. You are a shepherd
of no flock of savage citizens.

Dice

The dice of love are
shouting and madness.

The Vision of Love

On easy wings I glide to Olympos where
I seek my master Eros,
but he no longer lets me run down warm women
as in my doghood days:
he sees my graying beard and passes me by,

while I stand transfixed
in the wind made by his wings of quivering gold.

On an Old Lover

Eros, the blond god of lovers,
strikes me with a purple ball
and asks me to play with a woman
wearing colorful sandals,
but she is from beautiful
Lesbos, and scorns my white hair,
and turning her back runs gaping
behind another woman.

On a Virgin

My Thracian foal, why do you glare with disdain
and then shun me absolutely as if I knew
nothing of this art?

I tell you I could bridle you with tight straps,
seize the reins and gallop you around the posts
of the pleasant course.

But you prefer to graze on the calm meadow,
or frisk and gambol gayly—having no manly
rider to break you in.

Preparations for Love

Bring out water and wine and an armful
of flowers.
I want the proper setting
when I spar a few rounds with love.

Knockout

Eros, the blacksmith of love,
smashed me with a giant hammer
and doused me in the cold river.

The Plunge

Lord! I clamber up the white cliff
and dive into the steaming wave,
O dead drunk with love.

On a Conservative Lover

I love and yet do not love.
I am mad yet not quite mad.

Definition of a Whore

Given-to-all and
celebrated by the masses,
a carrier-of-peoples
and an apple orchard
of mad haunches.

On Streetwalkers

Although we call these women loose,
they tighten their thighs around thighs.

On the Fortunes of Artemon

Once he went about in filthy clothes and waspy hair,
with wooden rings on his ears, and wore around his ribs
an unwashed hairy oxhide from an old miserable shield.
Our con-man pimped a living from bakery girls and whores,
and got his neck bound to a whipping block where the
    leather
made raw meat of his back—and best, he rode the wheel
so that hairs could be torn from his beard and scalp.

But now the good Artemon rides like a generous lord
in an excellent coach or litter. He wears gold earrings
and carries a special ivory parasol like a grand lady.

Charioteer

O sweet boy like a girl,
I see you though you will not look my way.
You are unaware that you handle the reins
of my soul.

On Drinking Parties*

I do not like the man who sits by his bowl
and sobs about the sad wars
but the rake who loves to rave about fine feats
in the arts and art of love.

A Way to the Heart

Come swiftly
and rub aromatic myrrh on her breasts:
the hollow cave around her heart.

On the Origin of Mules or Half-Asses

The Mysians were first in perfecting the art
of coupling mare-hopping donkeys with horses.

Of Effeminacy

In the morning they were joined in marriage,
though later in the same chamber
the groom could not join with his wife.

December

We go through Poseidon's month.
Ponderous clouds sag with water
and furious storms break out
collapsing the rain earthward.

---

* Attributed to Semonides by Bergk.

On a Hoplite

Here, the tomb of Timokritos, a hero in the wars.
It is the coward whom Ares spares, not the brave.

On a Guardian Angel

Now I hang in Athene's gleaming temple.
It was I who brought Python safely home
from the dreadful wars:
I, his shield.

Vacillation

The bird flashes back and forth
between the black leaves of laurel trees
and the greenness of the olive grove.

On the Soldier Agathon

All members of this village have come to weep
at your funeral pyre, O courageous Agathon,
who died for Abdera.

In the chaos of the horrible battlefield,
blood-loving Ares never before slaughtered
a more fearless youth.

On Kleinorides, Lost at Sea*

You too, Kleinorides, were lost loving your country
as you confronted the wintry blast of the south wind.
In the spring season of your life you died unwed.
The seawaves washed away your graceful adolescence.

Encounter

I looked at her and took off
like a frightened cuckoo bird.

---

* Also ascribed to Leonidas of Tarentum.

Candor

Personally,
I hate those who are furtive and touchy, morose
in their ways. I have learned that you, Megistes,
are of the innocent, of the childlike ones.

On Death

My temples are white, my head largely bald.
Graceful youth has departed from my face,
and my teeth are loose teeth of an old man.
I have few years left of sweet life.

Therefore I tremble and fear the underworld,
for the lightless chasm of death is dreadful
and the descent appalling: once cast down
into Hell there is no return.

Preparation

Let us hang garlands of celery
across our foreheads,
and call a festival to Dionysos.

XENOPHANES

Born in 565 BCE in Kolophon (near Ephesos in Asia Minor), Xeno-
phanes fled from the Persian invaders and settled in Elea, in Italy.
He died sometime after 473 BCE. He seems to have been partly a
philosopher and partly a rhapsode (professional reciter of poems),
but the integration of the two roles is not a matter of common agree-
ment. On the philosophical side Xenophanes is remarkable for his
vigorous criticism of traditional myth and anthropomorphic reli-
gion, and for his espousal of a kind of pantheism. His works included
"Silloi" (satiric and parodic hexameters), a poem "On Nature" and
elegies. He wrote also two verse histories—of Elea and of Kolophon.

> When someone related to Xenophanes that he had seen eels
> alive in hot water, he said: "Then we can boil them in cold."
>
> PLUTARCH, *Common Notions against the Stoics*

> Consider Xenophanes' remark that it is just as impious to
> say that the gods were born as to say that they died. Both
> statements imply that at some time they did not exist.
>
> ARISTOTLE, *Rhetoric*

> You Xenophaneses, Diagorases, Hippons, Epikouroses,
> and the rest of that catalogue of odious god-for-saken
> wretches, go drop dead.
>
> CLAUDIUS AELIANUS

> Xenophanes says there are four elements in existing
> things, and an infinite number of separate worlds. Clouds
> are made from vapor of the sun carried upward into the
> air. The essence of god is spherical, in no way resembling
> man. He is all eyes and all ears but does not breathe. He
> is in his totality mind and thinking, and is eternal. Xeno-
> phanes was the first to have declared that all that exists
> is transitory and destructible, and that the soul is breath
> or spirit.
>
> DIOGENES LAERTIOS, *Lives of the Philosophers*

Banquet Decorum

Now the floor is scrubbed clean, our hands are washed
and cups are dry. A boy loops garlands
in our hair. Another passes round a phial
of redolent balsam. The mixing bowl
is bubbling with good cheer, and more fragrant wine
stands potent in the earthen jars.
Incense floats a holy perfume through the room.
Water is cold, crystal, sweet.
Golden bread is set near on a princely table
loaded down with cheese and rich honey.
The altar in the center is submerged in flowers
and the house vibrates with fun and singing.

Gracious men should first sing praises to God
with proper stories and pure words.
After the libation when we pray for strength
to act with rectitude (our first concern),
there is no sin in drinking all one can
and still get home without a servant—
unless too old. We commend the man who shows
good memory after drink, who seeks virtue
and not to harangue us with the ancient myths
of noisy wars of Titans, Giants,
Centaurs. These things are worth nothing. The good
lies in our reverence for the gods.

Cheerful Days in Asiatic Kolophon

They acquired useless luxuries out of. Lydia
while still free from her odious tyranny,
paraded to the market place in seapurple robes,
often in bright swarms of a thousand.
They were proud and pleased in their elaborate hairdo's
and hid body odor with rare perfumes.

The Nature of God

There is one God, supreme among gods and men,
who is like mortals in neither body nor mind.

Agnostic Credo

The truth is that no man ever was or will be
who understands the gods and all I speak of.
If you stumble on some rocks of the whole truth
you never know it. There is always speculation.

Pythagoras and the Transmigrated Soul

One day a dog was being thrashed in the street,
and behold, Pythagoras, philosopher of spirits,
was walking by.
His heart was in his mouth
for the poor pup.
"Stop! Stop!" he cried.
"Don't beat him any more.
This is my dear friend's soul.
I recognize the voice when I hear him bark."

Knowledge

The gods did riot: enrich man
with a knowledge of all things
from the beginning of life.
Yet man seeks, and in time
invents what may be better.

The Making of Gods

1
Man made his gods, and furnished them
with his own body, voice and garments.

2
If a horse or lion or a slow ox
had agile hands for paint and sculpture,

the horse would make his god a horse,
the ox would sculpt an ox.

3
Our gods have flat noses and black skins
say the Ethiopians. The Thracians say
our gods have red hair and hazel eyes.

On Waters and Winds

Sea is a source of water and source of wind.
With no great ocean there would be no wind,
no moving rivers nor rainwater from the sky.
Great ocean is father of clouds, winds, rivers.

The Physical Origin of the Rainbow

Whom they call Iris is also a raincloud
that we see as purple, scarlet and green.

The Nature of the Universe

Everything comes from the earth,
and everything ends in the earth.

First Principles

All that is born and grows
comes from water and earth.

Lampoon against Homer and Hesiod

Homer and Hesiod emblazoned the gods
with all that is shameful and scandalous
in man:
stealing, adultery and mutual deceit.

The Shape of the Earth

At our feet we see this end of the earth
where it rises to meet the firmament.
Below, the world sinks down unendingly.

Simonides

Pindar's stylistic antipode and sometime rival was born of good family on the island of Keos in 556 BCE. Like Anakreon he was one of the poets invited to Athens by Hipparchos as part of the program of cultural enrichment inaugurated under the Peisistratid tyranny. It was probably at Athens that he wrote the dithyrambs to which only one brief reference survives. After the fall of the tyranny—again like Anakreon—he went to Thessaly under the patronage of several leading houses. But he was back in Athens by 490, since he is reported to have defeated the dramatist Aischylos in a competition to write an epitaph for those fallen at Marathon. During the period of the Persian Wars he became as it were the poetic spokesman for the whole of Greece, as his ode on the fallen at Thermopylai would suggest. At Athens he became the friend of Themistokles. In 476 BCE at the age of eighty he went to Sicily, where he was welcomed both at Syracuse and Akragas. (Pindar was in Sicily at this same time.) Simonides died in Sicily in 468/7 BCE and was buried at Akragas. The tradition reports that he was ugly, and shrewd in money matters.

Simonides composed choral poetry in many genres, especially *threnoi* and *epinikia*. He also wrote elegies and elegiac epigrams. His dialect was a mollified Doric in choral lyric, and in elegy—as usual for this genre—predominantly Homeric. In contrast to Pindar, his style in choral poetry was on the whole direct and harmonious. His *epinikia* seem, unlike those of Pindar, to have been sportive and lighthearted. In outlook—political, ethical, religious—he was more "modern" and more adaptable by far than Pindar.

> "Still," I said, "I do not find it easy to disbelieve a wise and inspired artist like Simonides."
>
> PLATO, *Republic*

> When Simonides was discussing wisdom and riches with Hieron's wife, and she asked him which was better, to become wise or to become wealthy, he replied, "To become wealthy. For I see the wise sitting on the doorsteps of the rich."
>
> ARISTOTLE, *Rhetoric*

His chief excellence lies in his pathos. Indeed some con-
sider that in this quality he surpasses all other writers in
this kind of literature.

QUINTILIAN, *Guide to Oratory*

Men of the Front Ranks

Through their extraordinary courage, the wide
farmlands of Tegea
have not shot fire and smoke into the sky.
For they made their choice
to leave their children in a country green
and sweet with freedom,
and died for this in the wild ranks of battle.

On the Lakedaimonians Fallen at Plataia

These men left an altar of glory on their land,
shining in all weather,
when they were enveloped by the black mists of death.
but although they died
they are not dead, for their courage raises them in glory
from the rooms of Hell.

On the Greeks Fallen at Eurymedon

With mindless bravura Ares washed his long sleek
     arrowheads
in the crimson waters within their chests,
and dust now lies not on the living flesh
of javelineers,
but on the vivid remnants of lifeless bodies.

On Those Who Died at Thermopylai

Their tomb is an altar on which stand our bowls of
     remembrance
and the wine of our praise.
Neither mold and worms, nor time
which destroys all things, will blacken their deaths.

The shrine of the se brave men
has found its guardian
in the glory of Greece. Leonidas, the Spartan king,
lives in the great ornament he left behind
of unending fame and virtue.

Grave by the Water

We were slaughtered in a Dirphian gully, and our graves,
near Euripos, were paid for by our nation.
Justice. For in confronting the cruel clouds of war,
we gave away our years of lovely youth.

Arete*

Virtue lives on a high rock
painful to climb and guarded by
a band of pure and evasive nymphs.
No mortal may look upon her
unless sweat pours from his body
and he climbs the summit of manliness.

Inscription for Athenian Heroes
Who Fought at the Isthmos

When her fate rested on the razor's edge,
we gave away our lives to save all Greece.

Code of Honor at Thermopylai

Stranger, go back to Sparta and tell our people
that we who were slain obeyed the code.

Victory at Marathon

At Marathon the Athenians fought for all Greece
and broke the spearhead of Persia's crack troops.

* Arete: virtue, courage, achievement.

On Those Who Died with Leonidas

Leonidas, king of the open fields of Sparta,
those slain with you lie famous in their graves,
for they attacked absorbing the head-on assault
of endless Persian men, arrows and swift horse.

An Oracle's Death at Thermopylai

This is the tomb of famous Megistias, slain by
the Persians near the Spercheios River,
a seer who even when aware that death was near
would not desert his Spartan kings.

On Megakles

When I look at the tomb of Megakles
with its dead body,
I pity you, poor Kallia, his father.

Crossing the Gulf of Corinth

All these victors from the Tyrrhenian wars
were on their way to Apollo at Delphi
with their first plunder
when they found, their grave
on one night, in one ship, in one deep sea.

The Athenian Vanguard

Athenian sons demolished the Persian army
and saved their country from painful slavery.

Social Dictum

The city is the teacher of the man.

On Iphimenes

O Geraneia, tall-air mountain of evil,
I wish you faced the far Danube or Tanais,
river of distant Skythia;

that the Skeironian precipice did not rise
from the sea where Iphimenes sailed around
the broken rock of Molouris.
Now he is a frozen corpse in the gulf,
and this open tomb tells of his bitter voyage.

*Danaë and the Infant Perseus Imprisoned
in a Chest on the Sea*

A tilting sea and thundering winds
tossed the carved chest and filled Danaë
with terror; she cried
and placed her arm lovingly around
Perseus saying: "My child, I suffer
and yet your heart is calm; you sleep
profoundly in tie blue dark of night
and shine in our gloomy bronze-ribbed boat.
Don't think of the heaving saltwave
that seeps in through airholes and drenches
your hair, nor of the clamoring gale;
but lying in our seaviolet blanket
keep your lovely body close to mine.
If you knew the horror of our plight,
your gentle ears would hear my words.
But sleep, my son, and let
the ocean sleep and our great troubles end.
I ask you, father Zeus,
rescue us from our fate; and should
my words seem too severe, I beg you please
remember where we are, and forgive
my prayer."

On Lykas, a Thessalian Hound

Bitch-hound, hunter, even your dead white bones
terrify the beasts of the field,
for your bravery is common knowledge
from huge Pelion to far Ossa
and on the dizzying sheep-paths of Kithairon.

Halcyon Days*

During the winter solstice
Zeus orders fourteen days of peaceful weather,
and man has called this windless season holy
for then the mottled halcyon rears its young.

On a Statue of Philon

I am from the island of Corfu.
My name: Philon, son of Glaukos.
And I am here,
because down in Olympia, at the games,
I was champion in boxing two years running.

Victory Song for the Boxer Glaukos of Karystos

Neither the knockout king Polydeukes
nor even Herakles (iron boy of Alkmena)
would put up his guard to the mighty Glaukos.

A Modest Grave

Sir, you are not Looking at the tomb
of some great Lydian king,
for being poor my gravestone is small,
yet still too much for me.

On the Girl Gorgo

As she lay dying in her dear mother's arms,
Gorgo wept and whispered her last words:
"Stay with my father,
and on a better day bear a second daughter
who will care for you when you are old."

---

* "The halcyon nests about the time of the winter solstice, and
 that is why, when the weather is fine at that time of year, we call
 the days 'Halcyon days.'" Aristotle, History of Animals.

Encircled Woman

I am possessed by the fierce noise all around me
of the purple, tormented sea.

Human Bankruptcy

I who lie here, Brotachos of Gortyn, was born in Krete,
and I did not come here for death but weighty business.

Sacred Health

Not even lucid wisdom will give you joy
when sacred health is gone.

Flux

If you are a simple mortal, do not speak
of tomorrow or how long this man may be
among the happy, for change comes suddenly
like the shifting flight of a dragonfly.

Green

The birds of spring
are the green-necked
singing nightingales.

On Demigods

Born half-divine and sons of mighty gods,
not even these, living in ancient times,
came to old age unscorned and without painful
hardships, nor did they escape from doom.

On an Athenian Daughter Given to a
Foreign Prince in Lampsakos

This dust lies on Archedike, daughter of Hippias,
despot of Athens and most princely Greek of his day.
Although a daughter, wife, sister and mother of tyrants,
she never yielded to snobbery. Her heart was humble.

Passage of Time

One thousand years, ten thousand years
are but a tiny dot,
the smallest segment of a point,
an invisible hair.

Accomplishments

Without the gods
a man or city can do nothing.
Only God knows everything, and man
suffers for what he does.

There is no evil
man may not expect, and soon
God wipes away the few things
he may have done.

LASOS

Born about 545 BCE at Hermione in the Argolid of the Peloponnesos, Lasos lived at Athens under the patronage of Hipparchos, where he introduced competitions in dithyrambic composition and was rivaled by Simonides in this genre.

> The flute player Skopelinos taught Pindar the flute, and finding his pupil of exceptional ability, passed him on to Lasos of Hermione to learn the lyre.
>
> THOMAS MAGISTER, *Life of Pindar*

> Lasisms : sophistries as the sophistries or entangled arguments of Lasos.
>
> HESYCHIOS, *Glossary*

To the Hermionian Demeter

I sing of Demeter and the kore Persephone,
wife of Klymenos,
and I lead
a choral hymn of honey voices
with all the low notes in the Aiolian harmony.

THEOGNIS

Born in Megara in 544 BCE, Theognis was a member of the embattled aristocracy. He was in exile for part of his life, but returned home at some time. He lived until at least 480 BCE. The subjects of his poetry seem to have been chiefly two: the vicissitudes of an aristocrat fallen on evil populist times and the moral reflections appropriate to such experience, and the vicissitudes of the poet's affections—chiefly directed toward one Kyrnos. However much out-of-balance one may find Theognis' antediluvian social and moral views, his vivid expression of keen experience ranks him among the supreme elegists surviving from the Lyric Age.

The corpus of poems traditionally assigned to Theognis (about 1,400 lines) by no means wholly belongs to him. Much of it consists of imitations and copies of earlier poets (some of this may be by Theognis) and of Theognis himself. The collection may have arisen as a useful handbook of after-dinner poetry for the man who did not care to produce his own. The poems addressed to Kyrnos have the greatest likelihood of Theognidean authorship. The contents of the collection may be classified as follows: 1) autobiography; 2) preludes, hymns, epitaphs, etc.; 3) erotic and convivial verse; 4) gnomic or "wisdom" poetry: gather-ye-rosebud sermons, class propaganda, praise of wealth and dispraise of poverty, expression of aristocratic moral code—especially the virtues of courage, resignation and fidelity.

> We also have a witness in the poet Theognis, a citizen of Megara, Sicily, who said: "In a difficult dispute, a trustworthy man is equal to gold and silver."
>
> PLATO, *Laws*

> Theognis wrote exhortations; but scattered among them were disgusting, pederastic love poems and pieces repugnant to a virtuous life.
>
> *The Suda Lexicon*

This poet is concerned with no other matter than the virtues and vices of man, and his poetry is a study of man just as a treatise on horsemanship written by an expert horseman studies horses.

STOBAIOS, *Anthology*

The epic verse of Empedokles and Parmenides, the Theriaka (Venomous Bites) and the Gnomologies of Theognis are prose works which borrow from poetry the use of its meter and high tone, as if it were a carriage, to avoid going prosaically on foot.

PLUTARCH, *How the Young Should Listen to Poetry*

Shadows

Fools and children you are, mankind! You mourn
the dead and not the dying flower of youth.

Eugenics

In breeding donkeys, rams or horses, we seek out
the thoroughbred to get a good strain,
my Kyrnos. Yet now the noblest man will marry
the lowest daughter of a base family,
if only she brings in money. And a lady
will share her bed with a foul rich man,
preferring gold to pedigree. Money is all.
Good breed with bad and race is lost
to riches. Don't wonder our city's blood is polluted
when noble men will couple with upstarts.

Liberation

Death, friend Kyrnos, is better to the poor
than a life cursed with painful poverty.

Poverty

Nothing destroys a good man quicker than poverty:
not malarial fever, Kyrnos, nor old age.
Better to hurl oneself into the abysmal sea

or over a blunt cliff than be poverty's
victim. The poor man can do or say nothing
worthwhile. Even his mouth is gagged.

A Loose Vessel

A ripe young wife and an old husband
make a very sad conjunction.
She is a ship. Her wild rudder
doesn't respond to him.
Her anchors don't hold.
Often she slips her moorings altogether
to enter at night in another port.

To Kyrnos, a Reproach

I gave you wings to fly looming high and easy
over unboarded sea and the entire earth.
At every meal and banquet you will be present
on the lips of guests. Graceful young men
will sing of you in limpid lovely notes
to the clean piping of the flutes.
When you go under the dark vaults of earth
to the mournful chambers of sad Hell,
even when you lie dead you will not lose
your glory. Your name will be recalled
among men always, Kyrnos. You will wheel high
over the mainland and Greek islands
and cross the unharvested sea pulsing with fish,
not by horse but carried to those who love you
in the gifts of Muses capped in violet flowers.
You will be like a song to the living
as long as there is sun, earth. Yet you ignore me
and trick me as if I were a child.

A Seaman's Sorrow

I heard the sharp cry of the bird, O son of Polypas,
who came to men with the message to plow

in good season, and it wounded my heart black
that others own my flowering lands,
and not for me are mules dragging the curved plow,
now, in my exile, on the wretched sea.

Words of a Bearded Man Reclining on a Couch

O beautiful boy, I crave you more than any man.
Stand where you are and hear my few words.

Good Will Wasted

I knew it before and know it better now:
don't wait for thanks from the lower classes.

His Fairness

I will blame no enemy who is a good man,
nor praise a friend who may be vile.

Our Course

Best of all things is never to be born,
never to know the light of sharp sun.
But being born, then best
to pass quickly as one can through the gates of Hell,
and there lie under the massive shield of earth.

The Wanderer

I have spent long days in the land of Sicily, and walked
through the vineyards of the Euboian plain;
saw the city of Sparta shining by the reedy Eurotas.
Everywhere people took me into their homes
yet my heart found no pleasure in foreign kindness.
No place is as precious as one's homeland.

The Athlete

Blessed is the man who knows how to make love
as one wrestles in a gym,
and then goes home happy to sleep the day
with a delicious young boy.

Good and Evil

Easier to make bad out of good than good out of bad.
Don't try to teach me. I am too old to learn.

A City in Travail

Kyrnos, the city is pregnant, and I fear it will bear
a man who will clean up our outrageous pride.
The people are still well behaved, but the leaders
plunge along a course of vile corruption.

Apollodoros

Active during the late sixth century BCE.

> Under these omens Pindar turned to the art of poetry, his
> teacher being either Lasos, as said before, or the Athenian
> Agatholdes or Apollodoros. We are told about Apol-
> lodoros that when he was the leader of the cyclic chorus,
> he had to leave the city and entrusted the trailing of the
> chorus to Pindar, still a boy, who did so well as to become
> known throughout the area.

EUSTATHIOS, *Introduction to Pindar*

Who?

Who can be coming to the edge
of my gates
at this black hour of night?

HIPPARCHOS

Hipparchos was the younger brother of Hippias, Tyrant of Athens (who succeeded his father Peisistratos in 527 BCE). He was as it were the commissar of culture during his brother's reign, and was responsible for much of Athens' rapid advance in the arts. The frivolous decadence of his private life ended when he was assassinated by Harmodios and Aristogeiton in 514 BCE.

> Because of their esteem and age, Hippias and Hipparchos, not their half-brothers, held the reins of power, and since Hippias was the elder and by nature a clever politician, he was virtual ruler. On the other hand, Hipparchos was childlike, amorous and a friend of the arts. It was he who brought Anakreon, Simonides and other poets to Athens.
>
> ARISTOTLE, *Constitution of Athens*

> A great light was born in Athens when Hipparchos was slaughtered by Aristogeiton and Harmodios.
>
> SIMONIDES, *Inscription for Statues of Tyrannicides*

> Hipparchos set up statues of Hermes on the roads between the city and every community in Attica . . . so that his citizens would not most admire the wise sayings inscribed at Delphi, such as "Know yourself" and "Nothing in excess," but rather be guided by the wisdom of himself, Hipparchos. Thus they would read them and partake of his wisdom while going back and forth to their farms and homes, and so become enlightened men.
>
> PLATO, *Hipparchos*

Inscription from a Statue of Hermes

This will recall Hipparchos:
As you walk think of the good.

Inscription from a Statue of Hermes

This will recall Hipparchos:
Never doublecross a friend.

KORINNA

This Boiotian poet was probably a contemporary of Pindar, but it is also possible that she lived in the late third century BCE. Until the papyrus finds of this century, she was known only in the scantiest of fragments. Her works included narrative choral lyrics intended for an audience of women, on such subjects as the Seven Against Thebes. Her diction and meter are simple, her dialect chiefly Boiotian.

> Daughter of Acheloodoros and Hippokrateia, of Thebes or Tanagra; a pupil of Myrtis and a lyric poet. It is reported that she gained victory five times over Pindar in poetry competitions. She wrote five books as well as Inscriptions and Lyric Nomes.
>
> *Suda Lexicon*

> When Pindar the poet competed at Thebes he ran into ignorant judges, and was defeated five times by Korinna. To show the judges' bad taste, Pindar called Korinna a pig.
>
> CLAUDIUS AELIANUS, *Historical Miscellanies*

> When Pindar was still young and proud of his mastery of language, Korinna censured him for his poor taste.
>
> PLUTARCH, *Glory of Athens*

On Herself

I Korinna am here to sing the courage
of heroes and heroines in old myths.
To daughters of Tanagra in white robes,
I sing. And all the city is delighted
with the clean water of my plaintive voice.

The Contest of Helikon and Kithairon

Kithairon sang of cunning Kronos
and sacred Rhea who stole her son Zeus,
mighty among immortals.

Then the Muses asked the gods to put
their ballot stones in the urn of gold.
All stood up and Kithairon won

the greater part. Hermes shouted loud,
at once proclaiming sweet victory.
The gods adorned his brow with flowers,

and Kithairon rejoiced. But Helikon
was stunned with bitter rage, and tore
a massive boulder from the mountain.

Insanely he shouted and lobbed the rock
down on thousands of mortals below.

Hermes

When he sailed into the harbor
his ship became a snorting horse.
Hermes ravished the white city
while the wind like a nightingale
sang with his whirling battle axe.

Rout of the Eretrian Fleet

For you alone, Tanagra,
Hermes came to fight
with his naked fists.

On Myrtis

Although I was her pupil,

Even I reproach Myrtis
of the crystalline voice.

She was a mere woman poet,
yet she challenged Pindar.

On Herself

Will you sleep forever? There was a time,
Korinna, when you were not a loafer.

TELESILLA

Fifth-century BCE poet of Argos. She wrote hymns to the gods, mainly for women.

> No less renowned than these collective deeds is the battle in which the Spartan king Kleomenes was driven from Argos (with his men) by the poet Telesilla.
>
> PLUTARCH, *Feminine Virtue*

> Above the theater is a temple of Aphrodite. And in front of the pedestal of the goddess is a slab engraved with a figure of Telesilla, the writer of songs. . . . Telesilla was famous among women for her poetry but still more famous for the following deed: [her defeat of the Spartans].
>
> PAUSANIAS, *Description of Greece (Argos)*

Refuge from Rape

O Artemis and your virgin girls,
come to us. Run swiftly
to escape the hunter Alpheus.

Song to Apollo

O the sun-loving Apollo!

TIMOKREON

Born on Rhodes, active during first half of fifth century BCE. He sided with the Persian; in the wars and visited their king. Timokreon, who crossed poetic swords with Simonides, was reputed to be a glutton. He composed lyrics and elegies.

> When Timokreon became the guest of the Persian king, he took full advantage of the food offered him. Once, when the king asked why he was stuffing himself, he answered, "So I can give a great number of Persians a sound thrashing." The next day he defeated a large number of them, one by one, and then stood beating the air. He explained to his astonished host that he had all these blows to spare if any one would come on for more.
>
> ATHENAIOS, *Scholars at Dinner*

> After drinking and eating and slandering
> to my heart's content,
> I now lie here,
> Timokreon of Rhodes.
>
> SIMONIDES

The Source

Blind money, I wish you were banished
from coastal plains and the sea,
from the deep continent,
and made your home on Acheron's shore
in black Tartaros.
All the malevolence in man
is caused by you.

LAMPROKLES

Active at Athens in early fifth century BCE, he composed dithy-
rambs and hymns, and was an influential teacher of music.

> Pythokleides was a musician of solemn music, a Pythago-
> rian who taught Agathokles, the teacher of Lamprokles,
> the teacher of Damon.*
>
> SCHOLIAST, *On Plato*

> In the History of Harmony, Aristoxenos claims that the
> Mixolydian mode was invented by Pythokleides, the flute
> player. Lysis states that Lamprokles of Athens, under-
> standing that this mode has a disjunction . . . arranged it
> to proceed from B to B.
>
> PLUTARCH, *On Music*

On Athena

City-destroying Pallas,
wonderful captain in battle,
constant champion of war,
virgin, child of great Zeus,
you tame unbroken stallions.

---

* The teacher of Perikles and Socrates.

PINDAROS (PINDAR)

The prince of choral poets was born in 518 BCE at Kynoskephalai in Boiotia, of an aristocratic family. He was educated in his craft chiefly at Athens. In the course of his career he established connections with leading families in many parts of the Greek world. (The relationship between poet and patron during this period, remarks Hermann Fränkel, should be understood within the tradition of the exchange of gifts by guest-friends, rather than treated as a sheerly commercial link.) He went to Sicily in 476 BCE and was welcomed both by Hieron of Syracuse and by Theron of Akragas. At least from this time onward Pindar found himself on occasion in competition with Simonides and Bakchylides, and was not always the winner: Bakchylides was commissioned instead of Pindar to write an epinikion for Hieron in 468. Pindar died at eighty in 438 BCE.

The works of Pindar comprised seventeen books, including nearly all choral genres. Only the four books of his epinikian odes have survived in substantial completeness, but the fragments of others fill some eighty pages in Bowra's edition.

The style of Pindar is dense and highly personal, blended from several dialects. His viewpoint is that of an aristocratic conservative, both in religion and politics. The epinikion for Pindar is above all a religious celebration of the glories of god and hero, and (as it were incidentally) their reflection in the achievements of his aristocratic contemporaries.

Pindar has had deeper influence on subsequent literature than any other Greek lyric poet. The modern ode at its greatest is chiefly the descendant of Pindar. But, as Bowra says, "He was capable . . . at times, of a sublimity to which there is no parallel."

A delight to strangers and loved by friends, Pindar was servant of the sweet-voiced Muses.

PLATO

In lyric poetry would you prefer to be Bakchylides rather than Pindar? And in tragedy Ion of Chios rather than— Sophokles? It is true that Bakchylides and Ion are faultless and entirely elegant writers of the polished school, while

Pindar and Sophokles, although at time they burn every-
thing before them as it were in their swift career, are of-
ten extinguished unaccountably and fail most lamentably.
But would anyone in his sense regard all the compositions
of Ion put together as an equivalent for the single play of
the Oidipous [or all the works of Bakchylides as equal to a
single ode of Pindar's?]

"LONGINUS," *On the Sublime*

Whoever labors to be Pindar's equal,
Iulus, mounts on wings that are fastened with wax,
Daidalos-fashion, and will give his name to
glittering water.

As a river roars down a mountain, swollen
by showers of rain, spilling over its banks,
so Pindar rages and the deep of his voice
pours ever onward,

worthy of the laurel sacred to Apollo,
whither he is tumbling freshly minted words
through frenzied hymns, carried along on meters
free and unruly . . .

HORACE, *Odes*

Of the nine lyric poets Pindar is by far the greatest, in
virtue of his inspired magnificence, the beauty of his
thoughts and figures, the rich exuberance of his language
and matter and his rolling flood of eloquence, character-
istics which, as Horace rightly held, make him inimitable.

QUINTILIAN

Pindar lies in the earth, this Pierian trumpet, strong
forger of pure hymns, whose song when heard made
one think a swarm of bees had come from the
Muses to fashion it in the chamber of Kadmos'
bride, Harmony.

ANTIPATROS OF SIDON, *Palatine Anthology*

It was during the quadrennial festival [Pythian games]
with its procession of oxen that,
as a well-loved child, I was first wrapped
in swaddling clothes.

PINDAR, *Fragment*

A chosen herald of wise speech, I was raised by the Muses for Hellas. I am proud that my race and my home are in Thebes, a city of chariots.

PINDAR, *Dithyramb for Thebes*

Eclipse

God has in his power
to make dazzling unmixed light
spring from the somber depths
of evening. He can also
enclose the white explosion of day
under the gloom of black clouds.

Singing Dance*

Follow the curving line of melody,
and in contest
dance frenetically to imitate
the Amyklian hound or a wild unbroken horse.
And move your body
as a hound flies across the windy plain of Dotia
to kill a horned deer
who, in desperate dance,
bobs her head and neck convulsively
to either side.

Olympian Ode XII

For Ergoteles of Himera, winner of the long distance run,
  472 BCE, now
exiled from Knossos.

O daughter of liberating Zeus, I beseech you,
O saviour Fortune, guard the strength of Himera.
At sea you pilot our speeding ships,
and on land the Erupting wars and assemblies

---

* Also attributed to Simonides.

depend on your will. For men's hopes splash high,
break low as they toss through an ocean of lies.

No man of the earth has ever encountered
a sure sign from God of things to come. The future
is blind to him. It teases
his judgment as the reversal of delight,
or as after suffering a surge of pain
the sudden turning from gloom to meadows of joy.

Son of Philanor, like a cock who fights only at home,
even your legs' splendor might be dull
had civil strife among bitter men
not expelled you from your homeland, Knossos.
Now, Ergoteles, garlanded at Olympia
and twice festooned at Pytho and at the Isthmos,
you honor the Hot Springs of the Nymphs, here
at your new home, Himera.

Afterlife in Elysium

For them the sun shines at full strength while we here walk
      in night.
The plains around their city are red with roses
and shaded by incense trees heavy with golden fruit.
And some enjoy horses and wrestling or table games and
      the lyre,
and near them blossoms a flower of perfect joy.
Perfumes always hover above the land
from the frankincense strewn in deep-shining fire of the
      gods' altars.

And across from them the sluggish rivers of black night
vomit forth a boundless gloom.

Olympian Ode XI

To the Lokrian boy Agesidamos, winner in the boxing,
   476 BCE

There is a time when men most need winds.
There is a time for waters from the sky,
for raindrops, daughters of the cloud.
But if by effort a man is victorious, sweet songs
foretell later fame,
and are a pledge for remembrance of great achievements.

Abundant is the praise waiting for Olympian victory,
and my lips are pleased
to shepherd these words.
Yet only through God can wisdom blossom in a man's soul.
So know this, Agesidamos,
for you, son of Archestratos, for your boxing triumph
I will raise a sweet song to add radiance
to your olive wreath of gold,
and speak of the West Wind Lokrians, your people.
Let us acclaim him here, Muses. I warrant
you will not be received coldly like strangers,
nor find bluntness to lovely things,
but wisdom and excellent spearmen. For neither
the fiery brown fox
nor raucous lion can change his nature given from birth.

Lament

The stars and the rivers
and waves call you back.

Glorious Athens

O shining city, festooned in violets, draped in song,
you are the marble strength of all Hellas, glorious Athens,
   sacred citadel.

Olympian Ode III

To Theron of Akragas in Sicily, winner in the chariot race,
  466 BCE

I shall honor glorious Akragas and please the Dioskouroi,
Be kind to strangers and Helen of the lovely hair
when I have raised a hymn of Olympic victory for Theron
  and his stallions
of the never-tiring hooves. The Muses were faithful
as I found a shining virgin mode to link Dorian rhythms
  with the speech of celebration.
The olive wreath on his flowing locks moves me
to my God-appointed duty to blend clamoring flutes
and the lyre's supple voice with my pattern of words,
all for Ainesidamos' son. And Pisa bids me speak out. From
  Pisa
come heavenly songs to man
and to the victor. The upright Aitolian judge of Greeks,
obeying Herakles' ancient laws,
loops the gray glory of the olive over the hero's brow and
  locks.
Long ago Amphitryon's son carried the silver olive tree
from the shadowy springs of the Danube,
to be the handsomest symbol of the Olympian games.

With candid heart he persuaded the Hyperboreans, people
  of Apollo;
he begged them for a tree for Zeus' garden
to bring refreshing shade to all men, and crown their valor.
Already the altars were hallowed for his father;
and the mid-month moon,
riding in her gold cart, illumined the round eye of evening.
He established the fair judging for the great fifth-year
  games
by the overhanging banks of holy Alpheus River.
But the valley of Kronian Pelops was not yet verdant with
  beauty of trees.
He thought his garden, naked of green, must suffer the sun's
  dagger rays.

So his spirit moved him to journey to Istrian land.

There, Leto's daughter, driver of horses,

welcomed him as he came from ridges and mazy gullies of
    Arkadia

when, at Eurysteus' command, his doomed ties with Zeus

drove him on his mission

to bring back the gold-horned doe that Taygeta one day
    wrote down

to be sacrificed to Artemis Orthosia.

Chasing the doe, he saw the distant land behind the cold
    north wind

and stood in wonder at the trees.

A sweet desire burned in him to plant them at the
    finish-mark

of the twelve-lap track of horses.

And now he comes graciously to the festival, with the
    godlike

twin sons of deep-girdled Leda.

At Olympos he had charged those future stars to guide the
    wonderful games

where men's courage and chariot-speed are tested.

My heart impels me to say that glory has come to Theron

and the children of Emmenos as a gift from the horsemen
    Dioskouroi.

Among all mortals they drew near the gods through lavish
    feasts

and true reverence for the mysteries.

If water is best of all things, and gold the dearest possession,

then Theron's virtues touch the uttermost realm of
    excellence,

reaching Herakles' pillars. Beyond, the world is untracked

by wise or foolish. There I will not venture, being no fool.

BAKCHYLIDES

A contemporary, possibly younger, of Pindar, Bakchylides was born, like his uncle Simonides, on the island Keos in the Kyklades. He too took part in the dithyrambic competitions at Athens and accompanied his uncle to Sicily around 476 BCE. He was reportedly exiled to the Peloponnesos at some time in his life. Like Simonides and Pindar, he wrote for numerous patrons throughout Greece. Until 1896 there survived of Bakchylides only half as many lyric fragments as those of Simonides. But in that year a papyrus-find of fourteen epinikia and six dithyrambs was made in Egypt. Among lyric poets Bakchylides is now second only to Pindar in state of preservation. Fragments remain of other genres of Bakchylides' choral lyrics.

The language of Bakchylides is chiefly a combination of Homeric and Doric—a version of the "standard" international choral language. His style is on the whole much more direct and penetrable than Pindar's, but his diction is distinguished by an abundance of ornamental compounds, many of them newly coined.

> Pindar had a feud with Bakchylides, and compares himself to an eagle and Bakchylides to a jackdaw.
>
> SCHOLIAST, *On Pindar*

> In this ode (Pastor cum traheret) Horace imitates Bakchylides.
>
> PORPHYRIO, *On an Ode of Horace*

> There are nine Lyric Poets: Alkman, Alkaios, Sappho, Stesichoros, Ibykos, Anakreon, Simonides, Bakchylides, and Pindar.
>
> EUSTATHIOS, *Introduction to Pindar*

> It seems that the finest and most famous works of the ancients were also induced by exile. The Athenian Thucydides composed his history of the war between Athens and the Peloponnesians near Skapte Hyle in Thrace. Xenophon wrote at Skyllos in Elis. The poet Bakchylides (from Keos) wrote in the Peloponnesos.
>
> PLUTARCH, *On Exile*

Peace

Only great peace
brings wealth to men
and a flowering of honey-throated song,
and to the gods
ox-thighs burning and long-haired sheep
flaming yellow on the sculpted altars,
and to the young
a love of wrestling and the flute
and Bakchic dance.

In the iron-covered shield
the brown spider hangs his web.
The sharpened spear and double-edge sword
are flaked with rust.
The noise of the brass trumpet is dead,
and the honey of our dawnsleep
is not dried from our eyelids.
Streets clamor with happy outdoor banquets,
and the lovely hymns sung by children
spring like fire up into the bright air.

The West Wind

On his farmland Eudemos built this sanctuary to the
    Zephyr,
kind breeze among the harsh gales.
When the farmer prayed,
the wind awoke briskly
helping him winnow good wheat from the chaff.

Herakles

I must not sing of you now,
O Pythian Apollo (though
the lovely-throned Urania
sent me a gold ship from Pieria
cargoed with famous hymns) if you are hunting
far by the flowering bank of the Hebros

or delighting in the soft song
of the long-necked swan.
Before you come to cull
the bloom of paeans
which the Delphian dancers
chant loudly by your shining temple,
we will sing of Amphitryon's
brave son who fled the city
of Oichalia gutted by flames;
who came to that wavewashed cape,
where he was sacrificing nine deep-roaring bulls
to the Kenaian Zeus of the broad clouds,
a pair to the seagod who lifts
salt waters and punishes earth,
and a never-yoked high-horned ox
to chaste Athena of the fierce glance,

when a dread wargod wove
a terrible poisonous weapon of blood
for Deianeira : she had learned
the sorrowful news
that the fearless son of Zeus
was sending white-armed Iole
to his luminous rooms to become his bride.

O doomed insane wife! Why did she plot
disaster! Relentless envy
drove her against
the black veil of future
on that day, on the flowering bank of Evenos,
she took the star-cursed gift from the centaur Nessos.*

Idas Wins Marpessa

One day in spacious Sparta
goldhaired women

---

* The centaur's blood poisoned by Herakles' arrow in which jealous
  Deianeira dipped the shirt of her husband, Herakles, thinking it a
  love potion; the garment caused Herakles' death and her suicide.

danced to a song
when courageous Idas
led Marpessa of the violet braids
to his own rooms
after eluding death.
Poseidon the sealord
gave him a chariot
and horses equal to the wind,
and sent him to the handsome city of Pleuron
and to the son of Ares of the gold shield.*

Theseus

A blue-prowed ship was knifing the open sea
off Krete, carrying battle-fierce Theseus
and fourteen glorious
young Ionian men and girls.
The northerly winds slammed into
her white sails glittering far,
by grace of famous Athene of the war-aegis.
But the alarming gifts of Aphrodite,
who wears the headband of desire,
clawed at the heart of Minos,
and he could not keep his hand from a girl
and caressed her white cheek.
But Eriboia screamed
for Theseus the bronze-armored
offspring of Pandion; he looked
and his eye rolled black
under his brows, and angry pain
pierced his heart, as he spoke:
"O son of peerless Zeus,
here you are steering
a course of shameful behavior
within your heart.
Hero, control that wanton violence.

* Evenos, father of Marpessa.

Our powerful destiny comes from the gods,
and whichever way the scale of Justice
dips, we shall fulfill
our determined fate—whenever
it comes. So restrain
your heavy hand. Even if true
that you were conceived in the bed of Zeus
under the brow of Mount Ida
from the celebrated daughter
of Phoinix, yet I also came
into being when the daughter
of rich Pittheus lay with the sealord
Poseidon; and the violet-wreathed
daughters of Nereus gave her
a veil of gold. Therefore,
O war-king of the Knossians,
I ask you to hold back insolence
that will bring many tears.
I would never look on sweet light
of ambrosial dawn, were you to force
any of these youths or virgin
women. Rather, we shall match
the strength of our hands, and the gods will judge."

So spoke the spear-brave hero,
and sailors stood spellbound
before his defiant courage,
but Helios' son-in-law raged in his soul
and concocted new tricks,
and spoke: "Omnipotent Zeus, Father,
hear me. If I am your son by Phoinix' daughter,
your white-armed bride,
now break swiftly from the sky
a fire-haired flash of thunder,
a sign all will know. Theseus, if Aithra
from Troizen really bore you
as son to Poseidon the earth-shaker,
go leap into the deep pelagos,

your father's chambers,
and bring back this shining
gold ornament of my hand,
my ring. Now you will know
if Kronos' son, lord of thunder
and master of all, will hear my prayers."

Zeus, mountain of strength, listened to his pure
prayer and approved; and wishing to honor
his son in great public
display, spilled down
a flash of lightning. Minos, seeing
the welcome portent, raised his arms
to the echoing sky; the battle-fierce
hero spoke: "Theseus, now you see
how shining clear are my gifts
from Zeus. Come, dive into the roar
of the open sea, and your father,
the lord Poseidon, son of Kronos,
will lift you in transcendent glory
over the land of handsome trees."
He spoke, and Theseus did not flinch.
A heart of iron, standing tall
on the solid deck he sprang,
and the deep forest of the sea
took him down kindly. Zeus' son
was inwardly amazed,
and ordered the well-made ship
to sail before the wind.

But Destiny swept them on another course.
Pummeled astern by a northern blast
the rapid vessel shot ahead
and the group of Athenian
youths trembled in fear
as their hero plunged to the water.
Tears formed in their flower-bright
eyes, as they the tight of the grave danger.

But dolphins, roamers in the sea,
easily bore great Theseus
to the palace of his horseman father.
He entered the regal hall of gods.
There he looked with fearful wonder
at the beautiful daughters
of rich Nereus. From their
fabled bodies shone a glory
of fire, and ribbons of gold
were twined among their braids
as their nimble feet floated
in happy dance. He saw
in the pleasant palace
the ox-eyed Amphitrite,
his father's true majestic wife,
who wrapped round him a robe of purple linen,
and laid on his heavy mat of hair
an immaculate wreath
that one day at her marriage
cunning Aphrodite in rose garland gave her.

For men of sound mind
no labor by the gods is past belief.
Beside the ship's narrow stern Theseus came up
and how he amazed
the Knossian warlord
when he rose unwet from the sea,
a miracle to all, and on
his limbs gleamed the gift of the gods.
The bright-throned nymphs
shrieked in pristine triumph,
the sea clamored,
and those youths about him
sang a loud perfect paean!
O Lord of Delos, your heart
warmed with Keian chorales,
grant us godly blessings in all we do.

PRAXILLA

Poet active about 450 BCE at Sikyon in the Argolid. She wrote dithyrambs, drinking songs and hymns.

> Praxilla was portrayed in bronze by Lysippos, although she spoke nonsense in her poetry.
>
> TATIAN, *Against the Greeks*

> Only a simpleton would put cucumbers and the like on a par with the sun and the moon.
>
> ZENOBIOS

Of the Sensual World

Most beautiful of things I leave is sunlight.
then come glazing stars and the moon's face,
then ripe cucumbers and apples and pears.

Appearance

You gaze at me teasingly through the window:
a virgin face—and below—a woman's thighs.

Achilles

(You understood their words)
but they never reached the heart
buried in your chest.

The Coward

Under cover
a coward will strike from any side.
I warn you, friend:
watch out for his sting.
Under every rock is a lurking scorpion.

PARRHASIOS

A noted painter active at Athens probably in the second half of the fifth century BCE. His reported skill in details of facial expression and in outline drawing perhaps justified in part the *hybris* of the epigram given below. Parrhasios was represented as discussing painting with Sokrates in Xenophon's *Memorabilia,* and himself wrote on the art.

> Parrhasios so systematized all art that he is known as the lawgiver; the depiction of gods and heroes according to his manner is followed by other painters, as though by necessity.
>
> QUINTILIAN, *Elements of Oratory*

> Euenor was the father and teacher of the great painter Parrhasios.
>
> PLINY, *Natural History*

Perfection in Art

I say, even if those who hear are unbelieving,
I affirm that my hand has discovered the limits of art.
Though nothing is flawless in the world of men,
now the mark is fixed and cannot be surpassed.

On a Painting of Herakles for which the God Posed

Now you may see the god exactly as he was,
coming to me Parrhasios in my dream.

Hippon

Natural philosopher, probably from Samos, was active in the latter half of the fifth century BCE. He revived and modified the view that water was the source of all things.

> Kratinos also accuses Hippon of impiety.
>
> SCHOLIAST, *On Clement of Alexandria*

> Hippon of Rhegium in Calabria declared that the elements were cold (water) and heat (fire), and that fire, when made from water, overcame the power of its author and formed the world.
>
> HIPPOLYTOS, *Against Heresies*

> Because of the impoverished nature of his thinking, Hippon is not worthy of being included with those philosophers who hold water to be an element or first principle.
>
> ARISTOTLE, *Metaphysics*

On the Atheist Philosopher

Here is the grave of Hippon. When he died
fate made him equal to the eternal gods.

MELANIPPIDES

A famous dithyrambic poet of his time Born on Melos (and hence a Dorian) he was active during the middle of the fifth century BCE and died at the court of Perdikkas in Macedonia. A comic poet attributed to Melanippides the first innovations which led to the decadence of choral lyric. One innovation was the introduction of lyric solos into the dithyramb. In addition to dithyrambs, Melanippides wrote epics, elegies and epigrams.

> Like his grandfather he was a lyric poet. He made great
> innovations in the dithyramb and spent part of his life
> at the court of the Macedonian king Perdikkas, where he
> died. He wrote lyric poems and dithyrambs.
>
> *Suda Lexicon*

> "Tell me, Aristodemos," he asked, "are there any men
> whose art you esteem?" "Yes," he said. "Tell us their
> names," Sokrates asked. "For the epic I especially admire
> Homer, for the dithyramb Melanippides. . . ."
>
> XENOPHON, *Recollections of Sokrates*

The Danaïds

They were not shaped like handsome men
nor was their voice womanly,
but they trained naked
driving in chariots about the sunny
treelands. Often
they were happy in hunting;
often they sought the holy tear
of the dripping frankincense,
the good smell of dates
or smooth seeds of Syrian cassia.

Timotheos

Timotheos was born at Miletos around 450 BCE and died around 360 BCE, possibly in Macedon, whither he (like his friend Euripides) had been invited by King Archelaos. The most famous lyric poet of his time, Timotheos was also (according to some tastes ancient and modern) one of the most pernicious. His musical innovations were striking, and carried such weight (with Euripides, for example) that they contributed mightily to the decay of the verbal side of the ode. The language in his surviving fragments is often preposterously artificial and periphrastic. Yet the long papyrus fragment on the defeat of the Persians (published in 1903) includes a jarringly "realistic" imitation of a Persian speaking in broken Greek. His works included nomes, dithyrambs, hymns, encomia, etc.

> When Timotheos was hissed because he seemed to be an innovator and rebel against the laws of music, Euripides asked him to take heart, for soon the theater audience would acclaim him.
>
> PLUTARCH, *Should Old Men Govern?*

> Here the Spartans hung the lyre of Timotheos of Miletos, after censuring him for having added four new strings to the traditional seven in the art of singing to the lyre.
>
> PAUSANIAS, *On Sparta*

> If there had been no Timotheos, we would not have much of our lyric poetry, and if there had been no Phrynis there would have been no Timotheos.
>
> ARISTOTLE, *Metaphysics*

To Apollo

Sun, your phosphorescent rays pin fire
across the eternal firmament.
Snap a far-hunting arrow against our enemies,
O careering Healer to whom we cry!

PLATON (PLATO)

Born about 429 BCE in Athens and died in 347. He was a disciple of Sokrates, later the founder of the Academy, and in effect the father of Western philosophy. If he was in fact the author of the epigrams attributed to him, his *Phaidros* and *Symposion* may provide the spiritual link between his amatory epigrams and his philosophical works. "Hesperos" has been called the most perfect of all epigrams. Shelley prefixed it to hip "Adonais."

> You were the most accomplished stylist of the fine Attic tongue, and all Greek literature has no greater voice than yours. Inspired Plato, you were the first to contemplate ethics and life, looking to Gad and heaven. You combined the high thinking of Pythagoras with the cutting spirit of Sokrates, and were a beautiful monument of their solemn dissension.
>
> ANONYMOUS, *Palatine Anthology*

> If Apollo had not given Plato to Greece,
> how could he cure men's souls by writings?
> While Apollo's son Asklepios heals the human body,
> Plato heals the immortal soul.
>
> DIOGENES LAERTIOS, *Palatine Anthology*

> The golden bough of Plato's poems,
> forever divine, and shining with virtue.
>
> from the *Stephanos of Meleagros, 1st proem*

Hesperos

You were the Morning Star among the living.
In death, O Evening Star, you light the dead.

Love Poem

My child, Star, you gaze at the stars,
and I wish I were the firmament
that I might watch you with many eyes.

The Apple

I am an apple, and one who loves you
tossed me before you. O yield to him,
dear Xanthippe! Both you and I decay.

Lesson from the Academy

I throw this apple before you.
Take it—if you love me purely,
and give up your virginity.

Yet if you will not love me
keep the apple—and think
how long the beauty lasts.

Sokrates to His Lover

As I kissed Agathon my soul swelled to my lips,
where it hangs, pitiful, hoping to leap across.

*The Famous Courtesan Laïs Dedicates
a Mirror to Aphrodite*

I Laïs who laughed scornfully at Hellas,
who kept a swarm of young lovers at my door,
I lay my mirror before the Paphian,
for I will not see myself as I am now,
and cannot see myself as once I was.

On Loving Alexis

I barely whispered that Alexis was handsome
and now all the loose hounds goggle at him.
My heart, why do you show the dogs a bone?
Soon you'll suffer, as when you lost Phaidros.

Sokrates to Archeanassa

My girlfriend was Archeanassa from Kolophon
and her wrinkles are scars of a sour love.
Pain, horror. On her first voyage she loved
a graceful young man, and passed through fire.

Modesty

Aphrodite cried at Knidos when she saw Aphrodite:
O Zeus! Where did Praxiteles see me naked?

On Time

Time brings everything, and dragging years alter
names and forms, nature and even destiny.

Death at Sea

Sailors be free of disaster on land and sea,
for you are passing by a sailor in his grave.

Pindar

A delight to strangers and loved by friends,
Pindar labored for the sweet-voiced Muses.

Sappho

Some say nine Muses but count again.
Behold the tenth: Sappho of Lesbos.

In the Pine Grove

Sit below the long needles of the resonant pine
as its branches shudder in the western winds.
A shepherd's piping by the loquacious river
will lay heavy sleep on your spellbound eyelids.

Pan

Be still, green cliff of the Dryads. Be still,
springs bubbling among rocks, and confused noisy
bleating of the ewes.
For it is Pan playing on his honey-voiced pipe.
His supple lips race over the clustered reeds,
while all round him
a ring of dancers spring up on joyful feet:
Nymphs of the Water and Nymphs of the Oak Forest.

Aristophanes

When looking for an inviolable sanctuary,
the Graces found the soul of Aristophanes.

On a Doomed Settlement in Media

We lying here in the open plains of Ekbatana
once heard the throbbing waves of the Aigaian.
Farewell famous Eretria, once our country.
Farewell Athens, our neighbor by Euboia.
Farewell beloved sea!

Captivity in Persia

We are Eretrians of Euboia, but we lie in Susa,
and how remote, now, is our motherland!

On a Thief

You look upon a shipwrecked man. The sea killed
me but was ashamed to strip me of my last garment.
It took a man's inglorious hands to rob me naked,
a grave sacrilege for such a shabby
gown. Let the poor wretch wear it down in Hell
where King Minos may see him in my rags.

Equality of Death

I am a sailor's tomb. Beside me lies a farmer.
Hell is the same, under the land and sea.

Inscription for the Tomb of Dion, Tyrant of Syracuse

Tears were fated for Hekabe and Ilium's women
from the day of their birth,
but Dion, just when you triumphed with famous works,
all your wandering hopes were cast down by the gods.
Now dead in your spacious city, you are honored by
    patriots—
But I was one who loved you, O Dion!

Η ΠΕΡΙΟΔΟΣ ΈΛΛΗΝΙΣΤΗΣ

The Hellenistic Period

DIPHILOS

A comic poet of Athens, born before 340 BCE, died after 289 BCE. He wrote some one hundred plays. The passage below is in iambics, and was probably taken from one of his plays for inclusion in the *Greek Anthology.*

On the Argives

Argos may be a land of horses
but the inhabitants are wolves.

Anyte

Active about 290 BCE. Poet of Arkadiain the Peloportnesos, she wrote epigrams, mock-epitaphs and nature poems in the Doric dialect.

The many lilies of Anyte.

from the *Stephanos of Meleagros, 1st proem*

Repose

Lounge in the shade of the luxuriant laurel's
beautiful foliage. And now drink sweet water
from the cold spring so that your limbs weary
with summer toil will find rest in the west wind.

Epitaph of a Slave

Alive, this man was Manes, a common slave.
Dead, even great Darius is not his peer.

On a Statue in an Orchard

I am Hermes. I stand in the crossroads by a windy
belt of trees near the gray shore of the sea
where the weary traveler may rest: here a fountain
bubbles forth a cold and stainless water.

Kallimachos

Born about 305 BCE in Kyrene in North Africa. He became a school-master in Alexandria, and then cataloguer of the royal library (the most famous library of ancient times). He produced a systematic catalog of the library which has been called "the first scientific literary history." Kallimachos was the center of a controversy over the proper length of a poem; he claimed that the long poem was an anachronism. The typical "learned" poet composing for a narrow, sophisticated audience, he was versatile, experimental and prolific.

His known works include a long but episodic narrative-didactic poem in elegiacs, narrative hymns, iambics, miniature epics (epyllia), lyrics (of which little survives), elegies, dramas (lost) and—most important for lyric in the modern sense—epigrams.

> The sweet myrtle of Kallimachos is always full of harsh honey.
>
> from the *Stephanos of Meleagros, 1st proem*

Epitaph on Himself

You are walking by the tomb of Kallimachos,
who was accomplished in singing poems
and knew when to laugh over his wine.

KALLIMACHOS, *Palatine Anthology*

Epitaph of a Young Boy

Here Philippos the father buried his son Nikoteles,
a child of twelve and his dearest hope.

Twofold Grief

It was morning when we buried Melanippos
and by sundown Basilo his virgin sister
was dead by her own hand.
She could not bear to live
after she had placed him on the funeral pyre.

Their father's home displayed a double sorrow,
its lovely children gone,
and all Kyrene watched with downcast eyes.

On the Death of a Poet

They brought me word of your death,
Herakleitos,
and I wept for you
remembering how often we watched the sun
setting as we talked.

Dear Halikarnassian friend,
you lie elsewhere now
and are mere ashes;
yet your songs—your nightingales—will live,
and never will the underworld,
destroying everything,
touch them with its deadly hand.

Epitaph of an Enemy

Passerby, do not wish me well with your sour heart.
Go away. And I shall be well by your being gone.

A Sailor on the Beach

Who are you, O shipwrecked stranger?
Leontichos found your corpse on the beach,
buried you in this grave
and cried thinking of his own hazardous life.
For he knows no rest:
he too roams over the sea like a gull.

THEOKRITOS

The latest of the major Greek poets. An approximate contemporary of Kallimachos, he was born at Syracuse perhaps ca. 310 BCE. Active there, at Kos (an island in the Dodekanese), and at the court of Ptolemy II in Alexandria. He died perhaps ca. 250 BCE. As his best-known genre, the pastoral mime, suggests, he wrote for an audience of high sophistication. His Idylls (or "Little Forms") are for the most part on the borderline or outside the range of "lyric" poetry. They include works of the most diverse sort: pastoral and urban mimes (short quasi-realistic dramatic episodes), epyllia (short epic narratives), hymns, and love poetry after the manner of Sappho and Alkaios. Although "literary" Doric is his predominant dialect, Theokritos also used the Epic, Ionic and Aiolic dialects with skill. Some twenty epigrams are included in his surviving corpus. Pastoral art from Vergil to Picasso and Ravel is in his debt.

> I am not the other Theokritos from Chios.* I am Theokritos who wrote these poems
> and one of many Syracusans.
> Son of Praxagoras and noble Philinna,
> my muse is from my own native land.
>
> THEOKRITOS, *Introductory Poem to Idylls*

To the Goatherd

Goatherd, when you turn the corner by the oaks
you'll see a freshly carved statue in fig wood.
The bark is not peeled off. It is legless, earless,
    but strongly equipped with a dynamic phallus
to perform the labor of Aphrodite. A holy hedge
runs around the precinct where a perennial brook
spills down from upper rocks and feeds a luxuriance
of bay, myrtle and fragrant cypress trees.

---

* A fourth-century BCE orator and sophist.

A grape vine pours its tendrils along a branch,
and spring blackbirds echo in pure transparency
of sound to high nightingales who echo back
with pungent honey.
Come, sit down, and beg Priapos
to end my love for Daphnis. Butcher a young goat
in sacrifice. If he will not, I make three vows:
I will slay a young cow, a shaggy goat and a darling
lamb I am raising. May God hear you and assent.

Daphnis

Daphnis, you lie on the earth on some leaves
resting your tired body.
The hunting stakes
are newly set in the hills. Pan
is on your track, and Priapos comes with saffron ivy
tied about his forehead. They are heading
for your cave. Hurry!
Shake off your lethargy and run!

Offerings

These are gifts for Pan. And Daphnis
who pays country tunes on a warbling pipe—
he of the milk-white skin—gave them:

his double reel, a staff for hunting hare,
a fawn hide and keen javelin. And a pouch
of leather in which he once carried apples.

Sacrificial Goat

Morning-wet roses and the redolent thyme
are for ladies of Helikon.
But laurel trees
with black leaves
that grace the precipice at Delphi
are for you, Apollo: Pythian Healer.

The horned he-goat lowers his white body
as he grazes on the tips of sagging terebinth.
His blood will soon spill across the altar.

Late Summer

Many poplars and many elms shook overhead,
and close by, holy water swashed down noisily
from a cave of the nymphs. Brown grasshoppers
whistled busily through the dark foliage. Far
treetoads gobbled in the heavy thornbrake.

Larks and goldfinch sang, turtledoves were moaning,
and bumblebees whizzed over the plashing brook.

The earth smelled of rich summer and autumn fruit:
we were ankle-deep in pears, and apples rolled
all about our toes. With dark damson plums
the young sapling branches trailed on the ground.

Leonidas of Tarentum

Early third century BCE. "One of the greatest Greek epigrammatists," says Gilbert Highet of him. Author of about one hundred epigrams in an elaborate and artificial style, mostly about the life of the poor, to which class he belonged. Much admired by the Romans, and imitated by Vergil and Propertius.

> Far from my Italian soil I lie, far
> from my land of Tarentum; and
> this is more bitter to me than death.
> Such is the intolerable life of a
> wanderer. But the Muses loved me,
> and I have more honey than bitter
> fruits. The name of Leonidas goes
> unforgotten. His gifts from the
> Muses proclaim it as long as there
> is sun.

LEONIDAS OF TARENTUM, *Epitaph on Himself*

Fair Warning from Priapos

The season for sailing. Already the chattering swallow
returns with the slender west wind.
Meadows bloom, and the boiling waves of the sea,
whipped by gales, are smooth and silent.
Come then, sailor, haul in the anchors and loosen the
    hawsers
and sail with all the canvas flying.
It is Priapos, god of the harbor, who warns you now:
set out from this port for foreign cargoes.

Summer Thirst

Traveler, do not drink the warm water
from this pool,
all muddy from the quick mountain brook
and the intruding sheep.
Go a little further up the hill
where the heifers are grazing,
and there by a shepherd's pine
you will find
bubbling up through the porous rock
a spring colder than northern snow.

Asklepiades

Active about 270 BCE in Alexandria, Asklepiades was the originator
of much of the traditional imagery of love poetry, including Cupid's
arrows.

Snow in Summer

Snow in summer on a dry tongue is sweet,
and after winter sweet for the sailor
to see the spring stars,
but sweetest when one cloak shelters
two lovers,
and the Kyprian is praised.

Prudence

Save your maidenhead? What's the good?
My girl, down in Hades there are no lovers.
The pleasures of Kypris are for the living.
Once past Acheron, river of death,
we shall lie as bones and dust.

Black Woman

Didyme plunders me with her beauty.
When I look at her I am wax over fire.
If she's black, what of it? So are coals.
When kindled, they glow like blooming roses.

On a Man-Devouring Whore

Voracious Philainion bit me. The bite doesn't show
yet pain crawls in me, creeps to my very fingertips.
Love, I am drained, done in, dead! I fell half-dazed
on a viperous whore, and her embrace was death.

To Zeus

Snow, thunder, hail, blaze and blacken the earth,
shake the clouds,
kill me and I will stop,
but let me live
and I shall go on, a slave of love.
And Zeus, Aphrodite was also your master
when you stormed as gold rain through a bridal window
to shower down on lovely Danaë.

Mnasalkas

Of Sikyon, flourished about 250 BCE.

> The sharp needles of Mnasalkas' pines.
>
> from the *Stephanos of Meleagros, 1st proem*

At the Temple of Aphrodite

Let us stand on this low beach by the crashing surge
and gaze at the holy groves of the seaborn Kyprian;
at the bubbling spring under shadowy poplars
where a shrilling kingfisher dips its bill.

THEODORIDAS

Syracusan epigrammatist of the second half of the third century BCE.

Epitaph of a Sailor

I am the tomb of a drowned sailor. Sail on.
Even while we sank, the others sped away.

MOSCHOS

Of Syracuse, active around 150 BCE. Pastoral poet, to whom some half-dozen short pieces may be assigned. The *Rape of Europa* (a short narrative) and the Lament for Bion have also been attributed to Moschos, but chronology definitely excludes the latter.

Landlover

When wind dips calmly over the blue sea
my cowardly soul stirs. My love for land
becomes a craving for the vast salt waters.
But when the ocean bottom roars, and foam boils
spitting skyward on the wild crashing waves,
I gaze at the shore and its forests, and shun
the sea. Then I love black earth and shadowy
woods where even during a blasting gale
a pine tree sings. What a wretched life
the fisherman has—with his berth a home,
the sea his labor and fish his wandering prey!
I prefer to sleep under a leafy plane
and hear the plashing of a bubbling spring
which soothes the soul and never brings me pain.

ARISTON

Lived in time to be included in Meleagros' anthology.

A Poor Scholar's Warning

Mice, if you come for bread, go find another hole;
I live in a humble hut.
Go to some rich man's villa
where you can nibble on fat cheese and dried raisins
and make a feast out of scraps.
But if you come to sharpen your teeth on my books
your supper will be a dull poison.

MELEAGROS

Lived about 140–70 BCE, at Tyros and on Kos. As a philosopher, he wrote Cynic satirical sermons, now lost. He collected the first serious anthology of epigrams, and more than 130 of his own epigrams survive; these are mainly erotic, and written in the florid and complex "Asian" style.

Shining Foe

O morning star, bright enemy of love,
how slowly you turn around the world
while Demos lies warm with another
under her cloak,

but when my slender love lay on my chest,
how swiftly you came to stand above us,
drenching us with light that seemed to laugh
at our loss.

Love's Wages

Heavy soul, now you bellow fire,
now recover your cool breathing.
But why cry? When you harbored Eros,
you knew he would rise against you.

So be resigned to fire and snow.
You sheltered him, and this is your pay.
You must suffer now for being a fool
while you sizzle in boiling honey.

Myiskos

By Love, I swear it!
Tender are the boys whom Tyros nurtures.

Yet Myiskos is the sun,
and when he illuminates the world
bright stars fade under his light.

After Charybdis

Where are you driving me,
foul waves of love,
huge sleepless winds of jealousy,
turbulent sea of orgy?

The rudder of my heart is broken:
I drift.
Will I ever again see
the voluptuous Skylla?

Flowers for Heliodora

White, white violets
with myrtle and tender narcissus;
I shall weave laughing lilies
and soft crocus and purple hyacinths
with roses, flowers of lovers.
I shall come to decorate her brow
and brighten her perfumed hair
in a fine rain of flowers.

Light of Beauty

The flowers looped in Heliodora's hair darken
but she glows brighter as the flowers fade.

A Thieving Sky

Morning Star, herald of dawn, goodbye,
and come back swiftly as the Evening Star;
bring me clandestinely her whom you stole.

The Wine Cup

The wine cup is happy. It rubbed against
warm Zenophila's erotic mouth. O bliss!

I wish she would press her lips under my lips
and in one breathless gulp drain down my soul.

Love on the Blue Water

Asklepias adores making love. She gazes at a man,
her aquamarine eyes calm like the summer seas,
and persuades him to go boating on the lake of love.

Heliodora's Fingernail

Your fingernail, Heliodora, was grown by Eros
and sharpened by him. How else could
your mere scratching be a claw against my heart?

The Kiss

Your eyes are fire, Timarian, your kiss birdlime.
You look at me and I burn. You touch me and I stick!

Sole Tenure

Zenophila, my flowering tree, you are asleep.
Though wingless, I would come like Hypnos
and bury myself under your eyelids
so that even sleep might not intrude
and I alone possess you.

Hour of the Spring

Winter squalls are drained out of the sky,
the violet season of flowering spring smiles,
the black earth glitters under a green lawn,
swelling plants pop open with tiny petals,
meadows laugh and suck the dew of morning
while the rose unfolds.

The shepherd in the hills
happily blows the top notes of his pipe,
the goatherd gloats over his white kids.
Sailors race across the thrashing waves,

their canvas swollen on the harmless breeze.
Drinkers acclaim the grape-giver Dionysos,
capping their hair with flowering ivy.
Bees from the putrid carcass of a bull
work with intent care; bunched in their hive
they spill a limpid honey through the comb's perforations.
All tribes of birds clamor: kingfishers on the sea,
swallows in rafters,
swans by river banks, nightingales in groves.

When saplings blossom and dry meadows revive
or shepherds pipe and shaggy flocks meander
or fleets scud on the sea and drinkers dance
or bees labor and birds dazzle the sky with song,
why can a singer not praise the lovely spring?

The Last Victory

I'm on the ground, cruel god, so bury your heel in my neck.
I feel, God knows! your ponderous weight
and arrows of fire. Yet you can't burn me any more.
Hurl your torches at my heart. All is ashes.

I, Meleagros

My nurse was the island of Tyros,
and Attic land of Syrian Gadara was
my birthplace. I was sired by Eukrates
—I, Meleagros, friend of the Muses
and first to waken to the Graces of
Menippos. A Syrian? What if I am?
Stranger, we all live in one country: the world.

Out of one Chaos were all men born.
In my old age I traced these letters
on the slab before my grave,
knowing that old men are neighbors to death.
Passerby, wish me well, the talkative old man,
and you may also reach a loquacious old age.

BION

Born in Asia Minor. Active around 100 BCE, mostly in Sicily, where, according to tradition, he was poisoned by jealous rivals. Classed as a pastoral poet, though the pastoral element is not prominent in his surviving seventeen fragments. The *Lament for Adonis* is sometimes assigned to him.

> Nightingales mourning in the thick
> foliage, carry word to the Sicilian
> springs of Arethousa that the cow-
> herd Bion is dead. And with him
> song and Dorian poetry have likewise perished.
>
> UNKNOWN PUPIL OF BION, from *Lament for Bion*

Hesperos

Evening Star, gold light of Aphrodite born in the foam,
Evening Star, holy diamond of the glassblue night,
you are dimmer than the moon, brighter than another star.
Hello, good friend! I'm on my way to serenade
my shepherd love. Give me your rays in place of moonlight.
There was a new moon today, but quickly set.
I am no thief, no highway man to plague a traveler at night.
A lover I am. And those in love must be helped.

Polyphemos

What will I do? I'll just go my way
across to that distant hill and down
again to the sandpits on the shore.
And I'll sing quietly to myself
my prayer for Galateia, who doesn't care.
Yet till the shattering end of old age
I will never once abandon sweet hope.

THE ROMAN PERIOD

PHILODEMOS THE EPICUREAN

Lived about 110–40/35 BCE. A teacher and popularizer of Greek philosophy for the Romans, he was to influence Vergil and Horace. Approximately twenty-five of his epigrams survive in the Anthology.

The Private Life of Philodemos

Philenis, fill our silent confidant—
the lamp—with olive dew. Then go,
and lock the stout door behind you,
for love abhors a breathing witness;
and you, sweet Xantho, let us begin . . .
Only my couch, a friend to lovers,
will know the secrets of Aphrodite.

An Ageless Lover

Charito is more than sixty
yet her hair is still a dense forest
and no brassiere holds up the marble cones
of her high-pointed breasts.
Her unwrinkled flesh exhales ambrosia
and myriads of teasing charms.
Lovers, if you do not run from hot desire,
enjoy Charito and forget her many decades.

DIODOROS

The poems under this name in the *Anthology*, according to high-est authority (Wilhelm Schmid), can be attributed to any of three different men. At any rate they probably belong to the period 100 BCE–100 CE.

The Fall

A tiny child in the villa of Diodoros
fell headfirst from a little ladder
and broke his neck bones fatally,
but when he saw his much-loved master running up,
he suddenly spread out his baby arms to him.

Earth, do not lie heavy on the bones
of a tiny slave child.
Be kind to Korax, who died at two.

ANTIPATROS OF THESSALONIKI

Flourished at the beginning of the Christian era. Seine eighty of his epigrams are in the *Anthology*.

Morning Gray

Morning gray is here, Chrysilla, and long ago
the twilight cock began to herald jealous Dawn
and guide her by my window.
Go away, selfish bird!
You drive me out of home to the crowded chatter of young
    men.
Tithonos, you're getting old.
Why else have you chased your bedmate Dawn
so early from her couch?

A Double Grave

Neither the sea nor land may claim my body.
In this death they share me in equal parts.
The fish devoured all my flesh in the sea,
but my bones were washed up on this cold beach.

Marcus Argentarius

Lived at the beginning of the Christian era. He was probably a penniless speech teacher. "The liveliest of the Graeco-Roman epigrammatists," Gilbert Highet has said of him.

Dialogue

"Take a hard look at scrawny Diokleia.
She's a skinny Aphrodite but sweet."

"Then nothing will stand between us;
when I lie on her skinny breasts
I'll be pressing right against her heart."

Discreet Witness

As I lay clutching Antigone's body,
my chest throbbed against her bosom,
my lips pressed into her sweet lips—
for the rest you must ask the lamp.

Oxymoron*

Melissa, you do everything like a bee:
when you kiss, you drip sweet honey from your lips;
when you ask for money,
I feel the savage wound of your sting.

---

* Melissa is a name and also means honeybee.

Rufinus

Lived sometime between 50 BCE and 50 CE.

A Letter from Rufinus in Ephesos

I Rufinus wish my darling Elpis only pleasure,
if you are happy away from me.
Yet I swear before you: I am wracked with pain
without you in my lonely bed.
With moist eyes I go to the hill of Koressos
or the temple of great Artemis.
Tomorrow when my city receives me, I will fly
to greet you with a thousand blessings.

A Naked Bather

A silver-ankled girl was bathing in a brook,
letting the water flood down
on the gold apples of her milky breasts.

When she walked, her round hips rolled and flowed
more liquid than the water.
Her arm reached down to shield her swelling belly,
not all—but all her hand could hide.

Remorse

If women were as enticing after, as before,
no man would be bored with his wife's body.
But after love, all women are distasteful.

APOLLONIDES

Lived sometime between 50 BCE and 50 CE.

The Message

If you come to Apollo's harbor at Miletos,
bring Diogenes this desolate word:
off the island of Andros was a shipwreck,
and your son Diphilos, bloated with waves,
lies on the earth bottom of the Aigaian Sea.

Parmenion

Lived sometime between 50 BCE and 50 CE.

A Discreet Purchase

Zeus bought Danaë with golden rain
and I purchase you with a gold coin.
I can't, after all, pay more than Zeus.

NIKARCHOS

Alexandrian epigrammatist, probably of the first century CE. About forty of his epigrams are in the Anthology; they are humorous, and often vile.

On Nikon's Nose

Look, I spy Nikon's hooked nose, Menippos,
and the face itself cannot be far removed.
Be patient, friend, and let us wait,
for it stands no more than half a mile behind:
the parabolic snout leads the way
and if we climb a high hill
we may catch a glimpse of the face.

A Physician's Touch

Only yesterday the good Dr. Markos
laid his sure hand on a statue of Zeus.
Although he was Zeus and made of marble
we're burying him today.

Mistaken Identity

Your mouth and your ass, Theodoros,
smell so alike, only the supple mind
of men of science can tell them apart.
Really, you should label your mouth and your ass,
for when you speak I think you are farting.

Kissing*

If you kiss me you hate me; if you hate me
you kiss me,
but if you don't hate me, my sweet friend,
don't kiss me.

Enigma

Who knows when Diodoros is yawning or farting?
For above and below, his breath is the same.

Popular Singer and a Bird's Death

Deadly is the singing of the night-raven,
but when you, Demophilos, break into song,
even the night-raven croaks.

Big Women

A plump woman with beautiful limbs is always good:
whether she is just ripe or very old.
If young, she takes me in her arms and hugs.
If old and wrinkled, she licks.

* Kiss also means here copulate.

LUCILLIUS

Epigrammatist of the middle of the first century CE. He was expert at the sharply pointed joke and lampoon; Nero was his patron.

Shopping Tip

Lady, you went to the market
and picked up hair, rouge, honey, wax and teeth.
For a like amount
you might have bought a face.

Gossip

Some have passed the word you dye your hair.
They lie, Nikilla,
for in the open market
you bought it raven black.

On the Hard Luck of Diophon

Diophon was being crucified,
but when he saw another near him on a higher cross,
he died of envy.

Love of Learning

Zenonis gives a place in her home to Menandros
a bearded grammarian,
for she has delivered her son to his instruction;
and the bushy pedant even labors into night,
with the mother,
practicing their figures, her dangling participles
and his copulative verb.

A Moneylover

When miserly Kriton wants to ease his cramping stomach
he sniffs not mint
but a copper penny.

On Hermon the Miser

After spending some money in his sleep,
Hermon the miser was so hopping mad,

he hanged himself.

Contagion

Demostratis walks in a halo
of armpit aroma,
but worse,
she makes those who smell her
exhale the same he-goat fumes.

A Night Call

Diophantos went to bed and dreamed of
Dr. Hermogenes,
and though he was wearing a good-luck piece,
he never woke up.

On the Same Hermogenes

The barber is perplexed.
Where can he start to shave the head
of this hairy Hermogenes
who—from head to toe—
seems to be all head?

Epitaph of a Pugilist

We his grateful opponents erected this statue
To Apis a Thoughtful Boxer
who even when clinching never hurt any of us.

On Boxers

Here you see the ruins of a former Olympic star.
Once he had a real nose, mind you, a chin, forehead,
ears, and eyes (lids and all),
and then he went pro.

He scrambled everything,
even his share of his father's estate.
For his kid brother showed up
(a spitting image of the former champ)
and the pug
(who looked like an outsider now)
was quietly but sternly ushered away.

The Devout Boxer

Aulos the boxer dedicates his skull to the Lord of Pisa,*
having collected the bones one by one.
If he comes out alive from his match at Nemea,
he may, Lord Zeus,
honor you with any surviving ribs.

A Precaution

Lazy Markos dreamt he was running, running, running. . . .
Out of fear he might run again
Markos never went back to bed.

The Quest

We were searching for the giant Eumekios.
We found him sleeping with his arms outstretched,
all under a tiny saucer.

A Prostitute Bathing

A girl of a hundred and still in the métier,
Heliodora, you spend hours in the bath.

---

* Lord of Pisa: Zeus.

But I know your dream: you pray to grow young,
like old Pelias, by letting them boil you alive.

Inside an Atom

So skinny was the pin-head Markos
that he bore a hole
with his own skull
through an atom of Epikouros
and slipped inside.

Fidelity in the Arts

Eutychos the portrait painter got twenty sons,
but even among his children—never one likeness.

The Poet Descending

Eutychides the lyric poet is dead.
Escape! you who inhabit the underworld,
for he comes with odes,
and orders thirteen lyres and twenty crates of music
to burn beside him on his funeral pyre.
Now Charon has you,
for where can you escape
with Eutychides established in Hell?

Decorum

The miser Asklepiades finding a mouse
one evening in h is house, saluted it:
"My very dear mouse, what do you want from me?"
With its sweetest smile the mouse replied:
"My dear friend and ceremonious host,
put away your fears,
I did not come for board—merely a bed."

LEONIDAS OF ALEXANDRIA

Wrote between 55 and 85 CE. Nero and later emperors were his patrons. More than forty of his epigrams are in the Anthology. Thirty are composed in such a way that the letters of each couplet in a poem, if given a numerical value, produce the same total.

The Punishment

The grape-stealer Hekatonymos
    ran all the way down to Hades
        flogged with a stolen vine switch.

Traianus (The Emperor Trajan)

Lived from 53 to 117 CE. He was one of the best of Rome's emperors. For the ruling classes at Rome, Greek was, like French in modern times, a mark of one's sophistication.

A Natural Sundial

If you point your b i g nose sunward
and open your gaping
mouth,
all who pass by
will know the time of day.

Ammianus

Lived at the beginning of the second century CE.

On the Afterlife of Nearchos

May the dust lie lightly on you in your grave,
O wretched Nearchos,
that wild dogs may more easily drag you out.

LOUKIANOS (LUCIAN)

Born about 120 CE in Samosata in Syria; died sometime after 180. An itinerant teacher of rhetoric and Cynic philosophy, he was also the author of numerous satirical dialogues and other writings, including the fabulous *True History,* which influenced (among others) Rabelais and Swift.

On Magical Whiskers

If by growing a goatee you hope to come
upon wisdom,
then, O wise friend, any smelly goat in
a handsome beard
is at once Plato.

DIONYSIUS SOPHISTES

One of many poets, sophists, philosophers and miscellaneous writers of the same name who lived in the Roman period.

A Vendor of Flowers

You selling roses have a flowery charm.
But rose-girl, what are you selling me?
your roses? yourself? or both?

Julianus (Julian the Apostate)

332–363 CE. The Roman emperor who, among his other reforms, tried belatedly to stem the tide of Christianity and revitalize paganism. He wrote numerous prose works in Greek.

Calculation*

Konon is but two feet tall—his wife four.
When flat in bed
their feet touching the wall,
imagine where Konon keeps his lips.

---

* Attribution to Julianus is uncertain.

Aisopos

Ca. fourth century CE. (Not the semilegendary fabulist of a thousand years earlier.)

Futility

How can we escape from you, life, except through death?
Our sorrows are endless. Endure? Escape? Neither is easy.
Yes, the beauty of nature is sweet—the earth,
sea, stars, the orbit of the moon and sun.
But all else is fear and pain.
One day a bit of luck
and then we wait for inexorable Nemesis.

THE BYZANTINE PERIOD

PALLADAS

Active about 400 CE. An impoverished schoolmaster at Alexandria, a pagan among Christians, he wrote more than 150 epigrams, most of them hopeless and bitter.

Her Glorious Hour

A woman will gnaw at your bile
Yet she has two fine seasons:
one, in her bridal bed;
two, when she is dead.*

Heritage

A grammarian's daughter made love with a man,
and the poor creature gave birth to a child
who was, in orderly sequence:
masculine, feminine, and neuter.

On the Rhetor Mauros

I was thunderstruck
on beholding Mauros, Professor of Rhetoric,
raise his elephantine snout
and spew murder in a voice
made from lips weighing one pound apiece.

On Monks

If solitary, how can they be so many?
If many, how again are they solitary?
O crowd of solitaries feigning solitude!

---

* Occasionally, in Greek, such an example of internal rhyme as
  thalamo and thanato is used, especially for humor and satire.

The Slaughterhouse

We all are watched over and foddered for death
like a herd of pigs absurdly butchered.

A Pagan in Alexandria Considers Life under
Christian Mobs Who Are Destroying Antiquity

Is it true that we Greeks are really dead
and only seem alive—in our fallen state
where we imagine that a dream is life?
Or are we truly alive and is life dead?

Grave Warning

Sir, you talk a lot, and after a short span
are laid out in the earth.
Keep silent
and while you are alive, meditate on death.

Julianus (Julian the Prefect of Egypt)

Active during the sixth century CE.

On a Young Wife

O black winter of savage death
that froze the spring of your unnumbered charms.
The tomb tore you from brilliant day
in this, your bitter sixteenth year.
Your husband and father—blind with grief—
Think of you, Anastasia, who were our sun.

Gift from the Dead

Your dear husband, Rhodo, erects a monument
of shining marble to redeem your soul;
he gives money to the poor—for, kindest of wives,
you died early and gladdened him with freedom.

At Anakreon's Tomb

I often sang this, and even from the grave I shout:
drink, for soon you must put on this garment of dust.

On Anakreon

A. You died from filling your paunch with wine, Anakreon.
B. But I enjoyed it, and you who do not drink
will also find yourself in Hades.

PAULUS SILENTIARIUS

An official at the court of Justinian ca. 560 CE. He wrote about
eighty epigrams in the *Anthology*, including some of the liveliest
love poems.

Visions

A man bitten by a mad hound, they say,
sees an image of the beast in the water.

Is Eros then wild with rabies?
Did he gash me with his bitter tooth
and ravage my spirit with his heat?

For now I see your darling form mirrored
in winecup, river whirlpool and the sea.

Taboo

My fingers on her breasts, our mouths joined;
I graze with deep fury on her silver neck;
yet though I labor over Aphrogeneia
this virgin lets me go so far—and denies
me her bed. Her upper body she allows
to Aphrodite, but her under parts she commits
to chaste Athena. I waste away between.

Purity

Beautiful girl, let us cast off these garments.
Let our naked limbs be knotted
so that no space is left between.
To me the clothes you wear are as strong
as the great wail of Babylon.*
Let us press chest against chest,
mouth into mouth,
and plunge the rest into silence.
I cannot bear trivial chatter.

* Wall erected by Semiramis.

Agathias Scholastikos

Lived from 536 to 582 CE. He was a lawyer of Byzantium, and compiler of the epigram-anthology which was the basis for the existing *Greek Anthology*. Agathias was a friend of Paulus Silentiarius but not his poetic equal.

Intimate Dialog

A. What are you mooning about?

B. I am in love.

A. With whom?

B. A virgin.

A. Is she good looking?

B. Perfectly exquisite.

A. Where did you meet her?

B. At a dinner party. I found her lying on the same couch
   with me.

A. You think you'll get in?

B. Yes, yes, my friend, but I don't wish to broadcast it.
Actually I want it to be nice and discreet.

A. You mean you want to avoid marriage.

B. My friend, I found out she isn't worth a dime.

A. You know this already. You are not in love, dear friend.
You are lying. How can your heart be madly in love
when it calculates so well?

Damaskios

Ca. fifth–sixth centuries CE.

Epitaph of a Slave Girl

Zozime, you were a slave girl only in body
and now find freedom for your body too.

Julianus (Julian Antecessor)

Sixth century CE?

Winning Charm

Your face is the face of an ostrich.
Was it Circe in her island sanctuary
who made you drink her secret potion
to turn your sourpuss into a birdhead?

Harvesting

Tall and wavy are the crops
on your hairy face.
Scissors?
Never.
Throw them away and bring out a plow.

ΑΘΗΝΑ
ATHENA

AUTHORS AND ANONYMOUS WORKS OF INDEFINITE PERIOD

GLYKON

Little is known of Glykon. He is credited by Hephaistion with the invention of the Glykonic meter, but the Glykon of the *Greek Anthology*, where this single poem appears under that name, may be a later poet of the same name.

Life without Meaning

All is laughter and dust. And all is nothing,
since out of unreason comes all that is.

KALLIKTEROS

A poet known only through his poems in the *Palatine Anthology*.

A Skilful Thief

Rhodo removes leprosy and scrofula by drugs
and removes the rest with agile fingers.

Bartered Virtue

The unpurchased wheat in your home may inform you
that your dear wife has been a horn of plenty.

Ammonides

Known only through the *Palatine Anthology*.

A War Plan

Show off Antipatra naked to the Parthians,
and the enemy will flee beyond the horizon,
yes, beyond the pillars of Herakles.

Diophanes of Myrina

Known only through the *Palatine Anthology.*

For a Statue of Eros

Love is really a highway robber:
1) He waits in ambush through the night,
2) He is a desperado,
3) and in the end he strips us naked.

THE ANAKREONTEIA

These imitations, long attributed to Anakreon, were written between the first century BCE and the sixth century CE.

The Old Man

Anakreon, singer of Teos,
came to me in a dream
and laughingly called me.
And I ran up to him
and kissed and hugged him.
He was old but handsome
and wild over wine.
His lips smelled of grape.
Though old and tottery
he fed on love. He slipped
the wreath from his head
and offered it to me.
It smelled of Anakreon.
I stupidly took it
and stuck it in my hair,
and ever since, I can't
keep myself from loving.

The Well-Tempered Party

Bring Homer's lyre but mute
the chords of savage war.
Bring winecups and the laws
of proper revelry.
I shall get drunk and dance
at our party, and even
roar on my tinging lyre,

yet with a tempered fury.
Bring Homer's lyre but mute
the chords of savage war.

The Rub of Love

Once while plaiting a wreath
I found Eros among the roses.
I grabbed him by the wings
and dipped him in the wine
and drank him down.
Now inside my limbs
he tickles me with his wings.

Play before Death

"Anakreon, you are old,"
the women say to me.
"Look in the mirror, you
haven't one lonely patch
on your abandoned temples
or desolate pate." Yes,
I cannot boast about
my hair, but I know this:
an old man must have love
the closer he is to death.

Today

I don't care for Gyges's gold,
the king of fabled Sardis,
for money is repugnant.
I don't envy the despots.
I live to soak my beard
in perfume, and twine my hair
in roses. Day is my gold.
Who can tell the future?
So while sun is sweet, drink,
shoot dice and offer a toast

to Bakchos. Tomorrow
disease may cut your wine.

A Nuisance

What can I do to you,
verbose swallow? Shall I
clip your agile wings
or slit your sharp tongue
like a heartless Tereus?
Why do your morning cries
rip me from my dreams
of my tender Bathyllos?

Bargain

A young peddler was hawking
a wax replica of Eros.
I went to him and said:
"How much is the statue?"
He answered me in Doric.
"You name it. Just so
I can get rid of him.
I'm no sculptor in wax
and I am sick of living
with this grubby Eros."
Now Eros, make me burn
or I'll melt you in fire.

Arithmetic

If you can count the leaves
of trees, waves in the ocean,
I shall make you the sole
accountant of my loves.
Mark down 20 from Athens,
and throw in 15 more.
From Corinth a small army
(Greek women are splendid!)

From Lesbos and Ionia,
Karia and Rhodes: 2,000
satisfying affairs.
Do my numbers overwhelm you?
I haven't mentioned Syria
or love in Egypt and Krete
where in the cities love
is both refined and wild.
And shall I count up those
from Cadiz and from far
Afghanistan and India?

A Woman

Nature gave the bull horns
and nimble hooves to horses,
springing legs to the hare,
a chasm of teeth to lions.
She furnished fins to fish
and speckled wings to birds.
To man she offered wisdom.
Was nothing left for woman?
Yes, she gave her beauty
in place of shields and swords,
and beauty glides in victory
over virile swords and fire.

Stratagem

You chant of Theban battles
or the slaughter before Troy.
I tell of my disaster,
It was no horse or hoplite,
no black vessel in the port.
A new weapon hobbled me:
two eyes stuck me to the bone.

The Test

Eros came and struck me
with his hyacinth rod
and ordered me to come.
We crossed uncrossable
torrents; forests, cliffs.
We raced, dripping sweat:
my heart was in my mouth,
my body nearly dead.
Then Eros touched my forehead
with his deft wing, and spoke:
"Are you unable to love?"

Before the Shadows

Lying on a soft bed
of myrtle and lotus
I want to drink.
Eros, put your apron on
with the papyrus ribbon,
and pour my dark wine.
Like a swift wheel
our life speeds past
and soon we will lie:
dust of scattered bones.
Why waste those perfumes
on the soil by my grave?
While I live, bring flowers
and my lovely mistress.
Before my somber climb
down to death's choir,
I would forget my grief.

The Midnight Guest

Once in the frozen hours of night
While the Great Bear circled Arktouros
and mortals lay drugged with sleep,

Eros stood at my gate, knocking.
"Who is pounding on my door?" I said.
"You are splitting my dreams."
"Open up. I'm only a child.
Don't be alarmed," Eros called in.
"I'm dripping wet and lost
and the night is black and moonless."
Hearing his words I pitied him
and quickly lit a candle.
Opening a door I saw a boy
with bow, wings and quiver.
I sat him down by the fire
and warmed his hands with my own,
and squeezed water from his hair.
When he recovered from the cold
he said, "Let's test this bow.
Rain has weakened the string."
He drew and struck me square
in the groin like a gadfly.
He leapt up laughing with scorn:
"Stranger, let us be happy.
My bow is unharmed, but you
will have trouble in your heart."

Cicada

We bless you, cicada,
high in the branches.
You sip a dew drop
and whistle like a king.
What you see is yours:
all the soft meadows
and furry mountains.
Yet you do no harm
in the farmer's field,
and men exalt you
as the voice of summer.
You are loved by Muses

and Apollo himself
who gave you clear song.
Wise child of the earth,
old age doesn't waste you.
Unfeeling and bloodless
you are like a god.

Gold, Death, Wine

If gold could buy life,
I would guard my wealth
with jealous desire,
and when death came
he would take some
and leave me alone.
Yet being mortal
I cannot prolong
my life, so why
should I cry or moan?
If we must die,
what good is gold?
So bring sweet wine,
and when I've drunk
bring my good friends.
I'll lie on a soft bed
and be lost in love.

Reflection

How good it is to roam
on the ripe grassy meadows
where the sweet wind drifts;
look at the grapevines,
and lie under the leaves
with a soft girl in my arms
who is willing and warm.

Spring

Spring comes: see where
Graces leave the rose,
how the ruffled sea
smooths into peace,
the water-duck dives,
how the crane soars.
The hot sun burns up
the somber clouds;
fields shine with crops
and olive trees bud.
Everywhere the Flood
of swollen grapes
flowers in the vineyard.

Adaptability

Once the daughter of Tantalos*
became a stone on the Phrygian hills,
and the daughter of Pandion
flew into the sky as a swallow.
I wish I were a mirror
so you would look at me.
I wish I were a tunic
so you would always wear me.
I should like to be water
so I could bathe your body.
I would become myrrh
so I could anoint you.
I would gladly be a scarf
for your breasts, a pearl
for your throat, a sandal—
if you would be sure to step on me.

* The daughter of Tantalos was Niobe.

Drunkard

The black earth drinks
and trees suck rain.
The seas drink brooks
and sun the sea
and moon the sun.
Why do you rage, friends,
when I want to drink?

MISCELLANEOUS

On a Drowned Sailor

Do not ask, mariner, whose tomb I am,
but chance your life upon a kinder sea.

Pleasure*

To praise is the highest good, and censure
is the beginning of hatred,
yet to speak maliciously of one's neighbor
is, after all, Attic honey.

A Bitter Tale

After eating little and drinking less,
I suffered the pains of lingering disease.
I have lived long and now am dead. I say:
a curse on you all!

Metamorphosis

I wish I were a scarlet rose
so you might lift me in your hands
and pull me to your snowy breasts.

By the Sea

If I were the wind
you might walk slowly along the shore
and remove your dress
and, as I blow, take me to your naked breasts.

* Sometimes attributed to Palladas.

A Private Bath

Delicious girl of the bath,
why do you rub so fiercely
when you bathe me?
Before I am fully undressed
I feel the fire.

Prayer to Aphrodite

Kypris, if you save those from the pelagos,
save me: I founder shipwrecked on the land.

Dreams

Sthenelais (who is an expensive whore and burns
up the town, breathing a smell of gold
on all those who desire her)
lay naked with me and came and came
through my dreamy night,
all for nothing until the pleasant dawn.

Nor more will I crawl before that barbarous girl
nor sink into the sticky juice of self-pity,
for sleep gives me gratuit
my fill of sweet flesh.

On Gorgios

I am the head of the Cynic Gorgios—
no longer spitting or blowing my nose.

*Forest Music**

Come, sit under my pine tree which is shaking
pleasantly as it plays with the mild west wind,
and hear the gossipy riverlets where I finger
my lonely reeds—and merge into soft sleep.

* Similar to a poem ascribed to Plato, 454 BCE.

His Patience

You denied me your green grape.
When ripe, you sent me on my way.
Do you now begrudge me
a small bite of your dry raisin?

Proklos

Proklos cannot wipe his nose with his hand,
his arms being shorter than the wild snout,
and when the poor thing sneezes, he won't even say,
Zeus preserve us !
He cannot hear his nose,
his ears being O so far away.

At the Tomb of Anakreon

Stranger, passing near the tomb of Anakreon,
pour me a libation as you approach,
for in life I was a drunkard.

On Plato's Tomb

Apollo had two sons, Asklepios and Plato:
one to save the body; the other the soul.

Epitaph of the Philosopher Epiktetos

I was a slave: crippled in body and poor
as the beggar Iros, yet loved by the gods.

Her Unique Virtue

Under this slab I rest, famous among women,
having opened my legs for one man alone.

On Dionysios of Tarsos

At sixty I, Dionysios, lie in my grave.
I was from Tarsos,
I never married and wish my father had not.

The Expectation

I no longer mourn those gone from the sweet light
but those who live ever waiting for death.

Brevity

The rose blooms for a brief season. It fades,
and when one looks again—the rose is briar.

FOLKSONGS

The Owl

Send the screaming owl of night
away from our land, away
from our people. Send
the contemptible bird
to our enemy's fleet of quick ships.

*Aging Lover's Appeal**

Please—keep old age
away a while longer,
O beautiful Aphrodite.

Dawn

What happened to you? Don't betray me,
I beg you.
Before he comes, get up from the bed
so you won't hurt yourself or me.
I am unhappy!
It is already day.
Don't you see the light in the window?

The Sun

Shine on us,
friendly sun.

---

* Diehl attributes this song to Alkman.

SAPPHO

SAPPHO

SAPPHO: AN INTRODUCTION

In Sappho we hear for the first time in the Western world the direct words of an individual woman. It cannot be said that her song has ever been surpassed. In a Greek dialect of the Eastern Mediterranean, she became our first Tang dynasty poet, akin to one of those Chinese of the seventh century CE, whose songs were overheard thought and conversation, in strict form, and who were said to "dance in chains." In her seventh-century BCE Lesbos, Sappho danced in chains, singing of Kritan altars at night and fruit dreaming in a coma, and always in metrical patterns unseen but musically overheard like her thoughts, passions, and internal dialogues.

Time with its strange appetite has modernized these ancient voices, making the Tang writer Wang Wei and Aiolic Sappho fashionable and intimate. The East has preserved tons of the Tang poets—maybe ten thousand of those golden birds in the Middle Kingdom—since after the fires of the book-burner emperor Qin Shi Huangdi (ruled 221–206 BCE) China zealously preserved the work of its poets. But Sappho suffered from book-burning religious authorities, who left us largely scraps of torn papyrus found in waterless wastes of North Africa. Such maltreatment has especially modernized her into a minimalist poet of few but important words, connected often more by elliptic conjecture than clear syntax. But what a full living voice comes through those ruins! Every phrase seems to be an autonomous poem, including a fragment of two words describing Eros: *optais amme*—"you burn us."

One day, when the sorrows of war and hatred are weary and fade, many diggers will return to the sands of infinite Egypt, to those rich ancient garbage heaps in the Fayum and to the outskirts of Alexandria where Hellenistic grammarians arranged her strophes in the grouped lines still used today. There we will discover many books of Sappho as we have found the books of the gnostic *Nag Hammadi Library* in Egypt and the scriptures of the Dead Sea Scrolls in nearby Syria. And if we do not find more Sappho, what we have will still be an intelligible constellation of sparkling fragments filling the heavens from the Great Bear down to the Southern Cross.

Europe's first woman poet combined amazing metaphor with candid passion. But being a woman she wrote from her dubiously privileged position as a minor outsider in a busy male society. Outside the main business of the world—war, politics, remunerative work—Sappho could speak with feeling of her own world: her apprehension of stars and orchards, the troubles and summits of love, the cycles of life and death; and she chatted with Afroditi. She wrote, giving the impression of complete involvement, though even in her most intensely self-revealing poems her words have the jarring strength of detachment and accuracy. She wrote as one might speak, if one could speak in ordinary but perfectly cadenced speech. And suddenly, we hear her, half destroyed, revealing,

> I convulse greener than grass
> and feel my mind slip as I go
>   close to death,
>
>   *31*

In another poem she is one of the speakers,

> Honestly I wish I were dead.
> When she left me she wept
>
> profusely and told me,
> "Oh how we've suffered in all this.
> Psapfo, I swear I go unwillingly."
>
> And I answered her,
> "Be happy, go and remember me,
> you know how we worshiped you."
>
>   *94*

At times, as in the interior conversations of the English metaphysical poet George Herbert, we are the poet. We become Sappho as she is talking with her friend Atthis or, in the famous ode to Afroditi, conversing almost fiercely with her ally the love goddess. In each case she uses the device of speech in poetry to achieve both close intimacy and objectifying distance. We discover a Sappho who is a wholly distinctive personality as opposed to a voice construed by thematic and prosodic convention. Though clearly descending from a tradition of earlier singers, she is never other than herself. Her contemporary could be Constantine Cavafy, for time does not separate their use of conversation and the recollection of past happiness, or the objective and overpowering confessional voice of these two poets of modernity. Line by line, with relentless and sly frankness and outrage, they construct the biography of a voice.

By contrast, Homer, the first man in Western literary history, is but a shadow in his own poetry. By some he is considered two Homers, one of the *Iliad,* and one of the *Odyssey* and, by others, an editor whose composite voice combines elements of a bardic tradition. Sappho, despite scanty and often mythical biographical tradition, emerges as a realized figure through her poems. Homer was of the epic-heroic tradition, but it took a lyric age to produce the first major woman lyric poet. Or more justly, we can say that Sappho, along with Archilochos who lived in the early part of the seventh century BCE, created the lyric age of antiquity.* She talks, laughs, insults, speaks with irony or despair. As Longinos tells us, she knows how to assemble details from true life to give us the lightning force of sublimity. We will find such ecstatic transcendence in later poets, notably in the Sufi Persian poets, the English metaphysical poets, and the mystico-erotic poems of Saint John of the Cross. But Sappho also conveys another intensity—easy, spare, and piercing—in the meeting of two lovers, as in this very mutilated fragment, "Behind a Laurel Tree":

> You lay in wait
> behind a laurel tree
>
> and everything
> was sweeter
>
> women
> wandering
>
> I barely heard
> darling soul
>
> now you came
> first
>
> beautiful
> in your garments
>
> 62

---

* "Lyric" is a good word for Archilochos, Sappho, and many later lyric poets. Archilochos is associated with the iambus and elegy and Sappho with her own meters, under the general rubric of monody or solo song (as opposed to choral song). But none of these terms apply exclusively to one poet, and we cannot know how much heroic poetry, in addition to fragment 44, Sappho might have composed or what the versatile Archilochos might have been up to. "Solo song," however, literal meaning of "monody," is a perfect term to attach to Sappho—and to a myriad of later singers.

We know Sappho more intimately than any ancient poet, with the possible exception of Catullus, who was enthralled by Sappho's poetry, imitated and translated her, and addressed his lover and muse in his poems as "Lesbia." She has permitted us to overhear her longing and intelligence, her humor and anger, and her perception of beauty. Her conversations have the naturalness of a storyteller improvising in formal verse.* Though her poetry, with the exception of two complete poems, of which #58 was found in its complete form in 2004,† survives only as fragments (some substantial), her emerging portrait is precise and profound like a Vermeer or Goya. Yet that fresh image exists only in the poems, not at all in the unreliable testimonia, all from at least a century after her death.

A few essential facts can be drawn from external sources— where she was born, her approximate lifetime, a possible exile around 600 BCE, and that her fame as a lyric poet exceeded all others in Greek and Latin antiquity. As for her looks, character, family history, her profession and lifestyle, about which we have abundant assertions in later writing, they are contradictory and mythical, and often no more than pleasant aphoristic gossip. Her father's names are multiple, her husband's name Kerkylos may be true or a joke name, her daughter Kleis may be her daughter or a favorite young friend. But these uncertainties are what we have. Ovid's *Heroides* 15 on Sappho and Phaon is beautiful, fantastic, and has nothing to do with Sappho other than that its tale reveals and celebrates the poet's enduring fame. I regret that I cannot read about the poets from Lesbos as one can about the lives of extraordinary figures like Plotinos, Plato, or Pindar. But the absence of contemporary information should not trouble. The world's best-known writer, Shakespeare, wrote in a century of extensive documentation. However, his portrait derives only from what may be guessed from the poems, plays, and a history of the folio editions. Yet Sappho and William Shakespeare do very well, largely concealed from media fact and chronology but resonating in perfect pitch in their verse.

Sappho was born in Lesbos, an island in the Aigaian Sea, a few miles off the coast of Asia Minor. Lesbos was, as it is today, an

---

* Some of those forms that she invented were not visible on papyrus
    as lineated verse, because the words were jammed together to
    save space. Those distinctions of lines and stanzas were the work
    of Hellenistic grammarians in Alexandria centuries later.
† The earlier partial poem was first published in 1922. All, or perhaps
    "most" of the rest of the poem, was published in 2004 from a third-
    century BCE papyrus found in the Cologne University archives. Martin L.
    West first published the find in Greek in the *Zeitschrift für Papyrologie
    und Epigraphik* 151 (2005): 1–9, and in Greek along with his English
    translation in the *Times Literary Supplement* 2, no. 4 (June 2005): 1.

island of grains, grapes, redolent orchards, and salt flats, spotted with five coastal cities that commanded their harbors from a rocky acropolis. Greece is a country of light and sea rock—its source of beauty and too little farmland—and shows off its few precious valleys and plains of fertile land almost as rare tanagra, along with its many hills and mountains, which are often terraced for wheat and olive trees up to their steep tops. Lesbos was unusual in having a large part of its terrain tillable, along with its salt flats, dry hills then wooded, and a three thousand–foot mountain called Olympos, after the traditional abode of the gods in Thessaly. It was known in ancient times for its grains, fruit trees and, above all, the large valleys of olive groves. In 2,600 years the island has probably changed very little in its village architecture and landscape. As one should know Baeza and Soria to understand Antonio Machado, or Vermont and New Hampshire to know Robert Frost, so there is no better way to know the images of Sappho's poetry than to see today the light, sea, and land of Mytilini (Mytilene).

The biographical tradition of Sappho begins after her death and is a mixture of possible fact, contradiction, malice, and myth. Virtually all the testimonia are found in later grammarians, commentators, and historians such as Strabon, Athinaios, Herodotos, and Suidas (*The Sudas Lexicon*). From all this at least some statements of probable truth may be made. Sappho's birthplace in Lesbos was probably in Eresos on the western shore or possibly Mytilini; in any case, it was in Mytilini that she spent most of her life. She was born c. 630 BCE. Her name in Attic Greek (the language of Athens and of the bulk of ancient Greek literature) was Sapfo (Σαπφώ), by which she is known, but in her native Aiolic she called herself Psapfo (Ψάπφω). She wrote as she spoke, and the speech of Lesbos was Aiolic Greek.

Her father's name was given by Herodotos as Skamandronymos; but it also appears as Skamandros, Skamon, Eunominos, Eurygyos, Euarchos, Ekrytos, Semos, and Simon. Her mother's name was Kleis. Some suggest—and some deny—that Sappho married a rich merchant from Andros named Kerkylas, who may have been the father of her daughter Kleis. She had two brothers, perhaps three: Haraxos, Larihos, and possibly the more shadowy Erigyos. Several poems speak disapprovingly of Haraxos, a young man who paid for voyages abroad by trading wine off his estates and who had spent large sums of family money to buy the freedom in Egypt of a courtesan named Doriha. Larichos was a public cup-bearer in Mytilini. We know nothing of Erigyos, if indeed he existed. As for her personal appearance, there were no statues, coins, or vase paintings until long after her death. But she was frequently referred to as the "lovely Sappho," and with the same authority she was described as short, dark, and ugly, "like a nightingale with misshapen wings enfolding a tiny body." These are the words of the Scholiast on Lucian's *Portraits.* Yet the same Lucian, referring to her person, calls Sappho "the delicious glory of the Lesbians." In a poem ascribed to Plato from the *Greek Anthology,* she is called the "tenth muse." What are certainly Plato's words are in the *Phaidros,* in which he has Socrates speak of her as "the beautiful Sappho." In this, Plato was reflecting at least one contemporary belief in her feminine beauty; and in the existing statues and coins the "nightingale with misshapen wings" is depicted with the idealized features and beauty of Afroditi.

The evidence of her activities is not more conclusive. Sappho lived during the reigns of three tyrants in Lesbos: Melanhros, Myrsilos, and Pittakos, the Sage. When she was young, it appears that she and her family went, for political reasons while under Myrsilos, to the Lesbian hill city of Pyrrha, and later, about 600 BCE, to Syracuse in Sicily, probably in the time of Pittakos. To have left for political reasons implies that her family was important in city affairs. As for her own social position, there is no question that her wealth and class distinction gave her privilege and largely immunity from male domination. Her relationship with men was not, at least in the surviving verse, for political and social reasons, but rather a personal grievance in questions of affection and sexuality. In perhaps her most famous poem, fragment 31, she is pitted as an outsider woman, for the love of another woman, against a supremely fortunate competitor, a man who in her eyes seems godlike, and completely excludes her from the erotic agon. In this attitude she differs from her aesthetic cousin, the Shulamite of the Song of Songs, who is one of the earliest voices to speak eloquently and powerfully from a woman's vantage. The Shulamite celebrates erotic love and protests against the night guards of the city who have beaten her, "those guardians of the walls." Sappho is at least free from the bullying of such "night guards," but nevertheless confined by her sex to a parallel world of aristocratic women.

This should not suggest, however, that Sappho and other women were viewed, or viewed themselves, as equals. Although the Greeks did honor nine male poets—Pindar being first among them—we find Aristotle stating superciliously in the *Rhetoric* (1398b): "The Mytilinians honored Sappho although she was a woman."

The women mentioned in Sappho's poems as companions are Anaktoria, Atthis, and Gongyla; she loved them passionately and shared catalogues of happiness with them, which she recalls with pain and pleasure after they have left her. Other friends are Mika and Telesippa and Anagora; she was angry with Gorgo and

Andromeda, who had left her to become rivals. But of the widely held theory of Ulrich von Wilamowitz-Moellendorff and others that her relationship to all these women was that of high priestess in a cult-association (*thiasos*), or in a young lady's academy of manners, the most one can say is that she was probably known as a teacher of young women. As for using her position of teacher at any level (and surely "cult" is a stretch) as a means of explaining away her homoerotic poems, this is unpleasant nonsense and traditional bigotry, and has no basis in the ancient biographical tradition and no support in the existing remains of her poems. Unfortunately, the cover-up theory, born of moral desire to conceal Sappho's gay romances, remained dominant until the mid twentieth century.*

The ancient commentators have also told us that there were really two Sapphos, one a poet and one a prostitute who also wrote poems; or that Sappho herself was a prostitute; and Ovid recounts the legend that she threw herself from the Leukadian cliffs out of love for the ferryman Phaon. It should be remembered when considering these more extravagant tales about Sappho and her family that there were perhaps thirteen plays dealing with Sappho in later Attic comedy and that by then she had become a stock figure on the Athenian stage. It was on the stage, her modern apologists contend, that the black legend of Sappho originated. The black legend extended to her husband Kerkylas, whose name only appears in testimonia found in the late Byzantine Suda. The same wild Aristophanic imagination and comic nastiness that put Socrates as a fool standing on clouds and made Sappho into a babbling stage clown, surely took shots at her husband Kerkylas.

---

* Just how prevalent the disguisement was proved to me one day in June of 1962, in Burgos, Spain. I had been working in the archives of the Spanish poet Manuel Machado, brother of Antonio Machado, to find information about don Antonio. I came on a postcard to Manuel sent to him in the early thirties by Miguel de Unamuno. Unamuno was a foremost Spanish novelist, poet, and philosopher, and also a classical scholar, maverick journalist, and then rector (president) of the University of Salamanca. In intellectual thought Unamuno was and remains a grand world author, admired for his novelistic innovations that anticipate later postmodernism. His most famous exchange with history occurred in late August of 1936, when Franco's army took over Salamanca and its medieval university. At a meeting with the generals in his office, he denounced them saying, *Vencerán tal vez pero no convencerán* (You may win but not convince). The response was shouts of *¡Muera la inteligencia!* (Let the intelligentsia die!). The philosopher was placed under house arrest where he remained till his death. Despite all this enlightened academic, creative, and courageous baggage, Unamuno wrote in his card to Manuel Machado that he had recently been rereading his Greek Sappho, "not the one of the infamous reputation but the true Sappho in the poems." Unamuno's message was that whoever really knew Greek knew that Sappho was *not* a lesbian.

As we are told, Sappho's husband Kerkylas was from the island of Andros, meaning "man." In "Kerkylas" one can hear the common word *kerkís*, meaning "rod," "peg," or "weaver's spindle," which has led some scholars to speculate that both Sappho's husband's name and origin were an invention and "indecent pun" from one of the six later comedies entitled "Sappho" or from five entitled "The Leucadian," or two entitled "Phaon," all lost plays known to us only by their titles, but in which Sappho was a target for lampoon. So, according to ancient comedic reasoning, "Kerkylas of Andros" yielded "Penis of Man," or, in more fusty academic jargon, "Prick from the Isle of Man." See David A. Campbell, *Greek Lyric*, page 5, note 4.

Sappho is credited with certain technical innovations. She is said to have been the first to use the pectis (a kind of harp), and to have invented the Mixolydian mode and the Sapphic stanza, which was imitated by Horace and Catullus. Sappho was not the first Lesbian to contribute innovations to Greek poetry. Before her were the semi-legendary poets Arion and Lesches and then Terpandros, who invented and wrote poetry for the seven-string lyre, of whom we have four small and doubtful fragments, the earliest examples of lyric poetry in Greece. Her Lesbian contemporary Alkaios wrote Alcaics, which were also imitated by Horace and other Latin poets.

There is good reason to believe that Sappho was a prolific writer. We do not know how she recorded her work—whether on papyrus, on wooden tablets overlaid with wax, or orally through song—but centuries later, when the Alexandrian grammarians arranged her work according to meter into nine books, the first book contained 1,320 lines (330 four-line stanzas in Sapphics). Judging from this, we may suppose that the nine books contained a very extensive opus. Her work was well known and well preserved in antiquity. We have Athinaios's claim in the third century CE that he knew all of Sappho's lyrics by heart. But the best indication, perhaps, of the general availability of her works in the Classical Age is in the number of quotations from her poems by grammarians, even late into Roman times, which suggests that both commentator and reader had ready access to the corpus of the work being quoted.

Of the more than five hundred poems by Sappho, we have today about two thousand lines that fit into intelligible fragments, and these come from no single collected copy but are pieced together from many sources: from the scholia of ancient grammarians to the mummy wrappings in Egyptian tombs. Plato's entire work has survived virtually intact, having been both popular with and approved by pagan and Christian alike. Sappho's work did not lack popularity, but as one who, in Ovid's words, "taught how to love girls" (*Lesbia quid docuit Sappho nisi amare puellas?*), her popularity did not always win approval.

To the Church mind Sappho represented the culmination of moral laxity, and her work was treated with extreme disapproval. About 380 CE Saint Gregory of Nazianzos, Bishop of Constantinople, ordered the burning of Sappho's writings wherever found. She had already been violently attacked as early as 180 CE by the Assyrian ascetic Tatian: "Sappho was a whorish woman, love-crazy, who sang about her own licentiousness" (Orat. ad Graecos, 53).

Then in 391 a mob of Christian zealots partially destroyed Ptolemy Soter's Classical library in Alexandria. The often repeated story of the final destruction of this famous library by the Arab general Amr ibn al- 'Asand Caliph Umar is now rejected by historians. Again we hear that in 1073 Sappho's writings were publicly burned in Rome and Constantinople by order of Pope Gregory VII. Until late in the eleventh century, however, quotations from Sappho still appeared in the works of grammarians, suggesting that copies of her poems were still preserved. We shall never know how many poems by Sappho were destroyed in April 1204 during the terrible pillage of Constantinople by the Venetian knights of the Fourth Crusade, or by the Ottoman Turks at the fall of Byzantium in 1453.

But apart from official hostility, Sappho's works suffered equally from the general decline of learning in the early Middle Ages and the consequent anger of oxidizing time upon neglected manuscripts. It is probable that some of her work was lost in about the ninth century when Classical texts, preserved in uncial script, were selected and recopied in modern letters. No single collection of her poems, in whole or in part, survived the medieval period. Nevertheless, in the Renaissance, Sappho came back into light. Italian scholars found the essay *On the Sublime* by pseudo-Longinos and *On Literary Composition* by Dionysios of Halikarnassos, which contain two of her most important poems: "To me he seems equal to gods" (31) and the complete ode to Afroditi (Lobel and Page, 1). Every stanza, line, and isolated word by Sappho that appeared in the works of other Greek and Latin writers were assembled, including indirect poems, that is, summaries or retellings of her poems.*

---

* In the last few years our means of deciphering both papyri and parchment texts have dramatically increased as a result of X-rays and infra-red technology. At the Stanford Linear Accelerator Center at Stanford University, a particle accelerator is being used to read a hitherto unreadable tenth-century palimpsest, containing a 174-page book by the mathematician and astronomer

Very few fragments of original papyrus manuscripts have survived in continental Greece,* but in parts of rainless Egypt in the Fayum, an oasis semidetached from the Nile valley near Krokodilopolis, important papyrus manuscripts with poems by Sappho were discovered in 1879. The Egyptian expeditions by the Oxford University fellows B. P. Grenfell and A. S. Hunt, beginning in 1895, yielded a wealth of material found in the Graeco-Egyptian town of Oxyrhynchos, about 120 miles south of Cairo. These finds were known as the Oxyrhynchus Papyri. In addition to important poems by Sappho, parts of four plays of Menandros were found in a refuse heap near Afroditopolis (Atfih); at Oxyrhynhus, Alkman's maidensong choral ode, the first in Greek literature, and twenty odes by Bacchylides were discovered. Bacchylides ceased to be simply a name and became again a major poet of antiquity, rivaling Pindar.

But above all, the range of Sappho's work was dramatically expanded. The precious papyri had been used as papier-mâché in mummy wrappings. Unfortunately, many were torn in vertical strips, and as a result the Sappho fragments are mutilated at the beginning or end of lines, if not in the middle. The mummy-makers of Egypt transformed much of Sappho into columns of words, syllables, or single letters, and thereby made her poems look, at least typographically, like Apollinaire or e.e. cummings' shaped poems. The miserable state of many of the texts has produced surprising qualities. So many words and phrases are elliptically connected in montage structure that chance destruction has delivered us pieces of strophes that breathe experimental verse. Her time-scissored work is not quite language poetry, but a more joyful cousin of the

---

Archimedes that was originally written on the parchment. The original writing was erased in order to record a Christian prayer book. By shooting X-rays at the parchment, the iron in the ink of the "erased" ancient text glows, revealing a now perfectly legible mathematic treatise under the later prayer book.

A parallel technological breakthrough is being used to decipher the literary 10 percent of the some 400,000 Oxyrhynchus papyri fragments. Through multi-spectral imaging based on satellite imaging, the faded ink on ancient papyri comes clearly into view. English and American scientists and scholars have already deciphered lines from Sophocles' lost play "Epigonoi" ("The Progeny"), three pages in elegiac meter by seventh-century lyric poet Archilochos, and work by Euripides, Hesiod, and Lucian. There is realistic hope that in coming years the amount of significant ancient texts, including early Gnostic and Christian scripture, may be increased by more than 20 percent. Hopefully, this version of Sappho will soon be outdated when new strophes from the popular Lesbian poet are revealed. For extensive information, see POxy (Oxyrhynchus Online).

* In 1961, for the first time, a cache of eight original papyri, in poor condition, was found in continental Greece, at Dervani (Lagada). See Herbert Hunger, "Papyrusfund in Griechenland," *Chronique d'Egypte* 37, no. 74 (July 1962), Brussels.

eternal avant-garde, which is always and never new. So Sappho is ancient and, for a hundred reasons, modern.

Ezra Pound goes back full circle when he "antiques" the form of a poem in order to make it resemble a vertical strip of a Sappho papyrus. His brief poem "Papyrus," addressed to Gongyla, reads:

Spring . . .
Too long . . .
Gongula . . .

But Sappho aces him with an impeccable strip in which plenitude resides in the ruins of her script:

Return, Gongyla

A deed
your lovely face

if not, winter
and no pain

I bid you, Abanthis,
take up the lyre
and sing of Gongyla as again desire
floats around you

the beautiful. When you saw her dress
it excited you. I'm happy.
The Kypros-born once
blamed me

for praying
this word:
I want

22

In her minimalist Imagist period, H.D., and her descendents in the Black Mountains, learned from Sappho, copied her absences, and found themselves through her losses. William Carlos Williams translated her and Robert Creeley and the Brazilian concrete poets were her immediate kin. But despite this parenté d'esprit that truly helped generate our modernist movements, the price of the unwitting modernization of Sappho scripture, through the random damage of her poems, has resulted in the tantalizing loss of intelligibility of hundreds of her fragments, not to mention the disappearance of most of her work.

The cost was also high to the English and German scholars who undertook the labor of unraveling the damaged papyri (both literally and figuratively). The German scholar Friedrich Blass, who first deciphered important poems by Sappho in the Fayum desert, lost the use of his eyes, and Bernard P. Grenfell, the explorer and pioneer editor of Oxyrhynchus Papyri, during his intense labors for a while lost his mind. Most hurtful to Sappho were the majority of her defenders from the seventeenth to the early twentieth century, who in their eagerness to clean up Sappho's act, to create a morally sound "divine Sappho," quite lost their perspective of the poet and hopelessly muddled the poet's life with the poems.

While a thousand years of bigotry destroyed the greater part of Sappho's poetry, the zeal of later defenders, from Anna Le Fevée Dacier in 1682 to Wilamowitz, Snell, and Bowra,* to rehabilitate her moral character as a conventionally virtuous, innocent, and pure teacher, has not helped the poet's cause, nor has it contributed to our understanding of her work. It is no less than astonishing how otherwise temperate scholars became outraged and imaginatively unobjective at the slightest suggestions by others of moral frivolity on Sappho's part. Not Sappho's poems but Middle and New Comedy and Horace and Ovid are accused of incepting the black legend. Several arguments are offered and reiterated to justify her love poems to other women. The dominating cure was the *thiasos* remedy: Since Sappho was a priestess and head of a circle of young women, these poems did not mean literally what they say; her love poems to women were epithalamia written for ceremonial purposes; the poems castigating her brother Haraxos for his affair with Doriha prove her own high virtue; Alkaios once addressed her as agya (holy or chaste); she came from a noble and highly respectable Lesbian family. The arguments read like a brief—in an unnecessary trial.

In the nineteenth century denial of Sappho's homosexuality prevailed. There were exceptions to an illusory interpretation of her poems, but these were not apparently heeded. We find some notable exceptions in England and a tragic one in the instance of Charles Baudelaire, who paid bitterly for his candor. Perhaps the clearest statement of Sappho's sexuality appears in William Mure of Caldwell's *A Critical History of the Language and Literature of Antient Greece.* While the Scottish classicist condemns Sappho for her

---

* Bowra modifies his defense in the 1962 edition of his *Greek Lyric Poetry* by which time fellow scholars took a new line, acknowledging that Sappho's poems were indeed homoerotic.

"scandalous history" and her "taste for impure intercourse, which forms so foul a blot on the Greek national character," he pooh-poohs the standard notion of Sappho's higher "purity" and insists that her Lesbian "female association" had nothing less than the "pursuit of love and pleasure." He writes, commenting sharply on fragment 31:

> In several places, Sappho addresses certain of her female associates in terms of no less voluptuous passion than those employed towards her male objects of adoration. In one passage, equal in power and nearly equal in length to the ode to Venus already cited, her ardour is inflamed by the sight of a rival, a male rival it may be remarked, participating, however slightly, in the privileges to which she herself claimed an exclusive right. She describes it as "a bliss equal to that of the gods to sit by the music of her voice, and gaze on her fascinating smile." At the same time, in anger against her male rival she feels "mortification and jealousy."*

In his modern "right on" commentary, William Mure notes, "If Sappho did *not* mean or feel what she has expressed in the passage above, then the most brilliant extant specimens of her muse become comparatively unmeaning rhapsodies; if she *did* so feel, her sentiments were not those of maternal tenderness of sisterly friendship" (316).

A generation later, John Addington Symonds (who had "shocked" Walt Whitman in a letter sent to the American poet, assuming their common passion for men), speaks of Sappho's homoeroticism. He slightly tempers his view of Sappho as a practicing homoerotic by contrasting her "sating of the senses" with the cruder voluptuousness of Persian or Arabic art. He writes: "All is so rhythmically and sublimely ordered in the poems of Sappho that supreme art lends solemnity and grandeur to the expression of unmitigated passion."† He then laments the ruin of her literary remains: "The world has suffered no greater literary loss than the loss of Sappho's poems."

In mid- and late nineteenth-century France, official morality and hypocrisy reigned with respect to Sappho's lesbianism. While by the end of the century, there was a fad and rash of lesbian novels

---

* William Mure of Caldwell, *A Critical History of the Language and Literature of Antient Greece.* 2nd ed., vol. III (London: Longman, Brown, Green, and Longmans, 1854), pp. 315–16.

† John Addington Symmonds, *Studies of the Greek Poets* (London: Smith, Elder, & Co., 1873), p. 173.

and memoirs published under the guise of being "newly found nov-
els by the poetess Sappho," when Charles Baudelaire published his
Les Fleurs du mal in 1857, *Le Figaro* condemned the book as "the
putrescence of the human heart." In large part because of his inclu-
sion of six poems concerning Sappho and *les femmes damnées,* the
author and his publisher Auguste Poulet-Malassis were dragged to
court, convicted, and heavily fined. The six "lesbian" poems were
banned from the book, and Poulet-Malassis was sent to prison. An
appeal to the empress Eugénie resulted in the reduction of Baude-
laire's fines. Only in 1949 was the ban on the immoral poems of-
ficially lifted.

In the past century it is extraordinary that until mid-twentieth
century the myth of Sappho's chaste love remained standard fare. In
this cover-up there is an exact parallel with, it was claimed, the con-
fused and disturbed denunciations of those who dared to suggest
that the work of William Shakespeare was stained by the abnormal
emotions of Greek love. Such folly was expressed only by weak crit-
ics blind to the poet's metaphysical message and spiritual conven-
tion. Oscar Wilde was an obvious exception. He loved the *Sonnets,*
he tells us in letters, and he theorized that the young man who
received Shakespeare's relentless ardor was actually "a wonderful
lad" named Willie Hews, "a boy actor in his plays." On the third and
last day of his famous trial of "Gross Indecency" for a homosexual
act in 1895, he invoked the *Sonnets* in his defense, a declaration that
served to deepen his legal guilt.

In *Shakespeare's Sonnet* (1997), the editor Katherine Duncan-
Jones addresses historically the almost universal dissemblance of
Shakespeare's homosexual passions. Without sympathy she de-
scribes W. H. Auden's complex manner of reading *Sonnets,* saying
that interpretation becomes "entwined with the personality (and
sexuality) of the critic, as well as his or her cultural location." She
writes:

> This is the case of W.H. Auden. Though anyone with a
> knowledge of Auden's biography might expect him to cel-
> ebrate and endorse the homoerotic character of 1-126, he
> was absolutely determined not to do so, at least publicly.
> In his 1964 Signet edition Auden claimed—as G. Wilson
> Knight had done—that the primary experience explored
> in *Sonnets* was "mystical," and he was extremely scathing
> about putative readers of homosexual inclinations who
> might be "determined to secure our Top-Bard as a patron
> saint of the Homointern." Yet his public adoption of this
> position seems to have been a characteristic instance

of Auden's cowardice, for later in 1964 he confessed to friends that a public account of Shakespeare (evidently equated by Auden with the speaker in *Sonnets*) as homosexual "won't do just yet." Perhaps Auden was referring to the changes in legislation then under discussion: Parliament finally decriminalized homosexual acts between consenting adults in July 1967.*

By contrast with Auden's prudence, the Alexandrian poet Constantine Cavafy as early as the early 1900s fully presented his homosexuality in the poems, which, however, he printed privately to give to friends. Despite candor in verse, he too faced the reality of the impossible public plight of gays. Though he was in his lifetime (1863–1933) known as the foremost poet in the Greek language and T. S. Eliot published his poems in 1924 in his *The Criterion*, he could not permit a collection of his own poems, carefully ordered by his own hand, to be published while he was alive. We hear his own moving statement about public acknowledgment in his prescient "Hidden Things":

> From all I did and all I said
> let them not try to find out who I was.
> An obstacle stood before me and transformed
> my acts and my way of life.
> An obstacle stood before me and stopped me
> so often from what I was going to say.
> My most unnoticed acts
> and my most veiled writings—
> only from these will they know me.
> But maybe it's not worth it to devote
> so much care and effort to knowing me.
> Later—in a more perfect society—
> someone made like me
> will certainly appear and act freely. [1908]†

In England and America Sir Denys Page was the first major academic scholar to oppose all this posturing about Sappho's sexuality. Page, who with Edgar Lobel, produced the most authoritative edition of Sappho's works, chose to look at the texts and found that the poems gave no support whatsoever to the arguments. Page contends

---

* Katherine Duncan-Jones, *Shakespeare's Sonnets* (The Arden Shakespeare, 1997), 80–81.

† The translation is by Aliki Barnstone in her *The Collected Poems of C. P. Cavafy: A New Translation* by C. P. Cafavy (Norton: 2006), 76.

that Sappho was not a high priestess, that only a small portion of her poems might be considered epithalamia, and that Sappho herself, far from being a woman of unfailingly noble sentiments, was a common mortal concerned with common matters of love and jealousy. In deflating the contentions of her supporters, Page also deflates Sappho herself—not without a note of moral reproach.

I have spent some time reviewing the history of Sappho's usually violent encounter with the world, not because one must necessarily know something or anything about an author to appreciate the work, but because in Sappho's case the world has known—or assumed—too much, and this knowledge interferes with any fair appraisal of her poems. The question has been whether or not Sappho was indeed a lesbian in the sexual, along with the geographical—Lesbian, from Lesbos—sense of the word.

First, it should be stated that whatever Sappho was in her life has very little to do with the content of her poetry; whether she was indeed bisexual or merely ascetic like her contemporaries Jeremiah and Gautama Siddhartha will not change the meaning of her poems. It is not that an author's intention must be discounted, nor need we puristically fear the heresy of intentional fallacy or other critical sins, old and new, including historiological snooping into her time and culture. Yet if the author's intention is meaningful, it must be seen through the text, through the lyrical speaker in the poem, and not merely from outside sources. In Sappho's case the problem is more rudimentary. Even if we could accept outside sources, there is, in fact, no reliable authority outside the poems themselves to explain the author's intended meaning in her many poems dealing with love.

Nonetheless, the preponderance of recent literary research assumes an authoritative understanding of her culture and historical times, which runs the same risks of blunder and uncertainty as in the work of earlier literary critics, including my old heroes Bowra and Page. How helpful is the work of social historians in reading the poems of Sappho? As ever, there is much to be learned from serious investigation and much to be questioned. And new generations will question again. In these domains none of us is sinless, but as an amateur reader I prefer the less serious approach that sees Sappho mainly through her work, and reads her work not as document but as art.

To find Sappho, then, the Sappho of the poems, we may look long at the poems themselves. One fragment is addressed to her daughter Kleis. A few of them may have been addressed to men. The majority are love poems to women. They are passionate poems, self-critical, self-revealing, detached, and intense. If we are to believe what they say, we will conclude that the speaker in the poems experienced a physical passion for her beloved, with all the sexual implications that similar poems between men and women normally imply. (Much of the world's love poetry is homoerotic and in ancient Greek poetry, the majority of love poems by known male poets, from Ibykos to Pindar, are addressed to other men.) To give the poems meanings that the texts do not support, for whatever moral motive, is to dilute her language and to weaken and falsify her work. Even though the remains of her oeuvre are scant, the poems should be allowed a plain reading of unimaginative literalness. "Uninterpreted," they speak for Sappho more directly and eloquently than the countertexts of her old defenders.

In the fragments we have left, only a few lines give details of physical love: "May you sleep on your tender girlfriend's breast." Many speak of her passions. Sappho's best-known love poem, "Seizure" (31), is an example of her precision, objectivity, and cumulative power. The poem is direct, self-revealing, yet detached and calmly accurate at the moment of highest fever. She begins with a poised statement of her pain before the man sitting near the woman she loves, who, because of his envied position, appears godlike to her; she recounts the physical symptoms of her passion for the woman; and with full intensity, but without exaggeration, she uses the metaphor of green turning greener than grass to show her suffering, verging on death, because of a love not returned:

> To me he seems equal to gods,
> that man who sits facing you
> and hears you near as you speak
>   softly and laugh
>
> in a sweet echo that jolts
> the heart in my ribs. Now
> when I look at you a moment
>   my voice is empty
>
> can say nothing as my tongue
> cracks and slender fire races
> under my skin. My eyes are dead
>   to light, my ears
>
> pound, sweat pours from me. Trembling
> grabs all of me, I am greener than grass
> and feel my mind slip as I go
>   close to death,
>
> yet I must suffer all   even a poor man

31

The poem states a love relationship, but more, it states the poet's agony when, consumed by love, she is unable to compete with the rival—a man, a species with powers inaccessible to her as a woman, and who therefore appears equal to a god. She cannot reach the woman she loves. The woman affects her with paralyzing force, and she can in no way escape—except through words—from the solitude in which she is suddenly enclosed. Her senses are agitated and fail her. She can no longer see, speak, or hear.

As her bodily functions weaken, she moves close to death, her analogue of the *via negativa.* The mystics would describe this state as dying away from space and time. In Daoist terminology, she is moving to the open country of emptiness. There, as in Saint John of the Cross's dark sensory night of aridities, she reaches momentary detachment from bodily senses, which permits her to speak objectively of the symptoms of her passion. She too is "dying from love." And, like those who have had intense physical pain, at a certain threshold she becomes an objective self-observer. Unlike Saint John, however, the night of purgation is not, at least in this fragment, the moment before the joyful night (*la noche dichosa*) of illumination and union.

Sappho's desire is conveyed as a loss of self. She is exiled, as it were, from her desire, and remains in a darkness before death. In Saint John this darkness is described as "withdrawal ecstasy." In Sappho the movement from the self into an extraordinary condition of void and separation results in a violent failure of the senses, a seizure, the ekstasis of negative ecstasy (of being elsewhere, but in the wrong place). For the mystics the second stage is illumination, the discovery of a new self. However, in Sappho this second stage is blackness, the discovery of the loss of self. The catalogue of symptoms of her seizure is a universal condition that finds expression in varying diction and metaphors, secular or religious, from Saint Teresa's interior castles and Marvell's entrapment in the garden to Marghanita Laski's medical analyses* and Jorge Guillén's passionate merging in the circle of light. Hers, however, is love's lightless inferno, without union, and without the peace that follows union.

Unable to reach the object of her love, there is no fulfillment and no release except in the objectification of her passion in the poem. Yet in her poetry she does indeed reach the world, if not her beloved. Her words, used masterfully, make the reader one with the poet, to share her vision of herself. There is no veil between poet and reader. Here, as elsewhere in her art, Sappho makes the lyric poem a

---

* For an interesting and full examination of the condition of transport, see Marghanita Laski, *Ecstasy: A Study of Some Secular and Religious Experiences* (Bloomington: Indiana University Press, 1962).

refined and precise instrument for revealing her intensely personal experience. As always, through the poems alone, we construct the true biography of voice. In the poem in the *Greek Anthology*, Plato speaks of Sappho as the "tenth Muse." The ascription of the epigram to Plato, as of all thirty-seven poems ascribed to him, is surely false. What is certain is that these words reflect ancient opinion. Sappho's own expression of the continuity of her word appears in an astonishing line that contains neither silly phrases "worthy of a Muse," nor betrays any of the ambitious glitter and bay leaves in Petrarch's notion of fame. Rather, the intimate voice, serenely ascertaining its future, is prophetic:

> Someone, I tell you, in another time,
> will remember us.

> 14

Sappho is remembered despite the multiple violations of time. The fragments of her poems contain the first Western examples of ecstasy, including the sublime, which the first-century Longinos recognized and preserved for us. They also include varieties of ekstasis briefly alluded to in these pages: the bliss of Edenic companionship, dancing under the moon, breakfasts in the grass; the whirlwind blast of love; the desolation and rage of betrayal; the seizure and paralysis before impossible love; and, as all her ordinary senses fail, the movement near death—the ultimate negative ecstasy. Yet even when she has lost herself, her senses, her impossible love, Sappho is remembered. The diversity and clarity of her voice, the absolute candor, the amazing fresh authority of the poetry, whether in addressing a goddess, a Homeric marriage couple, the moon and stars, a sweet apple or mountain hyacinth, a lamb or cricket, a lover or companion, those qualities compel now as they did in antiquity.

ORDERING OF THE TEXTS WITH RESPECT TO CHRONOLOGY AND EDITIONS

The order of Sappho's poems in standard editions does not reflect chronology of composition or the author's implicit age. It may, as in the work by Edgar Lobel and Deny Page attempt to reflect Sappho's nine "books," or given the losses, the remnants of her collections. Lobel and Page fragments 1 to 117 are presented as clearly by Sappho, and fragments 118 to 213 (none of the longer poems) follow under the title *Incerti libri*, meaning that they are of uncertain ascription. The actual order or grouping within the books is mostly unknown, since Sappho's hand is not there. They were accomplished in Hellenistic times. This traditional presentation is thought to have been determined three centuries after Sappho by the Alexandrian scholar Aristophanes of Byzantium and Aristarchos of Samathrace, when her work was alive and well received.

In this edition the fragments have been ordered independently of their traditional numbering, under a logic that is a mixture of theme and implied chronology and event.

Here, the poem number of the Greek source text generally follows the number established in *Poetarum Lesbiorum Fragmenta*, edited by Lobel and Page (abbreviated here as LP), and the Loeb Classical Library *Sappho and Alcaeus,* edited and translated by David A. Campbell. The latter normally has the same numbering as Lobel and Page, though the Greek texts differ. So unless otherwise noted, the numbering standing alone refers to the LP Greek text.

My reading of letters and words tends to be closer to the more recent editions by Voigt, Treu, and Campbell than to Lobel and Page. Where the Greek text does not follow the numbering of Lobel and Page, I indicate which other text has been followed, usually Campbell. When Campbell ascribes a poem to Sappho that Lobel and Page ascribe to Alkaios, I also follow Campbell, who always notes the Lobel and Page ascription. I have also consulted the Denys Page transcriptions in *Sappho and Alcaseus.* When one of Sappho's fragments is not in Lobel and Page but is found in Campbell, Ernest Diehl (*Anthologia Lyrica Graeca,* Vol. 1), Eva-Maria Voigt (*Sappho et Alcaeus*), or Max Treu (who adds his own material to earlier Diehl), these differences in judgment are indicated. The judgment of authorship refers to texts of uncertain ascription—whether to Sappho, Alkaios, or to a late false attribution—and indicated by "incert."

While the numbering follows LP unless otherwise noted, the Greek is a composite based on Lobel and Page, and also Voigt and Diehl, but predominantly Campbell because of his selectivity.

With respect to Campbell's English renderings, I have found his strictly prose versions excellent and a benefit to all readers. I use the word "interpretation" because the Greek is so uncertain. He has also chosen, with exceptions, to reproduce those lines of Greek that lend themselves to intelligible translation and then his guesses in reading uncertain letters and words are chaste and selective. Even as a gloss and dictionary they are invaluable, and more so than the existing beautiful poetic versions.

The measure for determining which of diverse texts I draw from for each fragment has been their intelligibility for translation purposes. When unintelligible, the Greek is usually not given, which means that in a number of poems many lines are omitted

(Campbell generally follows this practice) and hence in this edition the Greek generally matches the English as parallel texts.

SOURCES AND TITLES

In the source section, I provide bibliographical source information for the poems translated in this edition as well as ancient commentary related to the poems. Sappho's fragments survive in papyri or in ancient commentaries. For almost every fragment, if an ancient commentary exists—prosodic, grammatical, or literary—it is provided here. First given is the ancient bibliographical source; any ancient commentary appears next in quotation marks. My own commentary sometimes follows.

The source and formal commentary normally provide the material from which the poem's title comes. Sappho did not title her poems. I have made use of "the free line," which is a poem's title, in order to give the reader information found in the source and commentary, or derived from a close study of a difficult or evasive fragment. A simple example: In the one-line fragment 54, the subject noun of the verb is missing. It reads: ". . . came out of heaven dressed in a purple cape." However, the lexicographer Pollux, in whose *Vocabulary* this line is cited and thereby preserved, states that Sappho is describing Eros. Hence we know the subject of the verb and have an informative title: "Eros." Some translators add titles, others do not. I add because a fine title can offer an immediate smooth opening into a mutilated text. It is preferable to obtrusive footnotes. If it illumines, good. Then the reader can choose, or not choose, to look for more end-of-book information.

In the event of translation there are many ways to reach a Sappho, and the history of ancient literatures globally, alas, abounds in literary remnants. Titles help give them sense. In what seems to be the most recent version of many of Sappho's fragments, in striking re-creations Sherod Santos provides appropriate titles. Barnard gives titles. Carson's elegant versions do not, but the poet and classical scholar more than makes up for any information gap by her abundant and fascinating end notes and commentary on the poems.

GREEK WORDS IN ENGLISH

The transliteration of proper nouns and common nouns from one language to another is universally transitional and vexing. One cannot be entirely consistent without being silly and awkward. Who is happy when the English render Livorno, Modigliani's birthplace, as Leghorn? However, there is radical change. In transliterating Chinese into English, in a generation we have gone from standard English Wade-Giles to standard Pinyin. At the beginning Pinyin was shocking and difficult. Now Pinyin is de rigueur for scholarship, dictionaries, and newspapers, though it remains a difficult replacement. Some commonly used words in common speech have quickly yielded to Pinyin, such as Peking to Beijing.* Canton (Kwangchow in Wade-Giles) is on the way to becoming Guangzhou, but that change is challenging.

Rendering the Greek alphabet in English is more challenging because there are so many interests that have imposed their spelling on Greek as it has slipped into other languages. Latin Rome conquered Greece and translated Greek gods into Roman ones. Artemis became Diana, Zeus yielded to Jupiter or Jove. Greek words were transliterated into Latin letters, not always close in sound or feeling. English and the Romance languages have followed the practice of Latinizing Greek names while Germany and Eastern Europe keep closer to the Greek.

While the ancient Alexandrian scholars preserved and fashioned Sappho, ordering and editing her poetry, since Horace and Quintilian there has been war between "grammarians" and "libertines" over the nature of translation itself, between *fidus interpres,* which the Latin writers mocked, and literary re-creation and imitation. In modern times the soft war goes on between translation as a literary art or a classroom language test, which is revealed in spelling. The combatants regularly have seats in the academy, and victory depends on which audience and publisher receives and acclaims them. As for the gods and their I.D.s, outside Romance tongues the Greek gods have regained their identity. As for the transcription of names, unlike Chinese where one power has enforced its system (notwithstanding holdouts in Taiwan and Singapore), there is no single rule book for regulating transliteration. This free-for-all mode reflects language flux, which is always with us, no matter who is emperor.

With no absolutes on the horizon, what is happening now? Despite the minor brawls, much happened in the twentieth century to return us to equivalents resembling the Greek scripture (though James Joyce did not get the word when he dropped the bomb of

---

* In Wade-Giles if one knew the rules, which neither people nor dictionaries did, Peking was supposed to be pronounced "Beijing" because the unvoiced consonants *p* and *k* were to be voiced. Fat chance. Only when ungainly Pinyin took over did we have a clue about transcribing Mandarin (*putonghua*) into English. We are still stuck with Tao instead of Dao, though not for long.

Ulysses). My own perplexities on the *how* (and here the quandary is not art versus gloss but simply on how to record the change of signs between tongues) at least is typical, and in my weathercock self I spin with each puff of revelation. I have been v with Classical Greek for many decades along with Koine Greek and biblical Hebrew. When I undertook the translation of the New Testament, a book from Asia Minor, I chose to restore, as far as one can know, the original Hebrew, Aramaic, and Greek names so that a reader might observe that most of the figures in the scriptures, including gods and demons, are Semitic, not European. So it is Yeshua the Mashiah, not Jesus the Christ. One may recognize that Saint James is not from London or China but a Jew from Jerusalem, and that it would be best to call him Yakobos as in biblical Greek, or better, Yaakov, reflecting his name in Aramaic and Hebrew. Similar convictions about reflecting original language and place have led me to a spelling I have presented, with variations, in rendering Greek lyric poetry and the philosophers Herakleitos and Plotinos.

The main lesson from all this is that whatever one does will make a lot of people furious. One cannot be consistent, and therefore one is an incompetent and worse. Any linguistic change troubles like new currency and stamps. Even God and his envoy Adam had trouble in naming and spelling in the Garden. In these often pained choices I have been helped hugely by a former colleague at Wesleyan University, William McCulloh, with whom I collaborated in ways like now for both *Greek Lyric Poetry* (1961) and *Sappho: Lyrics in the Original Greek and Translations* (1965). Now, as in the past, it is his scholarship against my amateurism. I learn from him, and when I don't he informs me he can live with it, uncomfortably. McCulloh is absolute in making me note all sins. So what you find here may be enervating but not slipshod. Not on McCulloh's watch, for which I am endlessly grateful.

In general I prefer to be closer to what Italians do with Cicero and Greeks with Euripides. They pronounce all common words and ancient names as they do Italian and Modern Greek and do not aspirate their φ. Hence, Greeks sitting in an ancient amphitheater or standing in an Orthodox church understand the old chanted Greek. Whatever script is used to record Sappho in another tongue, as she sings in Greek she must sing in English. The smallest of her surviving Greek fragments echoes with music.

If you hear some here, you may forgive the graphic signs.

Testimonia

1   Sappho was born on Lesbos and lived in the city of Mity-
lini. Her father was Skamandros, or, according to some,
Skamandronymos. She had three brothers, Ierigyos,
Larihos and Haraxos, the oldest, who sailed to Egypt and
was tied up with Doriha on whom he spent much money.
Larihos was the youngest, and Sappho loved him more.
She had a daughter named Kleis named after her mother.
She was accused by some writers of being irregular in her
way of life and a woman-lover. In appearance she seems
to have been contemptible and ugly. [Socrates called her
"the beautiful Sappho."] She had a dark complexion and
was very short. The same is true of . . . [Alkaios?], who was
smallish. . . . She used the Aiolic dialect . . . wrote nine
books of lyric poetry and one book of elegiac and in other
forms.

Oxyrhynhos Papyri 1800, frag. 1

2   Sappho was the daughter of Simonos or Euminos or
Ierigios or Ekrytos or Simon or Kamon of Etarhos or
Skamandronymos. Her mother was Kleis. A Lesbian from
Eressos and a lyric poet, she lived in the forty-second
Olympiad (612–608 BCE) when Alkaios, Stesihoros and
Pittakos were also alive. She had three brothers, Larihos,
Haraxos and Eurygios. She married Kerkylas, a very rich
man who traded from Andros and had a daughter by him
named Kleis. She had three companions and friends, At-
this, Telesippa and Megara, and she was slandered for
having a shameful friendship with them. Her students
were Anagora of Militos, Gongyla of Kolofon, and Eu-
neika of Salamis. She wrote nine books of lyric poetry and
invented the plectrum for playing the lyre. She also wrote
epigrams, elegiac iambic poems and monodies.

The Suda Lexicon 107 (iv 322s Adler)

3   The poet Sappho, daughter of Skamandronymos. Even
Plato, son of Ariston, calls her wise and skillful. I under-
stand that there was also another Sappho of Lesbos who
was a courtesan, not a poet.

AILIOS ARISTIDIS, *Historical
Miscellanies*, 12.19 (p. 135 Dilts)

5   The beautiful Sappho. Socrates liked to call her this be-
cause of the beauty of her song, although she was small
and dark.

PLATO, Phaidros, 235n in Maximus
of Tyre, Dissertation 24 (18) 7

6   Physically, Sappho was very ugly, small and dark, and
one can only describe her as a nightingale with deformed
wings enfolding a tiny body.

Scholiast on Lucian *Portraits*, 18

8   From the time Sappho sailed from Mitylini to Sicily when
she was exiled in the years. . . . [605/4 to591, perhaps for
second time). This was when Kritias was the archon at
Athens and during the rule of Gamori (landowners) at
Syracuse. [598 BCE]

Parian Marble Chronicle, Ep. 36 (p. 12 Jacoby)

10   Sappho was a Lesbian from Mitylini and a lyre player. She
threw herself down from the Leukadian Cliff out of love for
Phaon of Mitylini. Some say that she composed poetry.

The Suda Lexicon S 108 (iv 323. Adler)

11   You are a Phaon both in beauty and deeds. This proverb
is used for those who are handsome and proud. They say
that Sappho among many others, was in love with Phaon
but she was not the poet Sappho but another Lesbian,
who, having failed in winning his love, leapt from the
Leukadian Cliff.

The Suda Lexicon: Phaon

12   Phaon, a ferryman who made his living sailing back and
forth between Lesbos and the mainland, one day took
Venus in the guise of an old woman over for nothing. She
gave him an alabaster box of unguents which he used
daily to make women fall in love with him. Among them

was one who in her frustration was said to have jumped from Mount Leukates, and from this story came the present custom of hiring people once a year to jump into the sea from that place.

Servius on the *Aeneid*, 10.452

13   The temple of Apollo Leukates [has a rock] and a leap [from it] is believed to cure love. Menandros says,

> Sappho was the first to leap from the prominent rock
> in her madly amorous pursuit of the proud Phaon.

Although Menandros assigns Sappho priority in jumping, the more skilled authorities say it was Kephalos who was in love with Pterelas, son of Deioneus. It was an annual custom of the Leukadians to throw some guilty person from the cliff during the sacrifice to Apollo in order to avert evil; they tied all kinds of birds and wings to him so that they might brake his fall by their fluttering, and a large crowd waited for him underneath in small boats to save him, if possible, in that area outside the sacred precinct.

STRABON, *Geography*, 10. 2. 9 (ii 348 Kramer)

15   It is said that this pyramid tomb was built by her lovers as a tomb for a prostitute, who is called Doriha by the lyric poet Sappho. She became the mistress of Sappho's brother Haraxos when he visited Naukratis with a cargo of Lesbian wine; others call her Rodopis.

STRABON, *Geography*, 17. 1.33 (iii 379 Kramer)

16   Rodopis was brought to Egypt by Xanthous the Samian, to ply her trade, and Haraxos of Mitylini, son of Skamandronymos and brother of the poet Sappho, paid a large sum to redeem her from slavery." It seems that Naukratis must be a good place for beautiful prostitutes, for not only did Rodopis live there and become so famous that every Greek was familiar with her name. . . . When Haraxos returned to Mitylini after setting Rodopis free, he was ridiculed by Sappho in one of her poems.

HERODOTOS, *Histories*, 2.135

18   What else could one call the Lesbian's love was nothing else but that which Socrates practiced? Both seem to me

to have practiced love in their own way, she of women, he of men, and both said that they could fall in love many times and all beautiful people attracted them. What Alkibiades, Harmidis and Phaidros were to him, Gyrinna, Atthis and Anaktoria were to her; and his rival philosophers, Prodikos, Gorgias, Thrasymachos and Protagoras were to Socrates, so Gorgo and Andromeda were to Sappho, who sometimes rebuked them, at others refuted them and spoke ironically to them just as Socrates did to his rivals. For example, "Sometimes she censures them (Gorgo and Andromeda), sometimes she questions them, and just like Socrates she uses irony. Socrates says: 'Good day to you, Ion,' and Sappho says . . . [See Sources 155.]

MAXIMUS OF TYRE, *Orations*, 18.9 (p. 230s. Hobein)

19 The grammarian Didymus wrote four thousand books. I would pity anyone who simply had to read so many supremely empty works. Among his books he enquires about the birthplace of Homer, the real mother of Aeneas, whether Anakreon was more of a lecher than a drunkard, whether Sappho was a prostitute, and other things which you ought to forget if you knew them. And then people complain that life is short.

SENECA, *Letters to Lucilius*, Ep. 88

22 The beautiful Sappho.

MAXIMUS OF TYRE, *Orations* 24 (18)7

25 Sappho sang many contradictory things about Eros.

PAUSANIAS, *Description of Greece*, 9.27.3

37 Menaichmos of Sikyon in his *Treatise on Artists* declares that Sappho was the first to use the pectis [a kind of lyre], which he says is the same as the magadis [an instrument with twenty strings.

ATHINAIOS, *Doctors at Dinner*, 14, 635b (iii 401 Kaibel)

38 [She was called] "manly Sappho," either because she was famous as a poet, an art in which men are known, or else because she has been defamed for being of that tribe [of homosexuals]

PORPHYRIO, in Horace's *Epistles* 1.19.28. (p. 362 Holder)

40   The sweet glory of the Lesbians.

LUCIAN, *Loves,* 30

41   A contemporary of Pittakos and Alkaios was Sappho, a
     marvel. In all the centuries since history began I know of
     no woman who in any true sense came close to rivaling
     her as a poet.

STRABON, *Geography,* 13.2.3 (iii 65s. Kramer)

42   One evening, while drinking wine, the nephew of Solon
     the Athenian sang one of Sappho's songs, and Solon liked
     it so much that he ordered the boy to teach it to him.
     When one of the company asked why he was so eager to
     learn it, he answered, "I want to learn it and die."

STOBAIOS, *Anthology,* 3.29.58 (iii
638s. Wachsmuth-Hense)

43   Everybody honors the wise. The Parians honored Archi-
     lochos despite his slanderous tongue, the Chians honored
     Homer though he was not a Chian, and the Mitylinians
     honored Sappho although she was a woman.

ARISTOTLE, *Rhetoric,* 1398 b

44   "Don't you see," he said, "what charm the songs of Sappho
     have to hold the listeners spellbound?

PLUTARCH, *Pythian Oracles,* 6

46   It is fitting to mention Sappho in the presences of the
     Muses. The Romans speak of how Kakos, son of Hep-
     haistos, let fire and flames flow out of his mouth. And
     Sappho's words are truly mixed with fire, and through her
     songs she brings out her heart's warmth, and according
     to Philoxenos heals the pain of love with the sweet-voiced
     Muses.

PLUTARCH, *Dialogue on Love,* 18

49   The Mitylinians engraved Sappho on their coins.

POLLUX, *Vocabulary,* 9.84 (ii 171 Bethe)

50 The statue of Sappho stolen from the town hall of Syra-
cuse. . . . Not only was it beautifully done but it contained
a famous epigram on the base.

CICERO, *Orations against Verres*, 2.4

LITERARY CRITICISM

52 The polished and florid composition . . . has the follow-
ing characteristics. . . . It would be pertinent for me to
enumerate the people who excelled in it. Among the epic
poets Hesiod seems to me to have best worked out this
style, and among the lyrical poets, Sappho, and after
her, Anakreon and Simonides; among the tragic poets,
only Euripides; among the historians, no one, to be exact
but Ephoros and Theopompos somewhat more than the
others; among the orators, Isokratis. I shall now give
examples of this style, selecting Sappho among poets
and Isokratis among orators. I begin with the lyric poet.":
[There follows the complete poem "Prayer to Afroditi" 1]
The euphony and charm of this passage lie in the cohesion
and smoothness of the connecting phrases. For the words
are juxtaposed and interwoven according to the natural
affinities and groupings of the letters. . . .

DIONYSIOS OF HALIKARNASSOS,
Literary Composition, 23

53 For example Sappho takes the feelings that come over
you in love's madness are appropriate to true life. And
she shows her virtue when she takes the best and most
excellent events and expertly selects and combines them.
[There follows the poem "Seizure," 31] Is it not wonderful
how simultaneously she summons the soul, body, hearing,
tongue, sight, flesh, all as separate things distinct from
herself, and by contrary elements, she both freezes and
bums, is mad and sane, she is afraid or she is nearly dead;
thus not only one passion is evident but a whole assembly
of emotions; for all these things happen to lovers, and her
taking the most important of the emotions, as I said, and
joining them together, produces the excellence of this
passage.

PSEUDO-LONGINOS, *The Sublime*, 10

55 Hymns of invocation are like most of the hymns of Sappho [Prayer to Afroditi, 1] or Anakreon other poets, contain invocations of many deities. . . . The poetic hymns of invocation are long. They can summon the gods from many places, as we find in Sappho and Alkman: The poets summon Artemis from many mountains, many cities, and from rivers too, and Afroditi from Kypros (Cyprus), Knidos, Syria, and many other places. And they can also describe the places themselves: in the instance of rivers, the water and the banks, the near meadows and dances performed by the rivers, and so on. Similarly, if they call them from their temples, they must be long hymns of invocation.

MENANDROS, *On Oratorical Apology* (9. 132, 135s. Walz, 3.333, 334s, Spengel)

56 If we compare Sappho's poems with Anakreon's or the Sibyl's oracles with the prophet Bakis, then it is clear that the art of poetry or of prophecy is not one art practiced by men and another art when practiced by women. It is the same. Can anyone protest this conclusion?

PLUTARCH, *Virtues of Women*, 243 (ii 226 Nachstädt)

57 The rites of Aphrodite were left [by other poets] alone to the Lesbian Sappho for singing to the lyre and composing the epithalamium. After contests she enters the bridal room among the suitors, weaves the bower, makes the bridal bed, gathers the virgins in the bridal chamber and brings Aphrodite in her chariot drawn by Graces and a band of Eroses to join in the fun. She braids Aphrodite's hair with hyacinth, and except for the locks parted at the forehead, she leaves the rest free to float and ripple in the breezes. Then she adorns the wings and the curls of the Eroses with gold, and urges them on before the chariot, waving their torches in the air.

HIMERIOS, *Orations*, 9. 4 (p. 75s. Colonna)

58 Only Sappho among women loved beauty along with the lyre and so she dedicated all her poetry to Afroditi and Eroses, making a young woman's beauty and graces the subject of her songs.

HIMERIOS, *Orations*, 28.2 (p. 128s. Colonna)

59   Sappho loves the rose and always crowns it with praise,
     comparing the beautiful virgins to it; and she compares it
     to the fore-arms of the Graces when they have left them
     bare

PHILOSTRATOS, *Letters*, 51

62   Anakreon of Teos was the first poet after Sappho of Les-
     bos to make love the main subject of his poetry.

PAUSANIAS, *Descriptions of Greece*, 1.25.1

67   The grace that comes from her use of formal devices is
     evident and frequent, such as the use of repetition where
     the bride says to her virginity: "Virginity, virginity, where
     have you gone, leaving me / abandoned?" And she replies
     with the same formal device: "No longer will I come to
     you. No longer will I come." For more grace is evident
     than if it had been said only once and this formal device
     had not been used. And although repetition seems to
     have been invented in order to show force, Sappho even
     uses what is very forceful with great charm.

DIMITRIOS, *On Style*, 140 (p. 33 Radermacher)

73   Diotima says [in Plato's *Symposium*] that Eros (love) flour-
     ishes in abundance and dies in want. Sappho put these
     ideas together and called Eros (love) "bittersweet [literally
     "sweetbitter"]. See poem 130.

MAXIMUS OF TYRE, *Orations* 18.9gh (p. 232 Hobein)

92   You have given [the *Geography*] a literary distinction by
     prefixing it with the kind of iambic verses . . . which the
     beautiful Sappho chooses to go with her songs.

JULIAN, *Letters, To Alypios*, 30

FROM GREEK POETRY ON SAPPHO

92   This tomb contains the silent bones of Sappho,
     but her wise sayings are immortal.

PINYTOS, *The Greek Anthology*, 7.66

93   O stranger, when you pass my Aiolian tomb, do not say,
     that I, the singer of Mitylini, am dead.
     Human hands made this tomb, and mortal works fall
     quickly into oblivion. But compare me

to the sacred Muses, from each of whom I took one flower
for my nine books. You'll see I have escaped
from the gloom of Hades, and each dawn the sun
wakens the name of the lyric poet Sappho.

TULLIUS LAUREAS, *The Greek Anthology*, 7.17

94   The flowers of Sappho, few but roses.

Meleagros' proem, *The Greek Anthology*, 4.1

95   My name is Sappho. My song surpasses the song
of women as Homer's the song of men.

ANTIPATROS OF SIDON, *The Greek Anthology*, 7.15

96   Memory was astounded when she heard
the honey-voiced Sappho, and she wondered
whether mankind had a tenth Muse.

ANTIPATROS OF SIDON, *Greek Anthology*, 9.66

97   Aiolian land, you cover Sappho, sung as a mortal Muse
among the deathless Muses, whom Kypris
and Eros nourished. with whom Persuasion wove
an undying wreath of the Pierian Muses.
She was a joy to Greece and to you. You fates who twirl
the triple thread on your spindle,
why didn't you spin eternal life for the singer inventing
the enduring poems of Helikon's daughters?

ANTIPATROS OF SIDON, *Greek Anthology*, 7.14

98   Your poems, Sappho, are the sweetest pillow
for young lovers. Surely Pieria
or ivied Helikon honors you, whose breath is equal
to theirs, you Muse of Aiolian Eressos.
Hymen the wedding god is near ou when he, bright
torch in hand, stands by the bed
of the newlywed, or Aphrodite keeps you near as she
mourns the young offspring of Adonis
in the scared grove of the blessed. I greet you as a god.

DIOSKORIDES on Sappho of Mitylini,
Greek Anthology, 7.47

100 Some say there are nine Muses. Count again.
Behold the tenth: Sappho of Lesbos.

PLATO, *Greek Anthology*, 9.506

101 Stranger, if you sail to Mitylini, city of beautiful dances
      which kindled the fire of Sappho's beauty . . .

    NOSSIS, *Greek Anthology*, 7.718

102 And you know how the Lesbian Alkaios played
    many songs on the lyre about his warm love
    for Sappho. He was a poet who loved Sappho,
    the nightingale of song, but he annoyed Anakreon,
    poet of Teos, because of his eloquence.

    HERMESIANAX in Athinaios, *Doctors at Dinner*, 598 b

105 Portrait of Sappho
    Painter, creative Nature herself gave you the Pierian
    Muse from Mitylini to portray. Clarity is in her eyes
    and this plainly reveals an imagination full of intelligence.
    Her flesh is smooth and not painted unnaturally,
    showing her simplicity. Mingled in her face are joy,
    and intellectual spirit, showing the Muse joined with Kypris.

    DAMOHARIS, *The Greek Anthology*, 16.310

106 Sappho's kisses would be sweet; sweet the embraces
    of her snowy thighs and sweet all her body.
    But her soul is unyielding adamant. For her love stops
    at her lips and the rest she keeps virgin.
    Who can suffer this? One who can stand this,
    could easily endure the thirst of Tantalos.

    PAULUS SILENTIARIUS, *The Greek Anthology*, 5.246

107 Among Lesbian women with lovely locks of hair,
    Sappho is the jewel.

    ANTIPATROS OF THESSALONIKA, *The
    Greek Anthology*, 9.26

107 Fate granted you no small glory
    on the day you first saw the light
    of the sun, Sappho, for we Muses
    agreed that your words should be
    deathless; and the Father of All,
    the Thunderer, also concurred.
    You will be sung by all mortal men,
    and not be poor in glorious fame.

    ANONYMOUS, *Greek Anthology*, 9.521

109 Sappho was not ninth among men
     but rather tenth among the lovely Muses.

ANONYMOUS, *Greek Anthology*, 9.571

110 Come to the shimmering precinct of bull-faced Hera,
         women of Lesbos, your delicate feet
     spinning as you danced beautifully for the goddess.
         Sappho will lead, her golden lyre
     in her hand. You radiate as you dance. You seem
         to hear Kalliopi's thrilling song.

ANONYMOUS, *Greek Anthology*, 9.189

FROM LATIN POETRY ON SAPPHO

111 She was a woman of Lesbos too, who wrote
         lasciviously yet with such grace
         that she reconciles us to her outrageous speech
         through the sweetness of her songs.

APULEIUS, *Apology* 9 (p. 10 Helm)*

112 The love still breathes, the flame is still alive
     that the Aiolian woman girl sang to her lyre.

HORACE, Ode 4.9.11

113 The manly Sappho tames the muse of Archilochos
     through her prosody. . . .

HORACE, Epode 1.19.28

114 A girl more refined than the Sapphic Muse.

CATULLUS, 35.16

115 What did Sappho teach her girls
         but how to love women?

OVID, *Tristia*, 2.365–5119

SAPPHO TO PHAON

Say, lovely youth that dost my heart command,
Can Phaon's eyes forget his Sappho's hand?
Must then her name the wretched writer prove,
To thy remembrance lost as to thy love?

---

* I have lineated in verse the original Latin.

Ask not the cause that I new numbers choose,
The lute neglected and the lyric Muse:
Love taught my tears in sadder notes to flow,
And tuned my heart to elegies of woe.
I burn, I burn, as when through ripened corn
By driving winds the spreading flames are borne.
Phaon to Aetna's scorching fields retires,
While I consume with more than Aetna's fires.
No more my soul a charm in music finds;
Music has charms alone for peaceful minds:
Soft scenes of solitude no more can please;
Love enters there and I'm my own disease.
No more the Lesbian dames my passion move,
Once the dear objects of my guilty love:
All other loves are lost in only thine,
Ah, youth ungrateful to a flame like mine!
Whom would not all those blooming charms surprise,
Those heavenly looks and dear deluding eyes?
The harp and bow would you like Phoebus bear,
A brighter Phoebus Phaon might appear:
Would you with ivy wreathe your flowing hair,
Not Bacchus' self with Phaon could compare:
Yet Phoebus loved, and Bacchus felt the flame;
One Daphne warmed and one the Cretan dame;
Nymphs that in verse no more could rival me
Than e'en those gods contend in charms with thee.
The Muses teach me all their softest lays,
And the wide world resounds with Sappho's praise.
Though great Alcaeus more sublimely sings
And strikes with bolder rage the sounding strings,
No less renown attends the moving lyre
Which Venus tunes and all her Loves inspire.
To me what Nature has in charms denied
Is well by wit's more lasting flames supplied.
Though short my stature, yet my name extends
To heaven itself and earth's remotest ends:
Brown as I am, an Aethiopian dame
Inspired young Perseus with a generous flame:
Turtles and doves of different hue unite,
And glossy jet is paired with shining white.
If to no charms thou wilt thy heart resign
But such as merit, such as equal thine,
By none, alas, by none thou canst be moved;
Phaon alone by Phaon must be loved.

Yet once thy Sappho could thy cares employ;
Once in her arms you centred all your joy:
No time the dear remembrance can remove,
For oh how vast a memory has love!
My music then you could for ever hear,
And all my words were music to your ear:
You stopt with kisses my enchanting tongue,
And found my kisses sweeter than my song.
In all I pleased, but most in what was best;
And the last joy was dearer than the rest:
Then with each word, each glance, each motion fired
You still enjoyed, and yet you still desired,
Till all dissolving in the trance we lay
And in tumultuous raptures died away.
The fair Sicilians now thy soul inflame:
Why was I born, ye gods, a Lesbian dame?
But ah, beware, Sicilian nymphs, nor boast
That wandering heart which I so lately lost;
Nor be with all those tempting words abused:
Those tempting words were all to Sappho used.
And you that rule Sicilia's happy plains,
Have pity, Venus, on your poet's pains.

Shall fortune still in one sad tenor run
And still increase the woes so soon begun?
Inured to sorrow from my tender years,
My parent's ashes drank my early tears:
My brother next, neglecting wealth and fame,
Ignobly burned in a destructive flame:
An infant daughter late my griefs increased,
And all a mother's cares distract my breast.
Alas, what more could Fate itself impose,
But thee, the last and greatest of my woes?
No more my robes in waving purple flow,
Nor on my hand the sparkling diamonds glow;
No more my locks in ringlets curled diffuse
The costly sweetness of Arabian dews;
Nor braids of gold the varied tresses bind
That fly disordered with the wanton wind.
For whom should Sappho use such arts as these?
He's gone whom only she desired to please!
Cupid's light darts my tender bosom move;
Still is there cause for Sappho still to love;
So from my birth the Sisters fixed my doom,

And gave to Venus all my life to come;
Or, while my Muse in melting notes complains,
My yielding heart keeps measure to my strains.
By charms like thine, which all my soul have won,
Who might not—ah, who would not be undone?
For those, Aurora Cephalus might scorn,
And with fresh blushes paint the conscious morn:
For those, might Cynthia lengthen Phaon's sleep,
And bid Endymion nightly tend his sheep:
Venus for those had rapt thee to the skies,
But Mars on thee might look with Venus' eyes.
O scarce a youth, yet scarce a tender boy!
O useful time for lovers to employ!
Pride of thy age, and glory of thy race,
Come to these arms and melt in this embrace!
The vows you never will return, receive;
And take at least the love you will not give.
See, while I write, my words are lost in tears:
The less my sense, the more my love appears.

Sure 'twas not much to bid one kind adieu:
(At least, to feign was never hard to you.)
"Farewell, my Lesbian love," you might have said;
Or coldly thus, "Farewell, O Lesbian maid."
No tear did you, no parting kiss receive,
Nor knew I then how much I was to grieve.
No lover's gift your Sappho could confer;
And wrongs and woes were all you left with her.
No charge I gave you, and no charge could give
But this,—"Be mindful of our loves, and live."
Now by the Nine, those powers adored by me,
And Love, the god that ever waits on thee; —
When first I heard (from whom I hardly knew)
That you were fled, and all my joys with you,
Like some sad statue, speechless, pale I stood;
Grief chilled my breast and stopt my freezing blood;
No sigh to rise, no tear had power to flow,
Fixed in a stupid lethargy of woe.
But when its way the impetuous passion found,
I rend my tresses and my breast I wound;
I rave, then weep; I curse, and then complain;
Now swell to rage, now melt in tears again.
Not fiercer pangs distract the mournful dame
Whose first-born infant feeds the funeral flame.

My scornful brother with a smile appears,
Insults my woes, and triumphs in my tears;
His hated image ever haunts my eyes; —
"And why this grief? thy daughter lives," he cries.
Stung with my love and furious with despair,
All torn my garments and my bosom bare,
My woes, thy crimes, I to the world proclaim;
Such inconsistent things are love and shame.
Tis thou art all my care and my delight,
My daily longing and my dream by night. —
O night more pleasing than the brightest day,
When fancy gives what absence takes away,
And, dressed in all its visionary charms,
Restores my fair deserter to my arms
Then round your neck in wanton wreath I twine;
Then you, methinks, as fondly circle mine:
A thousand tender words I hear and speak;
A thousand melting kisses give and take:
Then fiercer joys; I blush to mention these,
Yet, while I blush, confess how much they please.
But when with day the sweet delusions fly,
And all things wake to life and joy, but I;
As if once more forsaken, I complain,
And close my eyes to dream of you again:
Then frantic rise; and, like some fury, rove
Through lonely plains, and through the silent grove,
As if the silent grove and lonely plains,
That knew my pleasures, could relieve my pains.
I view the grotto, once the scene of love,
The rocks around, the hanging roofs above,
That charmed me more, with native moss o'ergrown,
Than Phrygian marble or the Parian stone:
I find the shades that veiled our joys before;
But, Phaon gone, those shades delight no more.
Here the pressed herbs with bending tops betray
Where oft entwined in amorous folds we lay;
I kiss that earth which once was pressed by you,
And all with tears the withering herbs bedew.
For thee the fading trees appear to mourn,
And birds defer their songs till thy return:
Night shades the groves, and all in silence lie, —
All but the mournful Philomel and I:
With mournful Philomel I join my strain;
Of Tereus she, of Phaon I complain.

A spring there is whose silver waters show,
Clear as a glass, the shining sands below:
A flowery lotos spreads its arms above,
Shades all the banks and seems itself a grove;
Eternal greens the mossy margin grace,
Watched by the sylvan genius of the place:
Here as I lay, and swelled with tears the flood,
Before my sight a watery virgin stood:
She stood and cried,—"O you that love in vain,
Fly hence and seek the fair Leucadian main:
There stands a rock from whose impending steep
Apollo's fane surveys the rolling deep;
There injured lovers, leaping from above,
Their flames extinguish and forget to love.
Deucalion once with hopeless fury burned;
In vain he loved, relentless Pyrrha scorned.
But when from hence he plunged into the main
Deucalion scorned, and Pyrrha loved in vain.
Haste, Sappho, haste, from high Leucadia throw
Thy wretched weight, nor dread the deeps below."
She spoke, and vanished with the voice: I rise,
And silent tears fall trickling from my eyes.
I go, ye nymphs, those rocks and seas to prove:
How much I fear, but ah, how much I love!
I go, ye nymphs, where furious love inspires;
Let female fears submit to female fires:
To rocks and seas I fly from Phaon's hate,
And hope from seas and rocks a milder fate.
Ye gentle gales, beneath my body blow,
And softly lay me on the waves below.
And thou, kind Love, my sinking limbs sustain,
Spread thy soft wings and waft me o'er the main,
Nor let a lover's death the guiltless flood profane.
On Phoebus' shrine my harp I'll then bestow,
And this inscription shall be placed below: —
"Here she who sung, to him that did inspire,
Sappho to Phoebus consecrates her lyre:
What suits with Sappho, Phoebus, suits with thee;
The gift, the giver, and the god agree."

But why, alas, relentless youth, ah, why
To distant seas must tender Sappho fly?
Thy charms than those may far more powerful be,
And Phoebus' self is less a god to me.

Ah, canst thou doom me to the rocks and sea,
O far more faithless and more hard than they?
Ah, canst thou rather see this tender breast
Dashed on these rocks than to thy bosom pressed?
This breast, which once, in vain! you liked so well;
Where the Loves played, and where the Muses dwell.
Alas, the Muses now no more inspire;
Untuned my lute, and silent is my lyre:
My languid numbers have forgot to flow,
And fancy sinks beneath the weight of woe.

Ye Lesbian virgins and ye Lesbian dames,
Themes of my verse and objects of my flames,
No more your groves with my glad songs shall ring;
No more these hands shall touch the trembling string:
My Phaon's fled, and I those arts resign:
(Wretch that I am, to call that Phaon mine!)
Return, fair youth, return, and bring along
Joy to my soul and vigour to my song.
Absent from thee, the poet's flame expires;
But ah, how fiercely burn the lover's fires!
Gods, can no prayers, no signs, no numbers move
One savage heart, or teach it how to love?
The winds my prayers, my sighs, my numbers bear;
The flying winds have lost them all in air.
Or when, alas, shall more auspicious gales
To these fond eyes restore thy welcome sails?
If you return, ah, why these long delays?
Poor Sappho dies while careless Phaon stays.
O launch the bark, nor fear the watery plain:
Venus for thee shall smoothe her native main.
O launch thy bark, secure of prosperous gales:
Cupid for thee shall spread the swelling sails.
If you will fly—(yet ah, what cause can be,
Too cruel youth, that you should fly from me?)
If not from Phaon I must hope for ease,
Ah, let me seek it from the raging seas;
To raging seas unpitied I'll remove;
And either cease to live or cease to love.

OVID's "Heroic Epistle, XV," translated
by Alexander Pope, 1707

Like pensive cattle lying on the sand,
They turn their eyes to the sea's horizon,
Their feet and hands creeping slowly to band
And fuse in soft tremors and bitter abandon.

Some of these hearts beguiled by secrets shared
Deep in the woods where brooks chat noisily
Spell out their furtive love as children carve
Initials on green bark of a young tree.

Others are walking slow and grave like nuns
Across the rock fields filled with apparitions
Where once Saint Anthony saw lava stun
And surge like nude blue breasts of his temptation.

And some by torchlight of quiescent caves,
A resin smell in the old Pagan shrine,
Call for your help, Bacchus, healer who saves
And relieves them from screaming heat and pain,

Others wear scapulars round their throat,
Hiding a whip under their draping skirt,
And in dark forests and lonely night
Combine the foam of bliss with tearful hurt.

O virgins, demons, O monsters, martyrs,
Great spirits pondering reality,
Seeking the infinite, saints and satyrs,
Racked with sobs, breaking in ecstasy,

You whom my soul has followed to your hell,
Poor sisters, I love and pity you for your part
For desolate grief, for thirst your citadel,
And urns of love filling your great hearts.

CHARLES BAUDELAIRE (1821–67)
translated by Willis Barnstone

Spring . . .
Too long . . .
Gongula . . .

EZRA POUND, 1916

1   Ἱμέρρῳ
     Thy soul
     Grown delicate with satieties,
     Arthis.
     O Arthis,
     I long for they lips.
     I long for thy narrow breasts,
     Thou restless, ungathered.

     EZRA POUND, 1917

124 Taking us by and large, we're a queer lot
     We women who write poetry. And when you think
     How few of us they've been, it's queerer still . . .
     There's Sapho, now I wonder what was Sapho.
     I know a single slender thing about her:
     That, loving, she was like a burning birch-tree
     All tall and glittering fire, and that she wrote
     Like the same fire caught up to Heaven and held there
     And she is Sapho—Sapho—not Miss or Mrs,
     A leaping fire we call so for convenience . . .

     AMY LOWELL, from "What O'Clock?" 1925

125 Errana to Sappho
     You the wild far-hurling woman
     like a spear among common things,
     I lay with my sisters. Your song burst
     cast me somewhere. I don't know where I am.
     No one can bring me back.
     My sisters think of me and weave,
     and in my house familiar steps.
     Only I am far off and given away
     and tremble like a plea.
     The beauty goddess burns in her myths
     and lives my life.

126 Sappho to Eranna
     I want to crush your heart,
     I want to sword you with an ivy-wreathed staff.
     Like dying I want to pierce you
     and, like the grave, in all these things
     I want to pass you on

     From *New Poems (Neue Gedichte)* by Rainer Maria Rilke

Sources and Notes

(NB: The number at the start of the entry refers to the source number following each Sappho poem.)

1   *Papyri Oxyrhynchus,* 2288. Also, Dionysios of
Halikarnassos, *On Literary Composition,* 23 (vi. 114ss.
Usener-Radermacher).

     "I shall now give paradigms of this style [that is, polished
and florid], selecting Sappho among poets and Isokratis
among orators. I begin with the lyric poet." [There follows
the poem, and then again Diononysios] "The euphony and
charm of this passage lie in the cohesion and smoothness of
the connecting phrases. For the words are juxtaposed and
interwoven according to the natural affinities and group-
ings of the letters. . . ." See Dionysios of Halicarnassos, 40 in
Testamonia for a more complete context of the poem, being
with "The polished and florid composition. . . ."

     The poem to Afroditi (Aphrodite) is usually considered
the one of two complete poems that has survived of Sappho,
and therefore not a fragment, but by accepted convention
all lines of Sappho are identified by their fragment num-
ber, and here too we refer to frag. 1 and frag. 58. The other
complete poem, frag. 58, was published for the first time in
2005. There are fragments of other poems, however, which
have more lines than either of the complete poems, such
as frag. 44, "Wedding of Andromache and Hektor." Despite
the tone of intimate friendship and camaraderie, the poem
has the formal structure of a prayer, with the expected in-
vocation, sanction, and entreaty.

2a   Fragment 2 is preceded on the same *Ostracon Florenti-
num* (an ostracon is a potsherd or potshard, which is
a fragment of broken pottery) with a composite word
ranothenkatiou, which can be plausibly restored to mean,
"coming down from heaven."

2   *Ostracon Florentinum,* edited by Norsa, *Annali della reale Scuola normale superiore di Pisa, Lettere, Storia e Filosofia,* series 2, 6 (1937).

Kriti (Crete) was thought to be the original seat of worship of Afroditi, or so its inhabitants claimed. The scene described here is a real place in Lesbos devoted to the worship of Afroditi. Apples and horses were symbols of Afroditi, who was known as Afroditi of the Apples as well as Afroditi of the Horses. The prayer for epiphany in the poem is by no means proof that Sappho was a priestess or a poet of cult songs. Her concern with Afroditi was with a figure who represented beauty and love.

In Lobel and Page, there is word preceding the poem, which is not usually translated (not in Campbell's text, only in his note), which is σανοθεν κατιου, meaning probably "coming down from the sky," or "coming down from the mountain top."

Line 11 retains only the first two words, and line 12 is missing altogether. The English translation might retain obediently not indent line 11 and leave and extra blank line or brackets between the third and fourth stanzas. However, here as elsewhere I attempt to go partway in reflecting the abused Greek text (which can have its own delight and freshness in mirrored English). Normally I limit the mirror so the English can live. But sometimes in treating very brief fragments, I try to make the English wording correspond in spacing as close as possible. This device may still make the English conversion intelligible while giving it an interesting form based on the haphazard remains of the Greek text.

3   *Papyri Berlinenses,* 5006 + *Papyri Oxyrhynchus,* iii 424 (6–18).

4   *Papyri Berlinenses,* 5006 (see 3).

The text is obviously fragmentary, scarcely more than a column of words, yet the words are intelligible. The syntax and connective words present the main difficulty. Ezra Pound's early poem, imitating Sappho, suggests a similar scrap of papyrus:

Papyrus

Spring . . .
Too long . . .
Gongula . . .

5   *Papyri Oxyrhynchus,* 7 + 2289. 6.
        Sea nymphs in the Greek are Nereids or mermaids.
        The poem is to her brother Haraxos (Charaxos). The
        black torment is presumably Egyptian mistress, Doriha
        (Doricha), on whom Haraxos was "wasting" his fortune. In
        the mutilated lines that follow (not included here), Sappho
        seems to broaden her attack on Doriha. There are numer-
        ous attack poems against Doriha, or Rodopis (Rhodopis),
        which are mentioned much later in Herodotos and Strabo
        and Athinaios's *Doctors at Dinner.* This woman who is the
        object of Sappho's hostilities was a Thracian by birth, who
        later went to Egypt as a prostitute. She became the mistress
        of Sappho's brother Haraxos, who imported Lesbian wine
        to Naukratis. Sappho attacks her in several poems, presum-
        ably because Doriha captivated her brother and swindled
        him in commerce. Sappho wants his attention, and for him
        to reform and come back. For more, see the Testimonia,
        and Lobel and Page, 202, for the traditional poems against
        Doriha.

5a incert. Herodian, *On Anomalous Words,* 26 (ii 932 Lentz).

6   *Papyri Oxyrhynchus,* 2289 frag. 1 a + b.

7   *Papyri Oxyrhynchus,* 2289 frag. 2.

8   *Papyri Oxyrhynchus,* 2289 frag. 3.

9   *Papyri Oxyrhynchus,* 2289 frag. 2289 frag. 4.
        Another talk with Hera.

13 incert. Apollonios Dyskolos, *Pronouns,* 104c (I 81 Schneider).

15   *Papyri Oxyrhynchus,* 1231 frag. 1 col. i 1–12 + frag. 3.
        After "blessed" the goddess's name has not survived,
        but she was here, as elsewhere, addressing Afroditi.

16   *Papyri Oxyrhynchus,* 1231 frag. 1 col. i 13–34, col. ii +
        frag. 36.
        Sappho begins the poem with a paratactic trope (found
        also in Tyrtaios, frag. 9 Diehl, and Pindar, Olympian Odes,
        1) to compare the apparent splendor of military spectacles
        with the power of love. While she does not dull the public
        sparkle of the masculine world of war, to her all this bright
        clutter of history cannot match the illumination of love
        and physical beauty in her personal world. While Sappho

writes at least once in 44 in a Homeric voice, speaking of the wedding of Andromahi and Hektor, she has chosen to celebrate the wedding of Hektor and Andromahi, who are perhaps the two most developed and sympathetic characters in the *Iliad*, rather than a warring hero. Also, closer to the Troad and Lydia than to mainland Greece where the Achaean heroes largely come from, she also appears to show a preference for the Trojans over the Achaeans (the Greek—though Trojan and Achaean are all Greeks and Greek-speaking), which may also be Homer's preference as he finishes his epic with great sympathy for the fallen Hektor, his funeral, the bereaved Andromahi and the soon to be annihilated Trojans. So after stating how once the gaze of love and powers of Afroditi led Helen to choose lover before family, at whatever cost, she reaffirms the centrality of love by comparing chronicle event to personal circumstance. She Sappho would rather gaze at her beloved than to behold all the shining hoplites (foot soldiers) and chariots in Lydia.

16 Incert. Sappho or Alkaios, Hefaistion, *Handbook on Meters*, 11. 3, 5 (pp. 35–36 Consbruch).

"The Aiolians composed acatalectic Ionic a maiore trimeters in two ways, from two ionics and a trochaic metrical foot [verse follows] and others from one ionic and two trochaic metrical feet. In their tetrameters they sometimes begin with a short syllable as in their trimesters [verse follows]."

The poem is attributed to Sappho or Alkaios, but clearly appears to be Sappho's. It is similar in tone to LP 154 (with lines about women before an altar in Kriti), and to "Afroditi of the Flowers at Knossos" LP 2.

16 *P.S.I.* ii 123 3–12 + *Papyri Oxyrhynchus*, 1231 frag. 1 col. ii 2–21 + 2166a + *Papyri Oxyrhynchus* 2289 frag. 9.

18 *Papyri Oxyrhynchus*, 1231 frag. 1 col. ii 22–27.

19 *Papyri Oxyrhynchus*, 1231 frag. 2.

20 *Papyri Oxyrhynchus*, 1231 frag. 9; Addenda 2166(a)4^A.

The text is very fragmentary. "To Lady Hera" (17), as well as the other poems in this section, are poems related to shrines and goddesses. Sappho addresses many gods in her poems, but when asking for help from a friendly deity, she normally addresses a goddess. As can be seen the poem is a strip of papyrus. The poem by Sappho is one that has the sea storm qualities of Alkaios, but here there is less heroic symbolism and actual personal and immediate speech. It is a hint of the broadness of Sappho's vision and themes that were surely developed in other lost poems.

21 *Papyri Oxyrhynchus*, 1231.
    The text is very fragmentary.

22 *Papyri Oxyrhynchus*, 1231 frag. 12, 15.

23 *Papyri Oxyrhynchus*, 1231 frag. 14.
    Hermione was Helen's daughter.

24a *Papyri Oxyrhynchus*, 1231 frag. 13 + 2166(a)7a (*Ox. Pap.* 124); 24b *Ox. Pap.* 1231 frag. 17.

24c *Papyri Oxyrhynchus*, 1231 fragments 22 + 25.
    These strong fragments have the nostalgia of Constantine Cavafy's many memory poems, where youth is contrasted with the harshness of age.

25 Scholiast on Theokritos, 1. 55b (p. 50s Wendel).
    This line is attributed to Sappho or Alkaios but it is surely by Sappho.

26 *Papyri Oxyrhynchus*, 1231 f.16.

27 *Papyri Oxyrhynchus*, 1231 frag. 50–54 + 2166(a)5 (*Ox. Pap.* xxi p. 123).
    "Menelaos" can also be rendered "Meneleos."
"Meneleos."

30 *Papyri Oxyrhynchus*, 1231 frag. 56 + 2166(a)6a.
    This song sung by girls outside the window of the newlyweds humorously tells the groom to awaken and to go out and join his old friends. The taunting tone goes well with the happiness of the occasion.

31 "Pseudo-Longinos," *On the Sublime*, 10. 1–3.
    We owe the preservation of fragment 31 to the Pseudo-Longinos, probably first century CE. (The "real" Longinos was third century CE.) Pseudo-Longinos cited these lines as an example of the sublime and the ecstatic. See Fragment 31 is probably the most translated poetry by Sappho, from Catullus to William Carlos Williams. Catullus' fifty-first

ode to Lesbia—Lesbia after Sappho, but probably addressed to his lover Clodia. It is a close version of Sappho's poem and a precious document and major poem:

Ille mi par esse deo videtur,
ille, si fas est, superare divos,
qui sedens adversus identidem te
spectat et audit

dulce ridentem, misero quod omnis
eripit sensus mihi: nam simul te,
Lesbia, aspexi, nihil est super mi
. . . .

lingua sed torpet, tenuis sub artus
flamma demanat, sonitu suopte
tintinant aures, gemina teguntur
lumina nocte.
. . .

otium, Catulle, tibi molestum est:
otio exsultas nimiumque gestis :
otium et reges prius et beatas
perdidit urbes.

[To me that man seems like a god,
greater than a god, if that can be,
who sitting beside you steadily
    watches you,

hearing your soft laughter that rips
my senses away, hopeless, for as soon
as I gaze at you, Lesbia, nothing is left
    of me,

my tongue is broken, a thin fire
spreads through my limbs, my ears ring
inside, and my eyes are covered
    in darkness!

but Catullus your laziness hurts you,
you exult in laziness and lust.
In old times sloth ruined kings
    and rich cities.

Translation by Willis Barnstone

A recent tradition of scholarship holds this poem to be a wedding song to be sung before a bride and groom.

There is no internal evidence of this, and these verses of violent personal passion would be inappropriate at the ceremony. The poem is a marvel of candor and power in which Sappho states her hurt before the calm godlike man and describes with striking objectivity and detachment the physical symptoms of her passionate love for the girl. A few decades earlier, Archilochos, the first poet to speak of passions of the outsider and individual, had written:

I lie here miserable and broken with desire,
pierced through to the bones by the bitterness
of this god-given painful love.
O comrade, this passion makes my limbs limp
and tramples over me. (frag. 104 Diehl)

APOLLONIOS DYSKOLOS, *Pronouns*, 144a (I 113 Schneider)

Aiolic has the forms ἀμμέτερος and ἄμμος for "our,"
    ὔμμος for "your," and σφός for "their." See Sappho
    [verse follows]:
Literally, "the gift of their works."

33   Apollonios Dyskolos, *Syntax*, 3.247 (ii. 350 Uhlig).
        The grammarian Apollonios Dyskolos writes, "There are the adverbs that indicate prayer, as αἴθε: [verse follows]."

34   Eustathios 729. 21 on the *Iliad*, 8. 555.
        "In the expression, 'around the shining moon' one should not interpret this as the full moon, for then the stars are dim because they are outshone, for as Sappho says somewhere: [verse follows]."
        Probably Sappho's lines refer to the notion that one of her companions outshone all the others in beauty. As Anne Carson and others note, the Roman emperor Julian writes in a letter to his instructor the sophist Hekebolios: "Sappho says the moon is silver and so conceals all other stars from view." (*Letters*, 387a)

36   *Etymologicum Genuinum* (p. 31 Calame) = *Etymologicum Magnum* 485.41.
        "The Aiolic writers use ποθήω for ποθέω, "I long for."
        These four words in Greek crystallize one essential mood of Sappho.

37   *Etymologicum Gerninum* (p. 36 Calame) = *Etymologicum Magnum* 576. 23ss.

It is noted that Aiolic writers call σταλαγμός, pain, "a dripping," as if a pain "wounds."

For in Aiolic σσ is changed to ζ. ἐπιπλήσσω becomes ἐπιπλαζω. See Sappho [verse follows]:

38 Apolonios Dyskolos *Pronouns,* 127a (1100 Schneider).
Aiolic writers use ἄμμε, "us."

39 Scholiast on Aristophanes, *Peace,* 1174 (p. 205 Dübner).
"For the Lydian dyes differ . . . and Sappho states."
Pollus notes that Sappho speaks of a type of sandal.

40 Apollonios Dyskolos, *Pronouns,* 104c (i 81 Schneider) + incert. 13
σοί "to you," the Attic form, is used also in Ionic and Aiolic. See Sappho [verse follows]:
Other texts give a sequel to the LP 40 fragment, so it would read:

I leave you
the flesh of a white goat
and will pour wine over it

Presumably, the words refer to a sacrifice. Both lines are found in Apollonios Dyskolos's *Pronouns* 104c. Here, as in Voigt, the first line, 40, and for incert. are gathered together. The extra line spacing is to indicate that it is uncertain where in the original text that line was.

41 Apollonios Dsykolos, *Pronouns,* 124c.
A comment on the Aiolic form of the plural pronoun "to you."

42 Scholiast on Pindar, *Pythian Odes,* 1.10 (ii 10 Drachmann).
"Pindar has described a picture of an eagle perched on Zeus' scepter and lulled to sleep by music, letting both wings lie still . . . . On the other hand Sappho says of pigeons:"

43 *Papyri Oxyrhynchus,* 1232 frag. 1 col. i 5–9.
The reference is to a party or a night festival.

44 *Papyri Oxyrhynchus,* 1232 frag. 1 coll. ii, iii, frag. 2 +m2076 co. ii
Lobel and Page do not include this fragment. The poem ends with "End of the Second Book of Sappho's Poems." This hymeneal song, from the book of epithalamia, is

more narratively epic and Homeric in word and idea than any other existing fragment of Sappho. Because of these qualities not normally found in Sappho, Page casts some doubt as to her authorship. David A. Campbell and most scholars affirm her authorship. Campbell observes, "Sappho's authorship is confirmed by quotations in Athinaios, Bekker's Anecdota Graeca and Ammonios." Here is another voice, a Homeric voice, which reveals her breadth.

Latinized Paean is the normal English form of *Paian* in Attic Greek and *Paon* in Sappho's Aiolic Greek. Paean is Apollo's title and can be used alone to represent Apollo. In lower case a paean (paián) is a joyful song or hymn of praise and thanksgiving.

44a P 239, p. 7 Treu, 102 Diehl, 304 Alkaios LP.

This substantial fragment was copied in the second or third century CE and attributed to Alkaios, with uncertainty, by Lobel, and then Lobel and Page. Other scholars, however, including David A. Campbell assign it to Sappho. Max Treu made a strong and convincing case for Sappho's authorship in his *Sappho, 1958*. He cites the line "I shall always be a virgin" as Sappho's speech and rejects as insufficient the Page argument. More recently Campbell includes it among Sappho's poems, while recognizing Lobel and Page's ascription to Alkaios. This poem, which has the élan of 44, with its Homeric grandeur, adds a major woman deity to those whom Sappho admired. In its way it is a perfectly self-contained fragment, giving origin Artemis's origin, her own exuberant oath describing who she is, the name she has acquired among the gods and worshipers, and how in her life she won over the intrusions of *eros*.

45 Apollonios Dykolos, *Pronouns*, 119b (I 93 Schneider).

ὑμεῖς, "you," is ὔμμες in Aiolic.

Here the grammarian Apollonios Dyskolos cites Sappho's spelling of the word *you* (plural) in Aiolic.

46 Herodian, *On Anomalous Words*, b 39 (ii 945 Lentz).

The comment concerns the word τύλη (cushion), which was not used by Attic writers but by Sappho in Book 2.

47 Maximus of Tyre, *Orations*, 18.9.

The rhetorician Maximus of Tyre writes, "Socrates says Eros is a sophist, Sappho calls him a weaver of tales. Eros makes Socrates mad for Phaidros, and Eros shook Sappho's heart like a mountain whirlwind punishing the oak trees."

48   Julian, *Letter to Iamblichus*, 183 (p. 240s. Bidez-Cumont).

In his letter to Iamblichus (who is actually dead by the time Julian writes him), Julian refers to these words by Sappho. His playful letters begins: "You came, yes you came and so you write, even though you were absent."

49   Hefaistion, *Handbook on Meters*, 7. 7 (p. 23 Consbruch).

"Among the acatalectic types (that is, the types belonging to Aiolic dactylic verse), the pentameter is called the Sapphic 14-syllable, in which all of Sappho's *Book2* is written: [line one follows]."

PLUTARCH, 751d (4 343 Hubert).

In his *Dialogue on Love,* Plutarch puts the above line cited by Hefaistion together with a second line, which may, or more likely may not, have followed. Plutarch writes: "Speaking to a girl who was still too young for marriage, Sappho says: [both lines of fragment follow]."

Terentianus Maurus suggests that these two lines are consecutive.

Terentianus Maruus, *On Meters,* 6, writes what has been taken for a related indirect poem:

In those days when Atthis was small
my own girlhood was blossoming.

50   Galinos, *Exhortation to Learning,* 8.16s (I 113 Marquardt).

The author Galen, who wrote on medicine, philosophy, and grammar, says of Sappho,

"Since we know that the time of youth is like spring flowers and its pleasures do not last long, It is better to praise the Lesbian poet when she says: [verse follows]."

51   Hrysippos, *Negatives*, 23 (*S.V.F.* ii 57 Arnim).

52   Herodian, *On Anomalous Words*, 7 (2.912 Lentz).

Sappho [uses the form of ὄρανος, "sky"].

53   Scholiast to Theokritos, 28. arg. (p. 334 Wendel).

54   Pollux, *Vocabulary,* 10.124 (ii. 227 Bethe).

The lexicographer Pollux writes: "It is said that Sappho was the first to use the word χλάμυν (hlamys), 'mantle,' when she said of Eros: [verse follows]."

55 Stobaios, *Anthology (On Folly)* 3.4.12 (iii 221ls. Wachsmuth-Hense).

The fragment is from a poem in Stobaios's *Anthology (On Folly)*, prefaced with the phrase "Sappho to a woman of no education." Plutarch says that the verse is addressed to a rich woman, but he also says to "an ignorant, uneducated woman."

56 Hrysippos, *Negatives*, col. 8, frag. 13 (*S.V.F.* ii 55 Arnim).

57 Athinaios, *Scholars at Dinner*, 21bc (I 46 Kaibel).

58b Campbell 58b (lines 11–22) + Martin West (*TLS* 6.24.05).

The earlier segment of this poem was first published in 1922. All, or perhaps "most" of the rest of the poem, was published in 2004 from a third-century BCE papyrus found in the Cologne University archives. Martin L. West first published the find in Greek in the *Zeitschrift für Papyrologie und Epigraphik* 151 (2005), 1–9, and in Greek along with his English translation in the *Times Literary Supplement*, 21 June 2005, 1.

The English translation here, by Willis Barnstone and William McCulloh, differs substantially from the version deciphered by Professor West. The appearance of this "second" complete poem is a literary event, and, with the probability of more texts revealed through infra ray technology, it is reasonable to believe that there will be more significant finds, through the spade and through improved reading technology of papyri and later parchments.

Dawn (Eos) carried off Tithonos, who was the brother of Priamos (Priam) and Dawn's lover. Dawn asked Zeus to make Tithonos immortal, but she forgot to ask also for the gift of eternal youth. Tithonos became older and older and began to shrink, though he had the range of her palace, and Dawn could hear his weak voice. When he could not walk she locked him in a chamber and eventually turned him into a grasshopper. Because Tithonos did not retain his youth, the mention of his name evokes a decrepit old man.

58c *Papyri Oxyrhynchus*, 1787 frag. 1. 4–25, frag. 2.1 + frag. nov. (Lobel, 26).

Commenting on the last lines of the poem, Athinaios in *Doctors at Dinne,* 15.687, writes: "So you think that refinement without virtue is desirable? But Sappho, who was a real woman and poet, was loath to separate good from refinement, saying, 'Yet I love refinement and beauty and light are for me the same as desire for the sun.' It is therefore clear that the desire to live included for Sappho both the bright and the good, and these belong to virtue."

It is said that 58c may be from a separate poem or a part of 58b. However, 58c is contained as lines 25, 26 in the earlier found *Oxyrhynchos* 1787 frag. 1.4–25, frag. 2.1 + frag. nov. (Lobel Σ. μ., which confirms that the lines were part of our major ancient papyrus containing Sappho's poems. However, since West's new 58b does not contain these in the text he has published, they make a fine sequel as a separate fragment. I should note that both Treu's and Campbell's guesses in their editions of 58 have proved to be remarkably close to the full lines which are now disclosed in the discovery of the more coherent 58b.

60   P. Halle = *Papyri Oxyrhynchus,* 1787.
     Fragmentary text is from the right column.

62   *Papyri Oxyrhynchus,* 1787 frag. 3 col. ii 3–14.

63   *Papyri Oxyrhynchus,* 1787 frag. 3 col. ii 15–24.

65   *Papyri Oxyrhynchus,* 1787 frag. 4.
     Where the Greek text has Aheron (Acheron), the river of death running through Hades, I have kept Aheron, rather than Hades, since here "in Ahéron" indicates that it is used as a metonym for darkness and underworld Hades. If it signified the actual river, it would not say "in" since Afroditi is not in the river but in the place.

67a *Papyri Oxyrhynchus,* 1787 frag. 5.
     Daimon, daemon, or demon in line 2 can refer to a secondary god or deity, which is a later meaning. In Homer and the Lyric Age it generally refers to any divinity, especially a divinity that influences human life.

68a *Papyri Oxyrhynchus,* 1787 frag. 7 + frag. nov. (Lobel p. 32 + *Papyri Oxyrhynchus* xxi 135)71.
     The sons of Tyndareus or the Tyndarids are Kastor and Pollux. See Tyndareus in glossary. Megara is a friend of Sappho.

70 *Papyri Oxyrhynchus,* 1787 frag. 13.

Here *horon* (choron) means dance and also chorus or choir (from *horos*). The Greek chorus in a play danced as they chanted. The word *horos* persists in Modern Greek (and also in Romanian and Turkish for "round dance"). Greek Jews took their *horos* to Israel where it became the national dance, called the *hora* or *horah*.

Harmony may be the notion of harmony or Harmonia, goddess of harmony and concord, closely associated with Afroditi.

71 *Papyri Oxyrhynchus,* 1787 frag. 6 + frag. xxi Addenda p. 135.

Mika may be a shortened form for her friend Mnasidika. The house of Penthilos may refer to a rival school (thiasos) or, more likely, a rival political party and enemy of Sappho's family. Pittakos, the tyrant of Lesbos, married into the house of Penthilos, wedding the sister of a former leader, Drakon, son of Penthilios. It cannot be known what Sappho's intended word was in line 7. Ernest Diehl and Max Treu venture the reading of ἄη[δοι for nightingale, and Campbell reads ἄη[ται for "breezes."

3a *Papyri Oxyrhynchus,* 1787 frag. 11.

74 *Papyri Oxyrhynchus,* 1787 frag. novum a, b, c.

From three columns of a fragment. The fragment makes sense as haphazard words in a poetry word game may work together, but in this instance the fragments fit as a poignantly Sapphic description of the shepherd.

76 *Papyri Oxyrhynchus,* 1787 frag. novum.

78 *Papyri Oxyrhynchus,* 1787 frag. 10.

A short column of words, with no certainty of person or connections. Among many such incoherent splashes of words, this one is representative and delightful.

81 Athinaios, *Scholars at Dinner,* 15.674e (iii 491 Kaibel) (see 4–7) + *Papyri Oxyrhynchus* 1787 frag. 33 (see 1–5).

"Sappho gives a more simple reason for wearing garlands [her lines follow] in which she urges all who offer sacrifice to wreathe their heads, since being adorned with flowers makes them more pleasing to the gods."

82a Hefaistion, *Handbook on Meters*, 11.5 (p. 36 Consbruch).

84 *Papyri Oxyrhynhus*, 1787 frag.37, 41.
       Fragment 84 also resembles Ezra Pound's imitation of
   Sappho, which brought the Greek poet into his approved
   modernity. See Fragment 4.

85, 85A + 85B Voigt. See *Papyri Oxyrhynhus*, 1787 frag. 35 and
   38.
       Papyri Oxyrhynchus, 1787 frag. postmodo repertum
   = 2166(d)1.
       This fragment is probably a prayer to Afroditi, through
   Zeus of the Aegis (a goatskin shield or breast plate) is also
   mentioned in line two.

87e, f Voigt = 87 LP (16); *Papyri Oxyrhynchus*, 2166.

88b, a *Papyri Oxyrhynchus*, 2290.
       First two lines,[ν προ . . [ ]νως πρὸς πότ [,]ατον χάλα]
   ("before, toward, loosen) are omitted, since they don't add
   to the meaning of the fragment.

91 Hefaistion, *Handbook on Meters*, 11.5.

92 *Papyri Berlinenses*, 9722, fol. 1, *Berliner Klassikertexte*, 5.2
   p. 12 + Diehl A. L. G. 1. 4 p. 57s.
       Only line beginnings are preserved.

94 *Papyri Berlinenses*, 9722, fol. 2, *Berliner Klassikertexte*, 5.2
   p. 12ss + Lobel, p. 79.
       One of Sappho's longer and most important personal
   statements, here she invents her way of bringing herself,
   through a dialogue with a friend, into a poem, evoking
   exquisite love and sexual memories of an idealized youth.
   Again, the parallel with Cavafy is striking: recollection
   of youth, now gone. Of course Constantine Cavafy knew
   Sappho poems, as he did all ancient Greek poetry, but
   his recreation of antiquity was usually of late Hellenism,
   with certain obvious exceptions, such as his most famous
   poem "Ithaki," which retells, as a metaphor of instruction,
   Homer's tale of Odysseus the adventurer and his return
   to his island, which though poor, gave him the reason
   for his long adventures and his return." In all the paral-
   lel sensual poems, whether of immediacy or recollection,
   Sappho and Cavafy are utterly candid. But Sappho makes
   no excuses and reveals no self-consciousness of illicit or

immoral behavior for her love of women, in contrast to Cavafy, who was daringly candid, always with an awareness that his poems carried a dangerous message, which in his lifetime was sorrowfully epitomized by the nature of his publications, all private pamphlets and small collections, for friends, and not for a general public, which would in his lifetime (1863–1933) have been an unforgivable scandal. Though Sappho herself a hundred years later became a stock figure of Greek and later Roman comedy and satire, because of her lesbianism, it did not inhibit or color her own writing, and despite her detractors, she was still the favorite of Plato (that may be more tale than history), but she was still predominantly seen as the greatest lyric poet of Greek and Roman antiquity.

95 *Papyri Berlinenses*, 9722, fol 2, *Berliner Klassikertexte*, 5.2 p. 14s.
      Sappho is probably responding to Gongyla, whose name appears as the only word in line 1 of the extant papyrus. It is uncertain whom (or what) the sign may refer to in line 2 of the translation. The remaining lines of the fragment hang together. Letters are missing from his name, but Hermes is probably evoked here. His name appears in full in fragment 141. Hermes is the guide of the dead to the underworld.

96 *Papyri Berlinenses*, 9722 fol. 5, *Berliner Klassikertexte*, 5.2 p. 15ss + Lobel p. 80; lines 1–20, Campbell 96.
      It is presumed that this poem is addressed to Atthis. It has the outstanding qualities of fragment 94. It is not known who the "you" and "she" and "we" are. One can speculate that the "you" is Atthis, and that the "she" is Anaktoria because she was away in Sardis. In this mingling of Sappho and her friends, Sappho is the one who craves one who is far and one who is shining and there is an impossible triangle of love, typically Sapphic.

96 second half, lines 21–37, Campbell 96.
      See note on 96 for source. 96 second half may be a separate poem or a later part of fragment 96. It is placed here as a companion poem to others on Sappho's gods and goddesses. While the fragment does not continue the great sweep of the love triangle in 96, it is a powerful statement on its own, bringing in Adonis and Afroditi in words made evocatively mysterious by the chance remnants of

a mutilated papyrus. Though very fragmentary, it is important to be discarded as another unintelligible cache of Sappho's words.

98a and b from a third-century papyrus, *Papyri Oxyrhynchus, 1232*; Lobel and Page, 44, first published in Copenhagen by Vogliano in a booklet entitled *Sappho: una nuova della poetessa* (Milan, 1941).

In this intimate domestic poem addressed to her daughter Kleis, Sappho contrasts an artificial adornment with the natural, inexpensive ornament of a wreath of fresh flowers, which is more appropriate for one with light hair. It was necessary for a respectable woman to wear some kind of headgear.

Another reference to Kleis's hair is implied in fragment 98b, a poem of exile, when an elaborate headband was probably more than she could afford. Sappho and her family were apparently in exile around 600 BCE. The poem recalls the days when the Mytilinean ruler Myrsilos (who probably caused the exile of Sappho's family) may have been the tyrant of Lesbos. Headbands seem to be reminders of an island past not available because of banishment. The Kleanaktidai were of a family of rulers of Mytilini during Sappho's lifetime.

100 Pollux, *Vocabulary*, 7. 73 (ii 73 Bethe).
"In Book 5 of Sappho's lyric poem we find [line follows], which means that the material was of close-woven linen."

101 Athinaios, *Scholars at Dinner*, 9.410 e (ii 395 Kaibel).
"When Sappho in *Book 5* of her lyric poems says to Afroditi [the poem follows] she means the handkerchief as an adornment for the head, as indicated also by Hekataios, or some other writer, in the book entitled Guide to Asia where he writes: 'Women wear handkerchiefs on their heads.'"

The reading is difficult. Edmonds inserts Timas, gratuitously. Wilamowitz and Diehl find Mnasis in the poem. Page finds no specific friend. More recently, David A. Campbell also finds Mnasis in the jumble of letters that comprise the first word of line three. Though using "she" for the unknown friend would be safer, with uncertainty I follow those for Mnasis. One intertextual reason, perhaps a folly, on the side of Mnasis is that fragment 82a brings in *Mnasidíka*, who may be the same Mnasis sending gifts in 101.

101a Voigt, by Sappho, or 347b LP by Alkaios, Dimitrios, *On Style,* 142 (pl. 33 Radermacher).

"There are many examples of literary grace. Such grace comes due to the choice of words or metaphor, as in the lines about the cicada."

Older scholars attributed the fragment to Sappho, including H. L. Ahrens and U. von Wilamowitz, but as Denys Page points out in *Sappho and Alcaeus* (1955), p. 303, these lines also appear in a longer, more resolved poem by Alkaios, which is itself an imitation of a passage in Hesiod's *Works and Days.* Page reasons that it is too much to suppose that both poets imitated Hesiod. Yet how do we know what these friends did? While the first two lines are typical Alkaian drinking songs, the next three seem deeply Sapphic, and so, again, whoever is right about attribution, one camp or another, I think these haunting lines deserve their place among the fragments. Here is the longer poem 347a by Alkaios:

Summer Star

Wash your gullet with wine for the dogstar returns
with the heat of summer searing a thirsting earth.
The cicadas cries softly under high leaves, and pours
    down
shrill song incessantly from under their wings
the artichoke is in flower. Women are poisonous, men
feeble, since the dogstar parches their heads and knees . . .*

Alkaios's poem is itself a version of lines from Hesiod in *Works and Days.*

102 Hefaistion, *Handbook on Meters,* 10.5.

"The antispastic tetrameter catalectic is also common, in which only the second unit is antispastic, a meter in which Sappho wrote her songs at the end of *Book 7:* [verse follows]."

In this fragment Sappho seems to be stricken by desire for a young man. In the lines Afroditi, who caused the desire, is also brought in for her slender beauty.

103 *Papyri Oxyrhynchus,* 2294.

---

* The dogstar is not the morning star but the dogstar Sirius
that brings the heat and madness of the dog days.

103b   *Papyri Oxyrhynchus*, 2308 Voigt; incert. 26 LP.

104Ca, Cb Voigt and Campbell, 214 4.3.

104a   Dimitrios, *On Style*, 141 (p. 33 Radermacher).
   "Sappho also creates charm from the use of anaphora, as in this on the Evening Star: [her lines follow]. Here the charm lies in the repetition of the word 'bring.'"
   The Evening Star, son of Astraios or Kephalos or Atlas and Eos (Dawn), and father of the Hesperides.
   Many poets have imitated this fragment from Catullus's poem 62 (lines 20–37) to Byron in Don Juan, canto 3, stanza 107:

O Hesperus, thou bringest all good things—
Home to the weary, to the hungry cheer,
To the young bird the parent's brooding wings,
The welcome stall to the o'erlaboured steer;
Whate'er of peace about our hearthstone clings,
Whate'er our household gods protect of dear,
Are gathered round us by thy look of rest;
Thou bring'st the child too to its mother's breast.

   In *The Waste Land* T. S. Eliot hops around from London to Tiresias of Thebes, and ingeniously connects "the evening hour" with sailor home from the sea and typist home for tea. In his note on line 221, Eliot adds the fisherman to his list, writing: "This may not appear as exact as Sappho's lines, but I had in mind the 'longshore' or 'dory' fisherman, who returns at nightfall. The strange homage to Sappho reads:

At the violet hour, when the eyes and back
Turn upward from the desk, when the human engine waits
Like a taxi throbbing, waiting,
I Tiresias, through blind, throbbing between two lives,
Old man with wrinkled female breasts, can see
At the violet hour, the evening hour that strives
Homeward, and brings the sailor home from sea,
The typist home at teatime, clears her breakfast, lights
Her stove, and lays out food in tins.

104b   Himerios, *Orations*, 46.8 (p. 188 Colonna).
   "This song to Hesperos is by Sappho."

105a Syrianos on Hermogenis, *On Kinds of Style*, 1. 1 (Rabe).
"Some kinds of style have to do with one kind of thought only . . . Others . . . express things pleasing to the senses of sight, hearing, smell, taste, touch, such as Homer's *Iliad*, 347f., or Sappho's."

105b Himerios, *Orations*, 9–16.
"Sappho compared a virgin girl to an apple, allowing those who would pluck it before its time not even to touch it with their fingertips, but he who would pick it in the right season might watch its beauty grow; compared the bridegroom to Achilleus and his deeds to the hero's."

105c Dimitrios, *On Style*, 106 (p. 26 Radermacher).
"The epiphonema, as it is called, may be considered as a phrase that adds adornment, and elevates style. . . . For example, the sense is intensified by such a phrase as 'like a hyacinth' . . . while it is adorned by the succeeding words 'on the earth yet blooming purple.'"
Sappho's words also are echoed in Catullus, 11.21–24, and Virgil, *Aeneid*, 9.435.

106 Dimitrios, *On Style*, 146.
"Of this outstanding man Sappho says: [line follows]."

107 Apollonios Dyskolos, *Conjunctions*, 490 (I 223 Schneider).
"In all dialects except Koine and Attic ἄρα has the form ἤρα as in Sappho:"

108 Himerios, *Orations*, 9.19 (p. 84 Colonna).
"Then come and we will lead him into the bedroom urge him to encounter the beauty of the virgin bride."

110 Hefaistion, *Handbook on Meters*, 7.6. (p. 23 Consbruch).
"The Aiolic dactylic tetrameter catalectic."
Elsewhere the second-century scholar Pollux says that the doorkeeper kept the bride's friends from rescuing her.
Synesios in *Letters*, 3.158d.
"The man who is wronged is Harmonios, the father of the head doorkeeper, who, as Sappho would say (through in other respects he lived soberly and honestly), he claimed to be better born than Kekrops himself."
Dimitrios, *On Style*, 167 (p. 37 Radermacher) b. "In a different way Sappho ridicules the rustic groom and the

doorkeeper at the wedding, using prosaic rather than poetic language."

111 Hefaistion, *On Poems*, 7.1 (p. 70 Consbruch); Dimitrios, *On Style*, 148 (p. 34 Radermacher).

"There is a charm peculiarly Sapphic in its way when having said something, she changes her mind, as [poem follows], as if interrupting herself because she has resorted to an impossible hyperbole, for no one really is as tall as Aris."

112 Hefaistion, *Handbook on Meters*, 15.26 (p. 55s. Consbruch).

"The same poet uses the 3½-foot choriambic with an iambic close: [verse follows]."

Catullus has phrases reminiscent of these lines: mellitos oculos (48.1) and Pulcher es, neque to Venus neglegit (61.194).

113 Dionysios of Halikarnassos, *On Literary Composition*, 25 (vi. 127s. Usener-Radermacher).

"This Sapphic wedding song."

114 Dimitrios, *On Style*, 140 (p. 33 Radermacher).

"The graces who arise from the use of figures of speech are many and clear in Sappho. For example in the repetition when a bride addresses her virginity, and her virginity replies: [verse follows]."

See Testimonia for more.

115 Hefaistion, *Handbook on Meters*, 7.6. (p. 23 Consbruch).

"and the Aiolic dactylic pentameters, catalectic with a disyllabic ending."

116 Servius on Virgil, *Georgics* 1.31 (iii 1. 139s. Thilo-Hagen).

"Many say that *gener,* son-in-law, is used here for husband, as in *Sappho,* who in her book called 'Wedding Songs,' says" [line follows], "using γάμβρο," husband, instead of νυμφίος. Campbell notes that γάμβρ is used for any male relation by marriage.

117 Hefaistion, *Handbook on Meters*, 4.2 (p. 13 Consbruch).

"Meters are called catalectic when they have the final foot shortened, as in the iambic: [verse follows]."

118 Hermogenis, *On Kinds of Oratory*, 2.4 (p. 334 Rabe).

"The assignment of something deliberately chosen with respect to things that do not have the power of deliberate choice produces a sweet effect . . . as when Sappho questions her lyre and the lyre answers her: [verse follows]."

The statement is odd because it is certainly Sappho who is speaking to the lyre, not the lyre to Sappho.

120 *Etymologicum Magnum*, 2.43.

"Βάζω, 'I say' . . . from it comes ἀβακής, unspeaking, quiet, gentle, which Sappho uses in: [verse follows]."

121 Stobaios, *Anthology*, 4.22.112 (iv 543 Wachsmujth-Hense).

"In marriage it is best that the ages of the partners should be considered. Sappho"

122 Athinaios, *Scholars at Dinner*, 12.554b (iii 223 Kaibel).

"It is natural that those who think they are beautiful should gather flowers. That is why Persefoni and her companions are described as to gather flowers. Sappho says she saw: [verse follows]."

123 Ammonios, *On Similar Words That Also Differ*, 75 (p. 19 Nickau).

"There is a difference between ἀρτι and αρτίως. ἀρτι is an adverb of time, while αρτίως is applied to a completed action. So Sappho was wrong when she said: [verse follows]."

125 Scholiast on Aristophanes, *Thesmoforiazusai*, 401 (p. 267 Dübner)

"The young and people in love wove garlands. Here is a reference to the custom of those who women in old days wore garlands. As in Sappho: [verse follows]."

126 Etymologicum Gen. (papyri Calame) = Etymologicum Magnum, 250.10s.

daúo for *tò koimômai*, "sleep," in Sappho.

Herodian says that this word [for sleep] occurs only once in Sappho.

127 Hefaistion, *Handbook on Meters*, 7.7 (p. 23 Consbruch).

"Your gold house" may be the house of Zeus.

128 Hefaistion, *Handbook on Meters*, 9.2 (p. 30 Consbruch).

129 a and b   Apollonios Dyskolos, *Pronouns*, 66.3 (i 66 Schneider).

ἔμέθεν "of me," is often used by the Aiolic poets.

130 Hefaistion, *Handbook on Meters*, 7.7 (p. 23 Consbruch).

    These two lines may be followed by fragment 131.

    Diotima says (in Plato's *Symposium*) that Eros flowers in prosperity and dies in want. Sappho put these together and called him "sweetbitter." Maximus of Tyre, *Orations*, 18.9 (p. 232 Hobein).

131 Hefaistion, *Handbook on Meters*, 7.7 (see ad frag. 130); Plutarch, *Dialogue on Love*, 751d.

132 Hefaistion, *Handbook on Meters*, 15.18 (p. 53s. Consbruch).

    There follows before and after the fragment prosodic questions, especially concerning meter (four kinds of trochaic dimiters) and the use of caesura.

    It cannot be known what noun should follow "lovely" but Campbell and others have guessed "Lesbos."

133a, b   Hefaistion, *Handbook on Meters*, 14.7 (p. 46 Consbruch).

    "When the ionic is anaclastic (meaning, it has its syllables inverted), it is preceded by an iambic of six or seven short units, giving us: [2 lines follow]."

    Lines a and b are probably from the same poem, and "a" may have been first line of that poem. It is not known what verb connected the questioning "why" and Afroditi. Others have guessed "condemn" or "honor" or "neglect" or "summon," but we have no reasonable basis for this conjecture other than that a word is missing, indicating the here intended relationship between Sappho and Afroditi.

134 Hefaistion, *Handbook on Meters*, 12.4 (p. 39 Consbruch).

    "Among ionic *a* minore acatalectic trimeters is the acatalectic in Sappho's: [line follows]."

    The born in Kypros (Cyprus) is Afroditi.

135 Hefaistion, *Handbook on Meters*, 12.2 (p. 37s Consbruch).

    "Whole songs were written in ionics, as for example those by Alkman and Sappho: [line follows]."

    Irana is Sappho's Aiolic version of Eirana (Irini), Irana or, in English, Irene, which all also mean "peace."

136 Scholiast on Sophocles, *El.*, 149 (p. 110 Papageorgos).

    "The phrase messenger [or herald] of Zeus is used because the nightingale signals the coming of spring. Sappho writes: [line follows]."

Ben Jonson took from this fragment his line in *The Sad Shepherd*, act 2: "The dear good angel of the Spring, The Nightingale." He gave Sappho's word aggelos, herald, or messenger, its later biblical meaning of angel."

137   Aristotle, *Rhetoric,* 1367e (p. 47s Römer).
      "We are ashamed of what is shameful, whether it is said, done or intended; compare Sappho's answer when Alkaios said, 'I want to speak to you but shame disarms me.'"

      Diehl and Page assign the first line of part one to Alkaios 348 and the remaining lines to Sappho. The text in all cases is substantially the same. The poem is addressed to the fellow Lesbian poet Alkaios (Alcaeus in Latin), to whom is attributed the line: "Violet-haired, holy, honey-smiling Sappho." All this is uncertain, though there is little doubt that the rebuke of the poet is indeed by Sappho.

138   Athinaios, *Scholars at Dinner,* 13.56d (iii 244 Kaibel).
      "And Sappho also says to the man who is excessively admired for his beauty: [verse follows]."

139   Philon, *Papyri Oxyrhynchus,* 1356 fol. 4a 14ss + Lobel p. 55).
      "yielding to the good counsel of the woman poet Sappho."

140a Hefaistion, *Handbook on Metres,* 10.4 (p. 33 Consbruch).
      "Among antispastic tetrameters the following is the pure form of catalectic line."

      Kythereia is Afroditi. The verses are probably a dialogue between Afroditi and her worshipers. These lines addressed to Afroditi are probably by worshipers of an Adonis cult. See 168.

141   Athinaios, *Scholars at Dinner,* 10.425d (iii 425 Kaibel).
      "According to some versions the wine-bearer of the gods was Harmonia. Alkaios makes Hermes also the wine-bearer, as does Sappho, who says [verse follows]."

142   Athinaios, *Scholars at Dinner,* 13.571d (iii 259s. Kaibel).
      "Free women and young girls even today call their intimate and loving friends ἑταίρας (*hetaira*), hetaera, companions, as Sappho does: [verse follows]." See 160.

      In later Greek ἑταίρας (*hetaira*) took on the meaning of educated "courtesan" or "mistress."

143 Athinaios, *Scholars at Dinner*, 2.54f (I 127s Kaibel).

144 Herodian, *On the Declension of Nouns* (ap. Aldi *Thes.*
Cornucopia, 268; see Choerob. ii. lxv 43s. Hilgard) = cod.
Voss. g. 20 (Reitzenstein *Gesch. E.* 367).
  Gorgo is a rival of Sappho.

146 Tryfon, *Figures of Speech*, 25 (*Rhet. Gr.* viii 760 Walz); Di-
ongenianos *Proverbs*, 6 58 (I 279 Leutsch-Schneidewi).
  "[Sappho] said of those who are unwilling to take the
bad with the good."

147 Dio Hrysostom, *Discourses*, 37.47 (ii 29 Arnim).
  "'Someone, I tell you, will remember us,' as Sappho has
beautifully said. . . . The lines in brackets derive from Dio
Chrysostom's summary of Sappho's words. Up to now for-
getfulness has caused others to trip and be cheated, but
good judgment has not cheated anyone of worth, and for
this reason, stand upright for me like a man."

148 Scholiast on Pindar, *Olympian Odes*, 2.96f (i 85s.
Drachmann).
  "The meaning Wealth when not by itself but embel-
lished by virtue, opportunely enjoys its own benefits and
that of virtue [arete], and has a wise concern for the pursuit
of the good. Neither of these on its own is welcome."
  The text is uncertain. This wisdom saying is attributed
to Sappho and also to the later poet Kallimahos.

149 Apollonios Dyskolos, *Pronouns*, 126b (I 99 Schneider) and
151 *Etymologicum Genuinum* (p. 19 Calame) = *Et. Mag.*,
117. 14ss.
  And σφι, "to them," is used in Aiolic with an initial ἄ.

150 Maximus of Tyre, *Orations*, 18.9 (p. 232 Hobein).
  "Socrates blazed up in anger with Xanthippe for la-
menting when he was near death as Sappho did with her
daughter: [poem follows]."
  Maximus of Tyre seems to be making a parallel be-
tween the death of Socrates and Sappho's possible death.
See Testimonia 22.

151 *Etymologicum Genuinum.*
  "ἄωρος, a lengthened form of ὦρος, which has the same
meaning, 'sleep.' See Kallimahos (fr. 177.28 Pf.) and Sappho."
See frag. 149.

152 Scholiast on Apollonios of Rhodes, 1. 727 (p. 61 Wendel).

 ἐρευθήσσα, red, is used instead of πυσσα, flame-colored or ὑπέρυθσος, ruddy. This is contrary to Sappho's description: [verse follows].

153 Atilius Fortunatianus. *Ars,* 28 (vi 301 Keil) (*de metris Horatii*).

 In his comment on a poem by Horace, Ode 1.8 beginning *Lydia dic per omnes:* [verse follows], Artilius Fortunatinus cites this verse by Sappho.

154 Hefaistion, *Handbook on Meters,* 11.3 (p. 35 Consbruch) (On the ionic a major)

 "And there are brachycatalectic trimiters that are called Praxilleans. They have an ionic in the first meter and a trochaic in the second. Compare this example from Sappho."

155 Maximus of Tyre, *Orations,* 18.9d (p. 231 Hobein)

 "Sometimes she censures them (Gorgo and Andromeda), sometimes she questions them, and just like Socrates she uses irony. Socrates says: 'Good day to you, Ion' [opening words of Plato's *Ion*], and Sappho says: [verse follows]." See Testimonia 17.

156 Dimitrios, *On Style,* 161s (p. 37 Radermacher).

 "The charm of comedy lies especially in hyperbole, and each hyperbole is impossibility ... such as Sappho's."

 Dimitrios, *On Style,* 127 (p. 30 Radermacher).

 "Sappho's praise as in 'More gold than gold' is certainly an hyperbole and contains an impossibility, but is not without elegance. Rather, it derives its charm from the impossible. Indeed, the wondrous in holy Sappho is that she uses a device that is hazardous and difficult."

 Grigorios of Korinthos on Hermogenis, *Meth.* (*Rhet. Gr.* vii 1236 Walz).

 "The ear is lowly flattered by erotic phrases such as those by Anakreon and Sappho, as in 'whiter than milk,' 'gentler than water,' 'more melodious than lyres,' 'prouder than a mare,' 'more delicate than roses,' 'softer than a fine robe,' 'more precious than gold.'"

 Unfortunately, we do not know which of these comparisons are by Anakreon and which by Sappho, yet their statement here in Grigorios is somehow valuable as a lost glint of possibility.

157 *Etymologicum Genuinum.*
     "Αὐὸς, ἠώς. This is the Aiolic form. See Sappho: [phrase follows] and fragment 104a."

158 Plutarch, *On Restraining Anger,* 7.456e (iii 167 Pohlenz-Sieveking)
     "A man who is silent over his wine is boring but vulgar, and in anger there is nothing more dignified than tranquility, as Sappho advises."

158 Diehl *Greek Anthology,* 7.489
     Diehl includes three poems from the Hellenistic period, clearly in imitation of Sappho, though the prosody is of the epigrammatic style of the *Greek Anthology,* also called the *Palatine Anthology.* The first of the poems, beginning, "Children, "I am voiceless," is not remotely Sappho's in style and offers nothing about Sappho. Its only connection is the false ascription to Sappho and the mention of Aithopia, who is Artemis in a Lesbian cult.

159 Maximus of Tyre, Orations, 18.9g (p. 232 Hobein).
     "Diotima [in Plato's Symposium] tells Socrates that Eros is not the son but the attendant and servant of Afroditi, and in a poem Afroditi sings to Sappho."

159 Diehl *Greek Anthology,* 7. 505.

160 Athinaios, *Scholars at Dinner,* 13.571d (see fr, 142).
     "Free women and girls call a friend or acquaintance hetaira as Sappho does: [poem follows]." The verse shows that hetaira, as used by Sappho, signified comrade, not courtesan.

Wash your gullet with wine for the dogstar returns
with the heat of summer searing a thirsting earth.
Cicadas cry softly under high leaves, and pour down
shrill song incessantly from under their wings.

     Alkaios' poem is itself a version of lines by Hesiod in *Works and Days.*

161 *Papyri Bouriant,* 8 91ss.

166 Athinaios, *Scholars at Dinner,* 2.57 (I 134 Kaibe).
     "Sappho makes, ᾠόν, 'egg,' trisyllabic [oion], [verses follow]."

It is uncertain what flower the hyacinth was to the Greeks.

167 Athinaios, *Scholars at Dinner,* 2.57d (see frag. 166).

168 Marius Plotius Sacerdos, *Art of Grammar,* 3.3 (see vi 516 Keil).

"Sappho invented the adonius or catalectic dimeter, so it is also known as Sapphic. It is monoschematic, since it is always composed of a dactyl and a spondee." See 140a.

168b Campbell (Voigt) (= frag. adesp. 976 P.M.G.) Hefaistion, 11.5 *Handbook on Meters* (on ionic tetrameters acatalectic) (p. 37 Consbruch).

Although this is one of the two or three best-known poems attributed to Sappho, there is a lot of fuss about whether it is by Sappho, Alkaios, or by neither, and most recent editors deny her authorship, though it is included in most Greek editions under the epithet of incert. Apart from authorship, the poem is a simple yet impeccable example of images that spell the solitude of universal solitude.

Earlier scholars, including Arsenius around 1500, said yes, this is Sappho, and then later ones, from Wilamowitz to Lobel and Page, said no. My own thought is that it is quintessential Sappho, whatever the uncertainty of scholarship. I remember a fuming, hilarious letter to me from the formidable translator of Greek poetry and drama, Dudley Fitts, who was having a fit over this essential poem. So feelings arise.

168c Dimitrios, *On Style* (p. 37 Radermacher).

Grace is produced in keeping with ornamentation and by using beautiful words that contribute to it as in: [the lines follow].

The earlier scholar Wilamowitz attributed the lines to Sappho. Other modern scholars dissent, but literary translators have generally rendered it, and, whether Sappho or not, these exquisite lines fit the Sapphic fragments.

178 Zenobios, *Proverbs,* 3.3 (i 58 Leutsch-Schneidewin).

Zenobios cites then poem and then:

"This is a saying used about those who died prematurely, or of those who like children but ruin them by how they bring them up. Gello was a girl. She died prematurely and Lesbians say that her ghost haunts little children, and they blame premature deaths on her. Sappho mentions her."

ΛΕΞΕΙΣ ΚΑΙ ΟΝΟΜΑΣΤΙΚΟΝ
ΑΝΑΓΡΑΦΙΟΝ

Glossary and Onomastic Index

Proper nouns which are simply names of persons or places without historical reference are not included in the glossary.

ABDERA Greek city in Thrace founded by Herakles in memory of his attendant Abderos. Superstition held that the air of the city caused its inhabitants to be stupid and "Abderite" became a term of reproach. *112*

ACADEMY A grove of olive trees near Athens held sacred to the hero Akademos. Here Plato and his successors taught, hence the name "Academic philosophy." *159*

ACHELOODOROS Father of the Boiotian poet Korinna.

ACHERON One of the five rivers of the Aiolian underworld that dead souls must cross. *41, 138, 176, 302*

ACHILLES Son of Peleus and the sea nymph Thetis, he is the tragic hero of the *Iliad*. *37, 154*

ADMETOS King of Pherai in Thessaly. *97*

ADONIS A beautiful youth loved by Afroditi and lamented by the goddess after he was killed by a boar. His death was celebrated by women in a yearly festival. *47, 66, 186, 279–80, 286, 305, 313*

ADRIANOS Of Tyros, Sophist, pupil, and successor of Attikos Herodes at Athens. *4*

AELIANUS CLAUDIUS Author of Historical Miscellanies, a fourteen-volume book in Greek about political and literary celebrities, written in the second century CE.

AGAMEMNON King of Mykenai, son of Atreus and brother of Menelaos. Leader of the Greek forces against Troy. *97*

AGATHOKLES Teacher of Apollodoros. *139*

AGESIDAMOS Lokrian boxer celebrated by Pindar in his "Olympian Ode XI." *144*

AHERON/ACHERON The river of Death running through Hades. *41, 80, 81, 138, 176, 302*

AIAKOS Son of Zeus, father of Peleus and grandfather of Achilles, he was known as a just man and a judge in the underworld. *37*

AIETES King of Kolchis and father of Medeia. *90*

AIGAIAN (AEGEAN) SEA That part of the Mediterranean Sea between Greece and Asia Minor. *6, 162, 196, 216, 252*

AIGIALOS A city of Amorgos founded by the poet Semonides. *20*

AIGISTHOS (AEGISTHUS) Surviving son of Thyestes and lover of Agamemnon's wife, Klytaimnestra. *216*

AINESIDAMOS Father of Theron. *145*

AINOS Aiolic city at mouth of Hebros River. *36*

AIOLIC/AIOLIA/AIOLIAN Dialect of eastern Greece (Aiolia) in which Sappho and Alkaios wrote. *xxi, xxii, 25, 33, 43, 92, 126, 171, 249, 253, 272, 279–80, 282, 294, 298, 300, 309–12, 314, 316*

AIOLOS Father of Sisyphos. *41*

AISCHYLOS (AESCHYLUS) Greek tragic poet generally regarded as the founder of Greek tragedy. *118*

AITHRA Daughter of Pittheus, King of Troizen, and mother of Theseus. *151*

AITOLIA A division of Greece celebrated in mythology as the home of the Kalydonian boar hunt. *145*

AKRAGAS (AGRIGENTUM) A city on the southern coast of Sicily known for its splendor. *96, 118, 140, 145*

ALEXANDRIA/ALEXANDRIAN The capital of Egypt, founded by Alexander the Great, and the center of learning and culture during the Hellenistic period. The Library of Alexandria was said to have contained over half a million volumes. *89, 96, 156, 169, 171, 176*

ALKAIOS Lyric poet of Mytilene of Lesbos (fl. ca. 611–580 BCE). *xviii, xxvii, xxviii, xxx, 23, 33, 35, 37, 39, 41–43, 99, 100, 107, 147–71, 256–60, 268, 272, 276, 281, 294, 295, 299, 307, 313, 316, 317*

ALKESTIS (ALCESTIS) Daughter of Pelias and wife of Admetos. *23, 97*

ALKMAN Lyric poet of the second half of the seventh century BCE. His work is concerned mainly with Spartan feasts and festivals. *xvii, xxi, xxvii, xxviii, 23, 25, 27, 29–31, 96, 147, 244, 258, 278, 312*

ALKMENA Daughter of Elektryon, King of Mykenai, and wife of Amphitryon. Mother of Herakles by Zeus. *123*

ALPHEUS One of the largest rivers in Greece. As a hunter, Alpheus pursued the nymph Arethosia; he was transformed into a river, she into a spring. *See* Arethosia. *137, 141*

AMMIANUS MARCELLINUS Last of the great Roman historians, he wrote a history of the Roman Empire from 353 to 78 CE.

AMORGOS An island of the Aigaian Sea and the birthplace of Semonides. *xix, 20*

AMPHIPTOLEMOS Father of Asios. *95*

AMPHITRITE Daughter of Nereus and wife of Poseidon. *153*

AMPHITRYON Son of Alkaios, grandson of Perseus, and husband of Alkmena. Amphitryon's son refers to Herakles. *145, 149, 153*

AMYKLIAN Of Amyklai, an ancient town in Lakonia. *142*

ANAKREON Lyric poet of Teos (ca. 560 BCE). *xvii, xxiii, xxiv, xxvi, xxviii, 99, 100, 107–109, 111, 113, 118, 133, 147, 217, 231, 242, 275, 277–79, 281, 315*

ANAKREONTEIA Collected work by anonymous authors. *xxii, 107, 231–39*

ANAKTORIA One of Sappho's friends. One theory is that she left Sappho in order to marry a soldier stationed in Sardis. *xxix, 42, 59, 99, 254, 275, 305*

ANATOLIA The peninsula of Asia Minor. In Mimnermos Andromache—Daughter of Eetion, King of Thebes, and wife of Hektor. Her husband was killed by Achilles during the Trojan War, her son Astyanax was put to death, and she herself was taken prisoner by the Greeks. *89*

ANDROMAHI/ANDROMACHE She was the wife of Hektor, the Trojan hero, who was killed by Achilles. Homer is evenhanded in treating Achaeans and Trojans as tribes of the same people, portraying Andromahi as a noble figure. *42, 53, 54, 291, 294*

ANDROMEDA A rival of Sappho, perhaps a poet. *42, 61, 69, 70, 81, 218, 255, 275, 315*

ANDROS The most northerly island of the Kyklades. *196, 256, 272*

ANTHOLOGY *See* Palatine Anthology. *xxiv, xxv–xxviii, 4, 83, 103, 128, 141, 159, 167, 169, 181, 182, 191–93, 198, 204, 218, 220, 227–30, 254, 267, 276, 279–82, 301, 311, 316*

ANTIMENIDAS Brother of the poet Alkaios, who fought with the Babylonian army under Nebuchadnezzar in the early sixth century BCE. *35*

ANTIPATROS OF SIDON Greek epigrammatist who influenced Catullus and other Republican poets (fl. first century BCE). *141*

ANTIPATROS OF THESSALONIKE Greek epigrammatist of the Augustan Age whose work closely resembles that of Ovid. *193*

AFRODITI (APHRODITE, KYPRIAN, KYPRIS, KYTHEREIA, PAPHIAN) Goddess of love, beauty, and the sea. She was born in the seafoam (afros) off the shore of Paphos in Kypros (Cyprus) or near the island of Kythera. *5, 42–45, 47, 56, 66, 67, 69, 73, 78, 80, 81, 250, 254, 257, 277, 291–94, 302–307, 312, 313, 316;* APHRODITE, *xviii, xxii, 11, 29, 31, 42, 100, 137, 150, 153, 160, 161, 171, 177, 178, 186, 191, 218, 241, 244, 274, 278, 280, 291;* KYPRIAN, *98, 176, 178, 280;* KYPRIS, *72, 73, 100, 101, 176, 241, 280, 281;* PAPHIAN, *160*

APOLLO Son of Zeus and Leto, and

twin brother of Artemis, he was the ideal of young manly beauty and of civilized Greek man. God of medicine, music, the sun, archery, and prophecy. *xvi, 15, 23, 37, 64, 98, 131, 132, 137, 141, 145, 148, 158, 159, 172, 196, 237, 242, 274, 287*

ARCHEANASSA The girlfriend of Sokrates. *161*

ARCHEDIKE Daughter of the Athenian despot Hippias. *124*

ARCHELAOS King of Macedonia from 413 to 399 BCE. He obtained the throne by murdering his half-brother; he took a keen interest in Greek culture, and the poets Euripides, Agathon, and Timotheos frequented his court. *158*

ARCHESTRATOS Father of Agesidamos. *144*

ARCHILOCHOS Iambic and elegiac poet of Paros; lived in the seventh century BCE. *xvi, xix, 112, 116*

ARCHON The name given to the nine rulers of Athens after the abolition of royalty. *84, 118, 273*

AREIOPAGOS A hill at Athens where Ares was tried for the murder of Poseidon's son, the lover of Ares' daughter. Here the Council of State held its meetings. *84, 110*

ARES/ARIS The god of war. *11, 112, 119, 150;* ARIS, *56, 310*

ARETE Girlfriend of Hipponax. "Arete" also means goodness, virtue, courage, achievement. *xxiii, 103, 120, 314*

ARETHOSIA In order to escape the river god Alphaios, the nymph Arethosia was transformed into a fountain in Ortygia, which then bore her name. *186*

ARGIVES People of Argos. *167*

ARGOS/ARGOLID Argos is a city in Thessaly and the Argolid is the region around the city. *137, 167;* ARGOLID, *126, 154*

ARISTARCHOS Grammarian and great critic of antiquity. The founder of scientific scholarship. *4, 268*

ARISTODEMOS Pupil of Sokrates, one of the Seven Sages. *36, 157*

ARISTOGEITON Assassin, along with Harmodios, of the tyrant Hipparchos in 511 BCE. *See* Harmodios. *133*

ARISTOPHANES Greatest playwright

of comedy in antiquity (ca. 450–ca. 385 BCE). *162, 268, 298, 311*

ARISTOTLE Greek philosopher (384–322 BCE).

ARISTOXENOS Philosopher and musician (fl. ca. 318 BCE). *139*

ARKADIA A country in the middle of the Peloponnesos. The Arkadians regarded themselves as the most ancient people of Greece. *146, 168*

ARKESIME A city of Amorgos founded by Semonides. *20*

ARKTOUROS A bright star near the constellation of the Great Bear. *235*

ARTEMIS The twin sister of Apollo, daughter of Zeus and Leto. She was the goddess of chastity, the hunt, the moon, and childbirth. *31, 48, 53, 108, 137, 146, 195, 270, 278, 299, 316*

ARTEMIS ORTHOSIA Artemis was frequently identified with the Dorian goddess Orthia, who was worshiped at Sparta as Artemis Orthosia. *146*

ASKLEPIOS The god of the art of medicine. The son of Apollo and the pupil of Chiron, Asklepios was killed by Zeus because he could raise the dead. *159, 242*

ASTYPALAIA Sister of Europa. *95*

ATHENA (ATHENE, PALLAS) Goddess of wisdom, war, arts and sciences. The daughter of Zeus. *95, 96, 138, 139, 149, 218*

ATHENAIOS Greek grammarian (ca. 230 CE). *18, 95, 233*

ATHENIS A Chian sculptor satirized by Hipponax. *103*

ATHENS The capital of Attica. *xix, xxiii, 18, 84, 85, 87, 107, 118, 124, 126, 133, 135, 139, 140, 144, 147, 155, 159, 162, 167, 233, 253, 273*

ATREIDAI Sons or descendants of Atreus, usually referring to Agamemnon or Menelaos. *See* Atreus.

ATREUS King of Mykenai, son of Pelops and grandson of Tantalos. The gods cursed Atreus and his house because he dared to serve them the flesh of his brother's children. *41, 46, 81*

ATTALES Brother of Alyattes, King of Persia, whose tomb still exists. *104*

ATTALYDA Founder of city of the same name. *104*

ATTHIS One of Sappho's friends who

is treated with great affection. Like Anaktoria, she leaves Sappho. *42, 63, 66, 69, 85, 250, 254, 272, 275, 300, 305*

ATTICA/ATTIC A division of central Greece where Attic Greek was spoken. Its capital city was Athens. *86, 133, 321, 327, 330;* ATTIC, *85, 159, 185, 240, 253, 255, 298, 299, 309*

ATYS Mythical lover of Kybeles. *104*

BAKCHOS (BACCHUS, BACCHIS) *See* Dionysos. *34, 233*

BAKCHYLIDES One of the nine great Greek lyric poets. *xxiii, xxvii, xxviii, 140, 147, 149, 151, 153, 174*

BASILO Sister of Melanippos. *169*

BATHYLLOS A beautiful youth loved by the poet Anakreon. *233*

BATTOS Father of Kallimachos. *16*

BOIOTIA A district in Greece north of Attica. Boiotians were considered to be dull-witted despite the fact that Pindar, Hesiod, Korinna, and Plutarch were Boiotians. *xxiii, 135, 140*

BOUPALOS Sculptor suitor of Hipponax's girlfriend. *103*

BYZANTIUM A town of the Thracian Bosporos later renamed Constantinople. *xii, 220, 257, 268*

CALABRIA A region in southern Italy. *156, 182*

CATULLUS Outstanding Roman lyric poet (84–54 BCE). *4, 43, 252, 256, 295, 308–10*

CENTAURS A mythological race of creatures with the heads and torsos of men on the bodies of horses. *115*

CHALKIS Chief town in Euboia. *11, 203*

CHAOS The infinite space that existed before the creation of the world. *112, 185*

CHARAXOS/HARAXOS Brother of Sappho. *42;* HARAXOS, *72, 253, 260, 274, 293*

CHARON The boatman who ferried the dead across the rivers of the underworld. Also means "underworld." *11, 53, 203*

CHARYBDIS A giant whirlpool opposite the cave of Skylla off the coast of Sicily. *105, 183*

CHEIRON The wisest of the Centaurs, known for his skills in medicine, music, art, hunting, and gymnastics, accidentally killed by Herakles and later placed among the stars as Sagittarius. *37*

CHIAN Of Chios/Hios, a large island south of Lesbos near Asia Minor. Celebrated for its wine and marble, Chios was reputed to be the birthplace of Homer. *276*

CICERO Great Roman orator, statesman, and essayist (106–43 BCE). *271*

CIMMERIAN INCURSIONS Invasions into Assyria and Asia Minor in the eighth and seventh centuries BCE by barbarians from southern Russia.

CIRCE A beautiful witch famous for her magical powers, who held Odysseus captive on her island. Daughter of the sungod Helios. *182, 222*

CLEMENT OF ALEXANDRIA One of the early Greek Fathers of the church, important because of his extensive knowledge of literature and philosophy (ca. 160–215 CE). *156*

CUPID *See* Eros.

CYNIC Member of a school of philosophy founded by Antisthenes, pupil of Sokrates. The name is taken from the Kynosarges gymnasium where the school was established. *207, 241*

DAIDALOS Legendary Athenian craftsman who with his son Ikaros escaped from their prison tower with wings made of wax and feathers. Ikaros flew too near the sun and fell into the sea, hence the name Ikarian Sea. *141*

DAMON OF ATHENS Celebrated musician and Sophist, teacher of Perikles and Sokrates. *139*

DANAË A girl of Argos, whose father prophesied that her son would kill him. To prevent the conception of a son the father enclosed her in a chamber. Zeus penetrated the chamber in a shower of gold and begot Perseus. *xxiii, 122, 177, 197*

DANAIDS The daughters of Danaos. *157*

DAPHNIS A Sicilian shepherd, son of Hermes, and regarded as the inventor of bucolic poetry. *172*

DARIUS King of Persia (521–485 BCE).

During his reign the great war between the Persians and the Greeks began. *168*

DEIANEIRA Wife of Herakles. *149*

DELOS The center island of the Kyklades in the Aigaian Sea. The birthplace of Apollo and Artemis and an important center for their worship. *153*

DELPHI An ancient oracular shrine of Apollo in Phokis, and also a center for theatrical and athletic events. *37, 121, 133, 149, 172*

DEMETER Daughter of Kronos and Rhea and the mother of Persephone. She was the goddess of corn and a patroness of agriculture. *126*

DENTHIADES A town of Lakonia. *30*

DIAGORAS Poet and philosopher, known for his atheism. *114*

DIAGORASES Famous boxer of Rhodes praised in Pindar's "Olympic Ode VII." *114*

DIDYMOS Of Alexandria, nicknamed "brazen-guts" because of his great industry. This author of the first century BCE wrote a commentary on Homer. *108*

DIKA Probably short for Mnasidika, one of Sappho's friends. *76*

DIODOROS Poet of the Greek Anthology. *192, 199*

DIOGENES A Cynic philosopher (ca. 400 BCE) known in Athens for his pithy sayings. *196*

DIOGENES LAERTIOS Author of Lives and Opinions of Eminent Philosophers, an account of the principal Greek thinkers of his day (fl. 150 CE). *85, 115, 159*

DION Son of Hipparinos and son-in-law of the Syracusian tyrant Dionysios the Elder, Dion was a disciple of Plato and a statesman in Sicily. *163, 185*

DIONYSOS (BAKCHOS) Greek god of wine and fertility. The son of Zeus and Semele, Dionysos was the god of natural vitality also. *xvii, 46, 113, 185*

DIOSKOURI From the Greek "Dios Kouri," literally "sons of Zeus," or Kastor and Polydeukes. These twin sons of Zeus and Leda were regarded as both courageous gods and mortals and were later identified with the constellation Gemini.

DIRPHIAN/DIRPHYS Central mountain range of Euboia. *120*

DORIC/DORIAN Dialect of Greek used in Sparta. *xvii, xxi, 17, 25, 96, 99, 118, 145, 147, 157, 168, 171, 186, 233, 293*

DODEKANESE Twelve islands in the southeast Aigaian Sea. *171*

DORICHA Egyptian courtesan and lover of Sappho's brother. *293*

DOTIAN PLAIN Part of Pelasgiotis in Thessaly. *142*

DRYADS (HAMADRYADS) The nymphs of the trees. *162*

EKBATANA The capital of Media, a country of Asia near Persia. *162*

ELEA A town on the west coast of Lakonia. Here Parmenides founded the Eleatic school of philosophy. *114*

ELIS A state in the northwest of the Peloponnesos, which included the important site of Olympia. *147*

ELYSIUM In mythology, the residence of the blessed after death. *143*

EMMENOS Children of Emmenos refers to the family of Theron. *16, 128*

EMPEDOKLES Philosopher and scientist of Akragas (fl. ca. 460 BCE). The inventor of the art of rhetoric. *128*

ENYALIOS Epithet of the god Ares and later a different god of war. *10*

EPHESOS One of the principal Ionian cities on the coast of Asia Minor. *16, 103, 114, 195*

EPIKOUROS (EPICURUS) Greek philosopher (341–270 BCE) and founder of the Epicurean school of philosophy. *114, 203*

EPIKTETOS Stoic philosopher of first century CE. *22*

EPINIKION A victory ode, a form used by Pindar, Bakchylides, and Simonides. *17, 140*

ERETRIA A town of Euboia situated on the Euripos Strait. It was destroyed by the Persians in 490 BCE. *11, 136, 162*

ERGOTELES A political exile from Kriti and a victor in the Olympian games. Kriti enjoyed a reputation for its runners. *142, 143*

ERIBOIA Wife of Telamon and mother of Aias (Ajax). *150*

EROS (CUPID) The god of all striving toward union, particularly of sexual love. Usually regarded as the son of

Afroditi. *xxii, 15, 31, 47–49, 58, 59, 64, 82, 100, 108, 109, 159, 182, 184, 186, 218, 228, 230, 232, 233, 235, 236, 249, 269, 275, 278–80, 299, 300, 301, 308, 312, 316*

ERYSICHE A city of Arkanania. *29*

ERYTHEIA Birthplace of the monster Geryon, slain by Herakles. It was either Cadiz (Gades), the Balearic Islands, or islands off the coast of Epiros. *97*

EUBOIA The largest island of the Aigaian Sea and near the mainland. *11, 130, 162*

EUENOR Father and teacher of Parrhasios. *155*

EUKRATES Father of Meleagros. *185*

EURIPIDES One of the three great Attic tragedians (480–406 BCE). *158, 258, 271, 277*

EURIPOS The strait between Euboia and the mainland. *120*

EUROPA In mythology, Europa was kidnapped by Zeus in the disguise of a bull and carried off to Kriti where she became the mother of Minos. *120*

EUROTAS The chief river in Lakonia. *130*

EURYMEDON A river in Pamphylia; a proper name. *105, 119*

EURYALOS A young man loved by Ibykos. *101*

EURYSTEUS King of Argos for whom Herakles performed his twelve labors. *146*

EURYTION The Centaur whom Herakles slew. *97*

EUSTATHIOS Grammarian and historian of the eleventh century CE. *297*

EUTYCHIDES Proper name of a poet. *203*

EUTYCHOS Proper name of a portrait painter. *203*

EVENOS (EUENOS) A river of Attolia taking its name from Evenos, whose daughter was kidnapped by Marpessa. Evenos, being unable to rescue his daughter, threw himself into the river. *149, 150*

FIVE HILLS A town in Lakonia. *30*

GADARA A city in Syria. *185*

GALATEIA Sea nymph, daughter of Nereus and Doris, and loved by Polyphemos. *186*

GERANEIA The mountain range between the territories of Megara and Corinth. *121*

GERYON A monster with three heads and three bodies joined together, living on the island of Erytheia. *96, 98*

GIANTS The sons of Ge produced from the blood of the mutilated Uranus. Beings of great size with serpent feet, the Giants were eventually destroyed by Herakles and the other gods and were buried beneath volcanoes. *115*

GLAUKOS Proper name. *xx, 7, 12, 123*

GONGYLA/GONGULA One of Sappho's intimate friends. *64, 80, 254, 259, 272, 289, 292, 305*

GORGIOS Sicilian rhetorician and orator of the fifth century BCE. A leading Sophist, his writings influenced much of Attic prose, especially the writings of Isokrates. *241*

GORGO A rival of Sappho's; perhaps a poet. *42, 69, 123, 254, 275, 314, 315*

GORTYN An ancient city in Kriti famous for two groups of inscriptions about social institutions written on the interior wall of the courthouse. *124*

GRACES Goddesses of grace and charm, associated with the Muses. *53, 73, 74, 76, 98, 101, 162, 185, 238, 278, 310*

GREEK ANTHOLOGY *See* Palatine Anthology. *xxiv, xxix, 83, 167, 220, 227, 254, 267, 279–82, 316*

GYARA An island of the Kyklades in the Aigaian Sea.

GYGES King of Lydia whose wealth became proverbial. *11, 104, 232*

GYRAI Some rocks off the island of Mykonos. *7*

GYRINNO One of Sappho's companions. *76*

HADES God of the underworld, or sometimes a name for the underworld itself. *80, 86, 98, 103, 176, 204, 217, 280, 286, 302*

HAGESICHORA Leader of Alkman's chorus of girls. *27, 28*

HALIKARNASSOS Birthplace of Herodotos. This city of Asia Minor stood in the southwestern part of Karia, opposite the island of Keos. *257, 291, 310*

HARMODIOS Assassin, along
with Aristogeiton, of the tyrant
Hipparchos in 511 BCE. *133*

HARMONY Daughter of Ares and
Afroditi, the wife of Kadmus. *78,
126, 139, 141, 303*

HEBROS Chief river in Thrace. It is
frequently mentioned in the wor-
ship of Dionysos. *36, 148*

HEKATE Earth goddess associated
with sorcery, magic, and ghosts, and
worshiped by night at crossroads.

HEKTOR Son of Priam and husband of
Andromache, Hektor was the hero
of the defense of Troy. He was killed
by Achilles in Homer's *Iliad. xvi,
42, 53, 54, 291, 294*

HELEN Daughter of Zeus and Leda, a
goddess of extraordinary beauty. As
wife of Menelaos, she was seduced
and taken to Troy by Paris and so
came the overt cause of the Trojan
War. *xxi, xxviii, 36, 37, 59, 65, 96,
97, 145, 294, 295*

HELIKON Mountain in Boiotia named
after a legendary man. *135, 136,
172, 280*

HELIODORA Girlfriend of
Meleagros. *183, 184, 202*

HELIOS God of the sun. *91, 98, 151*

HELLAS/HELLENES The Greeks called
their country Hellas and themselves
Hellenes. *6, 7, 142, 144, 160*

HEPHAISTION A writer on prosody in
the second century CE. *6, 37*

HEPHAISTOS God of fire and metal-
work. *8, 91, 276*

HERA Queen of the Olympian gods,
daughter of Kronos and Rhea,
and mother of Hefaistos and Aris.
In Rome she was Juno. Hera was
the patron goddess of marriage
and childbirth, and, beginning at
Minoan Kriti, she was worshiped
in all ancient periods throughout
Greece, and many temples were
built to adore her. Her husband and
brother was Zeus.

HERAKLES Son of Zeus and Alkmena
(whose husband was Amphitryon).
Herakles was a strongman and the
performer of the Twelve Labors. *96,
98, 99, 101, 123, 145, 146, 148, 149,
155, 229*

HERMES/HERMIS Herald of the
gods. Patron of heralds, travelers,
and thieves. Also guide of the souls

to the underworld. *55, 80, 104, 133,
134, 136, 168, 201, 305, 313*

HERMESIANAX Greek elegiac poet of
the fourth century BCE. *89, 281*

HERMIONE/HERMIONI Daughter of
Menelaos and Helen. Hermione's
beauty, as a demigod, did not
match the beauty of her mother,
Helen. *64, 126, 295*

HERMIONE Birthplace of Lasos in the
Argolid of the Peloponnesos.

HERMOS A river of Asia Minor. *91*

HERO One of Sappho's friends.

HERODOTOS (fifth century BCE)
The first author to make the events
of the past the subject of research
and verification. According
to Cicero, he is the "Father of
History." *85, 253, 274, 293*

HERONDAS A writer of mimes and
a native of Kos or Miletos (ca.
300–250 BCE). *103*

HESIOD Early Greek poet of the eighth
century BCE, and author of *Works
and Days* and the *Theogony. 117,
258, 277, 307, 316*

HESPERIDES Divine maidens, guard-
ians of the golden apples in the gar-
den of the gods. *91, 308*

HESPEROS The evening star, the son
of Astraios or Kephalos or Atlas
and Eos (Dawn) and father of the
Hesperides. *49, 159, 186, 308*

HESYCHIOS Greek grammarian of
Alexandria whose chief literary
work was a Greek lexicon. He lived
in the fourth century CE. *126*

HIERON Tyrant of Syracuse and vic-
tor in the Olympic and Pythian
games. *118, 140*

HIMERA A Greek city on the north
coast of Sicily. Probably the birth-
place of the poet Stesichoros. *96,
142, 143*

HIPPARCHOS Brother of the Athenian
despot Hippias. He was murdered in
54 BCE. *107, 118, 126, 133, 134*

HIPPIAS Son of the despot
Peisistratos, Hippias was despot of
Athens from 527 to 510 BCE. *107,
124, 133*

HIPPOKRATELA Mother of the
poet Korinna and wife of
Acheloodoros. *135*

HIPPOLYTOS A Christian writer (fl.
200 CE). *156*

HIPPONAX Of Ephesos, a Greek iambic poet (fl. 546–520 BCE). *6, 20, 103–105*

HIPPON A physical philosopher (fl. 430 BCE). *ix, 156*

HOMER First epic poet of Greece. His poems were the basis of Greek literature and education. The author of the *Iliad* and the *Odyssey*. *xv–xvii, xxiii, xxix, 3, 4, 16, 18, 22, 25, 33, 43, 96, 97, 105, 117, 118, 147, 157, 231, 251, 267, 275, 276, 280, 294, 299, 302, 304, 309*

HORACE One of the main Roman lyric poets (65–8 BCE). *xviii, 4, 33, 89, 107, 141, 147, 191, 256, 260, 270, 275, 282, 315*

HYMEN God of marriage, a handsome youth whom it was customary to invoke at Greek weddings by singing "Hymen, O Hymen" in the hymenal or bridal song. *xvi, 56, 280, 298*

HYPERBOREANS A fabulous people living in a land of perpetual sunshine somewhere beyond the North Wind. Poets use "Hyperborean" to mean most northerly. *37, 145*

HYPERION A Titan, son of Uranus (Heaven) and Ge (Earth), and father of Helios (Sun), Selene (Moon), and Eos (Dawn). Sometimes refers to Helios himself. *98*

HYPNOS God of sleep. *184*

IBYKOS Greek lyric poet of Rhegium, Ibykos lived at the court of Polykrates at Samos. *xxi, xxii, xxv, xxviii, 96, 99, 100, 101, 107, 147, 265*

IDA In Homer, Ida is the summit from which the gods watched the battle of Troy. Zeus was said to have been brought up in a cave in Mt. Ida, in central Kriti. *151*

IDAS The kidnapper of Apollo's beloved Marpessa. *149, 150*

IDYL, IDYLL "A little picture," or a short poem depicting a pastoral scene. *171*

ILOS Son of Tros, father of Priam, and founder of Ilium (Troy). *25, 53*

ILIUM Another name for Troy. *37, 163*

IOLE Daughter of King Eurytos. Herakles sought to marry her. *149*

IONIA/IONIAN A district on and off the west coast of Asia Minor, colonized by the Ionians. In this region early Greek literature and philosophy developed. *xxi, xxii, 51, 86, 89, 96, 107, 126, 150, 234*

IONIC The Greek dialect of Ionia. *3, 20, 171, 294, 298, 312, 315, 317*

IRANA/EIRANA One of Sappho's friends. Irana can be a friend's name or mean "peace." *58, 75, 312*

IRIS (THAUMANTIAS) The goddess of the rainbow and a messenger of the gods. She is the wife of Zephyros, the West Wind. *6*

IROS A beggar in the house of Odysseus. *242*

ISMARIAN Of Ismaros, a town in Thrace which produced excellent wine. Poets use the term "Ismarian" as equivalent to "Thracian." *10*

ISOKRATES Fourth of the "Ten Attic Orators," he was a great teacher of rhetoric.

ISTHMOS The isthmus at Corinth separating the mainland from the Peloponnesos. *120, 143*

ISTRIA The Istrian land was by the Istros or Danube River. *146*

IULUS (ASCANIUS) Son of Aeneas. *141*

JASON Leader of the Argonauts who set sail in the Argo to find the Golden Fleece. *75*

JUSTINIAN Roman emperor at Constantinople (527–565 CE). *218*

KADMOS Son of Agenor and founder of the Greek city of Thebes. *141*

KALLIA Father of Megakles. *121*

KALLIMACHOS Alexandrian grammarian and poet of the third century CE. *169, 171*

KALLINOS Of Ephesos. The earliest Greek elegiac poet (fl. 700 BCE?). *xi, 16–18*

KARIA A district of western Asia Minor. *234*

KARYSTOS A town of Lakonia. *30, 123*

KASTALIA A nymph who, when pursued by Apollo, threw herself into a spring on Mount Parnassos. The spring was henceforward held sacred to Apollo and to the Muses. The latter were often called Kastalides. *37, 38*

KASTOR *See* Dioskouri. *29, 34, 74*

KEAN Of the island of Keos.

KENAIAN ZEUS Of the temple to Zeus in Kenaion. *149*

KEOS An island of the Kyklades and birthplace of Simonides. *118, 147*

KEPHISSOS Chief river in the Athenian plain. *37, 38*

KERES Spirits of death. *91*

KERKIDAS Greek poet of an uncertain date. Wrote in lyric meters on ethical subjects. *103*

KERKYLAS Husband of Sappho. *42, 253, 255, 256, 272*

KITHAIRON A mountain in Boiotia named after a legendary man. *22, 135, 136*

KLAZOMENAI City of Asia Minor where the poet Hipparchos wandered as a beggar. The birthplace of Anaxagoras. *103*

KLEÏS (CLEIS) Name of Sappho's daughter, also her mother, and perhaps a friend. *42, 52, 72, 252, 253, 264, 272, 306*

KLEOMENES King of Sparta, 520–489 BCE. *137*

KLYMENOS A god of the nether world. *137*

KLYTAIMNESTRA Wife and murderess of Agamemnon and mistress of Aigisthos. Murdered in turn by her son Orestes. *97*

KNIDOS City of Asia Minor and the home of the famous astronomer Eudoxos. *161, 278*

KNOSSOS An ancient town in Kriti. "Knossian" is the equivalent of "Kretan." *44, 142*

KOIOS Father of Leto, the mother of Apollo. *48*

KOLOPHON One of the twelve Ionian cities of Asia Minor and said to be the birthplace of Homer; the site of the oracle of Apollo Klarios.

KORESSOS A hill. *185*

KORINNA Greek lyric poetess (fl. ca. 500 BCE). Believed to have been the instructor of Pindar. *27, 35, 135, 136*

KOS One of the islands called Sporades, home of Hippokrates and a favorite place for men of letters. Theokritos lived there at one time. *16, 171, 182*

KRATINOS Athenian poet of the Old Comedy. *156*

KRITI (CRETE) A large island in the Mediterranean where Minoan civilization flourished. *44, 292, 294*

KRITON Rich citizen of Athens and friend of Sokrates. *201*

KROISOS The last king of Lydia. His wealth and power attracted the poet Solon to his court. Kronian Pelops—Pelops was the great-grandson of Kronos. *85*

KRONOS Father of Zeus. *41, 48, 135, 152*

KYKLADES A group of islands in the Aigaian Sea lying in a circle around the sacred Island of Delos. *147*

KYLLENE The highest mountain in the Peloponnesos, sacred to Hermes, who had a temple on the summit. Hermes is sometimes called "Kyllenios." *104*

KYNOSKEPHALAI "Dog Heads," two hills in Thessaly where Flaminius defeated Philip of Macedonia (197 BCE). *140*

KYPRIAN/KYPRIS/KYTHEREA See Afroditi.

KYPROS/CYPRUS An island in the Mediterranean and one of the chief seats of worship of the goddess Afroditi. *31, 48, 53, 64, 77, 81, 85, 259, 278, 312*

KYRENE A Greek city of North Africa between Carthage and Alexandria. *169, 170*

KYRNOS Friend of the poet Theognis; also the Greek name for Corsica. Poems which specially mention Kyrnos by name are considered authentic poems of Theognis. *127, 128, 129, 131*

LAÏS A famous courtesan of Corinth, known for her beauty. *160*

LAKEDAIMONIANS Spartans. In mythology Lakedaimon, a son of Zeus and Taygete, married Sparta and named his city after her. *119*

LAKONIA A region of the Peloponnesos. Sparta was its capital. *23, 28, 30*

LAMPSAKOS City of Asia Minor celebrated for its wine. The chief seat of worship for Priapos. *124*

LASOS A poet and teacher of Pindar. *126, 132*

LEDA Mother of Helen and Klytaimnestra, Kastor and Polydeukes. Wooed by Zeus in the disguise of a swan. *xi, 34, 146*

LEIANTINE WAR A war between Chalkis and Eretria for possession of the plain watered by the Leiantos (ca. 690 BCE). *11*

LEONIDAS King of Sparta, 487–480 BCE, died heroically at

Thermopylai, fighting against the invading Persians. *120*

LEONIDAS OF ALEXANDRIA A Hellenistic poet who wrote many hilarious epigrams that survive in the Anthology. *204*

LEONIDAS OF TARENTUM Early third century BCE, author of elaborate epigrams, many based on numbers. *12, 112, 174, 175*

LESBOS An island in the Aigaian Sea off the coast of Mysia in Asia Minor. Birthplace of the poets Terpandros, Sappho, and Alkaios. *xxii, 23, 33, 40–43, 109, 161, 234, 249, 252–54, 264, 272, 274, 279, 280, 282, 292, 303, 306, 312*

LETHAIOS A small tributary of the Maiandros River in Asia Minor. *108*

LETO Mother of Apollo and Artemis. Leto was worshiped in connection with her children. *23, 93, 98, 146*

LEUKADIAN ROCK Promontory on the island of Leukas from which suspected criminals were cast into the sea. Birds were attached to them in order to break their fall. This rock gave rise to the story that lovers leapt from it to escape the pangs of love. *See* Phaon.

LOKRIA Greek city in southern Italy, known for its laws. *144*

LONGINUS/LONGINOS Greek philosopher, literary critic, and grammarian of the third century CE. Teacher of Zenobia.

LOUKIANOS/LUCIAN Greek writer of the second century CE. *207*

LYDIA A district in Asia Minor between Mysia and Karia. An early seat of Asian civilization, exerting an important influence on the Greeks. *11, 25, 27, 39, 52, 59, 65, 76, 90, 104, 105, 115, 123, 139, 256, 294, 298, 315*

LYKAMBES Nobleman, father of Neoboule, loved by Archilochos. *3, 12, 15*

LYSIPPOS Famous Greek sculptor, contemporary of Alexander. *154*

LYSIS Pythagorean philosopher and teacher of Epaminondas. *139*

MACEDON/MACEDONIA A region of northern Greece; birthplace of Alexander the Great. *157, 158*

MAIA Daughter of Atlas and Pleione.

The eldest and most beautiful of the Pleiades. Mother of Hermes. *104*

MARATHON Village in Attica and the site of the crucial battle between the Persians and the Athenians in 490 BCE. *118, 120*

MARPESSA Daughter of Evenos and wife of Idas. *149, 150*

MEDIA North of Persia, its inhabitants were the Medes. When Media was conquered by Persia, Mede and Media became synonymous in Greek for Persian and Persia. *162, 252, 259, 269*

MEGALOSTRATA Loved by Alkman. *29*

MEGARA Capital of Megaris, a district of Greece. One of the four divisions of Attica. *62, 127, 272, 302*

MEGASTRYS Lover of King Gyges. *104*

MEGISTIAS An Akarnanian seer who at Thermopylai refused to return to the rear and died in battle. *121*

MELANCHROS Tyrant of Lesbos in 610 BCE. Overthrown by Pittakos. *33*

MELANIPPOS Friend of Alkaio. *41, 169*

MELISSA Nymph, discoverer of honey, and from whom bees received their name. Here used as a proper name. *194*

MELOS An island in the Aigaian and the most westerly of the Sporades. *157*

MENELAOS Son of Atreus and younger brother of Agamemnon. The rape of his wife, Helen, by Paris, caused the Trojan War. *81, 97, 295*

MENIPPOS Cynic philosopher of Gadara in Syria (fl. 250 BCE). *185, 198*

MENISKOS Father of Pelagon. *83*

MESSENE Country in Peloponnesos, defeated three different times by Sparta in the Messenian Wars (seventh century BCE). *18*

MIKA Probably a shortened form of "Mnasidika," a rival who had gone over to the rival house of Penthilos, ruling nobles of Mytilene. *70, 254, 303*

MILETOS A great city of Asia Minor. Birthplace of Anaximandros, Anaximenes, and Thales. *93, 158, 196*

MIMNERMOS Greek elegiac poet and

contemporary of Solon. *16, 89, 91, 93*

MINOA City in Amorgos founded by Semonides. *20*

MINOS Son of Zeus and Europa, Minos was a mythical king of Kriti, ruling at Knossos. Later he was one of the judges of the underworld. *150, 152, 162*

MNASIDIKA A friend of Sappho's who appears to have deserted her. "Mika" is probably a shortened form of "Mnasidika." *76, 303, 306*

MOLIONE The twins of Molione were the Aktoridai; they were killed by Herakles. *101*

MOLOURIS A rock on the coast near Megara, from which Ino and Melikertes threw themselves into the sea.

MUSES Daughters of Zeus, the nine Muses lived on Mount Helikon where they presided over the arts and sciences. *4, 23, 25, 43, 53, 74, 79, 82, 101, 129, 136, 140–42, 144, 145, 161, 174, 185, 225, 227–29, 236, 276, 280–83, 288*

MYKONIANS/MYKONOS Of Mykonos, an island in the Aigaian Sea. The place where Herakles defeated the Giants. *13*

MYRSILOS Tyrant of Mytilene who probably caused the exile of Sappho and Alkaios. *33, 55, 254, 306*

MYRSILOS Teacher of Korinna. *33, 41, 254, 306*

MYSIANS Of Mysia, a district in the northwest corner of Asia. *111*

MYTILINI/MITYLENE The city in ancient Lesbos (now called Mytilini) where Sappho spent much of her life. *33, 39, 40, 42, 71, 253, 254, 306*

NANNO A flute-girl to whom Mimnermos addressed his elegies. *27, 89*

NAXOS An island in the Aigaian. *10, 14*

NEBUCHADNEZZAR King of Babylon from 605 to 562 BCE, who captured Jerusalem. *33*

NELEIAN PYLOS Neleus of Pylos, son of Poseidon and king of Pylos in the western Peloponnesos. Brother of Pelias. *92*

NEMEA Valley in Argolis where Herakles slew the Nemean lion,

and where the Nemean games were held. *202*

NEMESIS The Greek goddess of retribution for sinful excess; also of compensation for good fortune. *210*

NEOBOULE Daughter of Lykambes, loved by Archilochos.

NEREIDS Sea nymphs. Fifty in number, they were the daughters of Nereus. *72, 293*

NEREUS The god of the sea. His empire is the Aigaian Sea. Sometimes he is called the Aigaian. *37, 151, 153*

NERO Emperor of Rome (54–68 CE). *15, 110, 200, 204*

NESSOS A Centaur who tried to seduce Herakles' wife Deianeira. *149*

NIOBE Daughter of Tantalos, wife of Amphion. Niobe once boasted that her family was larger than Leto's. To avenge this insult Leto killed twelve of Niobe's children. Niobe is a stock figure of bereavement. *238*

NYMPHS Female divinities of a lower rank represented as beautiful girls living in the mountains, forests, meadows, and waters. *120, 143, 153, 162, 173, 283, 284, 287, 293*

OICHALIA City of Euboia. *149*

OINEOS Father of Perimede. *95*

OINOS Town of Lakonia. *30*

OLYMPIA/OLYMPIANS A plain in Elis where the Olympian Games were held. This plain was sacred to Zeus. *xii, 8, 85, 123, 142–45, 272, 293, 314*

OLYMPIAN GAMES Athletic events celebrated at Olympia from earliest times in Greece every four years.

OLYMPOS A range of mountains separating Thessaly and Macedon. The home of the gods. *54, 108, 146, 253*

ONOGLA A town in Lakonia. *30*

ORESTES Son of Agamemnon and Klytaimnestra and avenger of his father's murder by Klytaimnestra and Aigisthos. *96*

ORTHRIA (ORTHIA) A goddess. Later Artemis Orthia. *27*

ORTYGIA An island near Syracuse, claimed as birthplace of Artemis. Ortygia was also a name associated with Artemis, and hence another name for Delos, where Artemis, according to most accounts, was born. *102*

OSSA A mountain in the north of Thessaly associated with the war of the Giants. *122*

OVID Roman poet (fl. ca. 23 BCE). *xx, 28, 43, 252, 255, 257, 260, 282, 288*

PALATINE ANTHOLOGY (GREEK ANTHOLOGY) Collection of Greek epigrams started by Constantine Cephalas and finished by Planudes. *xxvii, xxviii, 4, 103, 122, 141, 159, 169, 228–30, 316*

PAN Goat-footed god of shepherds and flocks. *162, 172*

PANDION Father of Prokne, who became a swallow, and Philomela, who became a nightingale. Reputed grandfather of Theseus. *75, 150, 238*

PAPHIAN Of Paphos, and therefore of Afroditi. Afroditi was born in the foam near the city of Paphos in Kypros. *160*

PARMENIDES Philosopher of Elea and founder of the Eleatic school of philosophy. Born ca. 510 BCE. *93, 128*

PARNASSOS A mountain in central Greece thought to be the dwelling place of Apollo and the Muses. Also sacred to Dionysos. *37*

PAROS An island in the Aigaian Sea. Birthplace of Archilochos. *3, 7*

PARRHASIOS Painter and poet, second century BCE in Parrhasios. *155*

PARTHIANS Of Parthia, a country of Asia. The Parthians were a warlike people and their savagery became proverbial. *229*

PASIPHILE Proper name meaning literally "lover of everybody." *9*

PAULUS SILENTIARIUS (PAUL THE SILENTIARY) An officer of the Justinian household (fl. 540 CE) and a Greek poet of epigrams. *xxiv, 218–20*

PAUSANIAS Greek travel writer of the second century CE. Author of Hellados Periegetes, a guide to the cities and monuments of Greece. *95, 137, 158, 275, 279*

PEISISTRALOS Despot of Athens, 561–527 BCE, with intervals of exile.

PEITHO Personification of persuasion, the goddess of seductive charm. *101*

PELAGON A fisherman. *83*

PELEUS King of the Myrmidons at Phthia in Thessaly. The father of Achilles and the husband of the Nereid Thetis. *37*

PELIAS Son of Poseidon and Tyro. Ordered Jason to search for the Golden Fleece and was later butchered by his own daughters, and boiled. *203*

PELION A mountain of Thessaly. *122*

PELOPONNESOS The southernmost part of Greece, connected with the central region by the Isthmus of Corinth. *127, 147*

PELOPS Son of Tantalos. When he was a child his father killed him and served him as food for the gods. He was later restored to life by the gods and Tantalos was punished in Hades. Pelops murdered his wife's suitor, Myrtilos, and brought about a curse on his two sons, Atreus and Thyestes. *34, 145, 226*

PENTHILOS A rival family of ruling nobles in Mytilene. The tyrant Pittakos was the son of Penthilos. *70, 303*

PERDIKKAS King of Macedonia (454?–413 BCE).

PERIKLES Great Athenian statesman. Under his direction the Parthenon and Propylaea were constructed. *157*

PERIMEDE Wife of Phoinix and daughter of Oineos. *95*

PERSEPHONE (KORE) Wife of Hades and queen of the underworld. Daughter of Zeus and Demeter. *126*

PERSEUS Son of Danaë and Zeus. He was cast away with his mother so as not to fulfill the prophecy that he would kill his grandfather, Akrisios, whom he actually killed later. *xxiii, 122, 283*

PHALARIS Tyrant of Akragas in Sicily in the first half of the sixth century BCE. He commissioned the "brazen bull," a torture device, whose inventor was the first to be put to death by it. *96*

PHAON Legend says that Sappho leaped from the Leukadian rock out of love for Phaon, but there is no evidence for this story. *42, 252, 255, 256, 273, 274, 282–88*

PHILANOR Father of Ergoteles. *143*

PHILETAS Greek grammarian and poet of the Alexandrian Age. His amatory poems were imitated by Ovid. *169*

PHILINNA Mother of Theokritos. *171*

PHILIPPOS Poet of the Greek Anthology (second century CE). *169*

PHILOCHOROS Greek historian of Athens (fl. third century BCE). *18*

PHILODEMOS Epicurean philosopher and an epigrammatic poet. A contemporary of Cicero. *xxiv, 191*

PHILON Son of Glaukos, and champion in boxing for two years at the Olympian Games. *123*

PHOIBOS/PHOEBUS An epithet of Apollo, meaning "shining." *48, 283, 287*

PHOINIX Father of Europa, according to one version. *95, 151*

PHOKAIA A city of Ionia in Asia Minor. *76*

PHOKYLIDES A poet, contemporary with Solon. *93*

PHOTIOS A lexicographer and literary critic. *16*

PHRYGIA A country in Asia Minor associated with the worship of Dionysos and Kybele (Rhea), mother of the gods. The Roman poets used the term "Phrygian" as an equivalent of "Trojan." *75, 98, 238, 286*

PHRYNIS A dithyrambic poet (fl. 430 BCE). *158*

PIERIA Home of the Muses. It was the region in Thrace where the Muses were first worshiped and often the word "Pierian" means simply "of the Muses." *53, 80, 148, 280, 281*

PINDAROS/PINDAR Greek lyric poet of the fifth century BCE. Most of his extant poems are those written in commemoration of victories in public games. *xii, xv, xvii, xviii, xxiii, xxiv, xxvii, xxviii, xxx, 4, 23, 82, 96, 118, 126, 132, 135, 136, 140–43, 145, 147, 161, 252, 254, 258, 265, 293, 298, 314*

PISA A city in Peloponnesos, near Olympia and often identified by poets with it. *145, 202, 292*

PITTAKOS A contemporary of Sappho and one of the "Seven Sages of Greece." He was the same tyrant of Lesbos against whom Alkaios rages in his poems. *33, 40, 41, 43, 254, 272, 276, 307*

PLAKIA A river near Thebe, near the area of Troy.

PLATIA A city of Boiotia where the Greeks defeated the Persians in 479 BCE. *53*

PLATO The famous Greek philosopher (497–347 BCE). *xxiv, xxvii, xxx, 16, 43, 97, 118, 127, 133, 139, 140, 159, 163, 207, 241, 242, 252, 254, 256, 267, 273, 279, 280, 305*

PLEIADES The seven daughters of Atlas and Pleione. Pursued by Orion, they were turned into stars. *27, 58*

PLEISTHENES Son of Atreus and father of Agamemnon and Menelaos. *97*

PLEURON An ancient city in Aitolia. *150*

PLINY (THE ELDER) Roman author of *Natural History* (23–79 CE).

PLUTARCH Famous Greek biographer and moral philosopher. *300, 301, 312, 316*

POLYDEUKES *See* Dioskouri.

POLYKRATES Tyrant of Samos in the second half of the sixth century BCE. He maintained a sumptuous court at Samos where Anakreon and Ibykos lived. *99, 107*

POLYPHEMOS A Cyclops and son of Poseidon. *186*

PORPHYRIO Neoplatonic philosopher (fl. 270 CE).

POSEIDON The brother of Zeus and the lord of the sea and of earthquakes and horses. *15, 150–52*

PRAXAGORAS Father of Theokritos.

PRAXINOA Friend of Sappho. Praxiteles—a famous Greek sculptor of the fourth century BCE.

PRIAM/PRIAMOS King of Troy at the time of the Trojan War and husband of Hekuba. The father of fifty sons and daughters, including Paris. *36, 53, 301*

PRIAPOS God of fertility and of the herds. Son of Afroditi and Dionysos, he is represented as a grotesque character with a phallic symbol. It was customary to inscribe short poems on his statues. *172, 174*

PRIENE A city of Ionia near Mount Mykale. *9, 172*

PROPERTIUS Roman poet of the first century BCE, rivaled only by Catullus as a love poet. *xx, 174*

PTOLEMY II King of Egypt in the second century BCE. Patron of literature and science. The Holy Scriptures were translated into Greek by his command. *171, 257*

PYGELIA A city in Ionia near Ephesos. *105*

PYRRHA A town of Lesbos. *33, 254, 287*

PYTHAGORAS Celebrated Greek philosopher and mathematician. *116, 159*

PYTHIA/PYTHIAN HEALER A surname for Apollo.

PYTHO Older name for Delphi, where the Pythian priestess gave her ambiguous answers and where Pythian games were held. The Apollo of Delphi was the Pythian Apollo. Pythokleides—a Pythagorian musician of the sixth century BCE. *143*

QUINTILIAN Roman rhetorician. His greatest achievement was a complete system of rhetoric. *270*

RHEGIUM A Greek town on the coast of Bruttium in the south of Italy. This was the crossover point for Sicily. *99, 100, 156*

RHEIA (RHEA) Greek earth goddess, daughter of Ge and Uranus, wife of Kronos and mother of Demeter, Hestia, Zeus, Hera, Hades, and Poseidon.

RHIPE A legendary mountain range in northern Greece. *29*

RHODES The most easterly of the islands of the Aigaian. *138, 234, 315*

ROME Capital of modern and ancient Italy. *xi, xxiv, 89, 205, 257, 270*

SALAMIS An island off the coast of Attica, where the Greeks defeated the Persian fleet of Xerxes in 480 BCE. *84, 85, 87, 272*

SALMYDESSOS A town in Thrace on the coast of Euxine. The name originally referred to the whole coast. *6*

SAMOS An Ionian island off the southwest coast of Asia Minor. Birthplace of Pythagoras. *20, 95, 99, 107, 156*

SAMOSATA Capital of the province of Commagene, north of Syria. Birthplace of Loukianos. *207*

SAPPHO/PSAPPHO Lyric poet of Eresos or Mytilene in Lesbos. In Ionian Greek she was Psapfo. *xi, xii, xv, xvii, xxii, xxv, xxvii, xxix, xxx, 23, 42–44, 83, 99, 107, 108, 147, 161, 171, 246, 247, 249–317*

SARDIS Ancient city of Asia Minor, capital of Lydia. *25, 29, 51, 65, 107, 232, 305*

SCHOLIAST Refers to an ancient commentator whose scholia, marginal commentaries of a Greek text, have been preserved.

SEMELE Mother of Dionysos.

SEMIRAMIS Assyrian queen known for her beauty, reputed founder of Babylon. *219*

SENECA (LUCIUS ANNAEUS) Roman philosopher and playwright born in the first century BCE. Convicted in a conspiracy to assassinate Nero, Seneca was ordered to commit suicide. *108, 275*

SEVEN AGAINST THEBES Polyneikes and six other warriors in a force against Eteokles in Thebes. *135*

SICILY A large island separated from Italy by the Straits of Messina. Birthplace of Stesichoros and Theokritos, it was one of the principal points of contact between Roman and Hellenistic cultures. *xxi, 6, 42, 96, 118, 127, 130, 140, 145, 147, 186, 254, 273*

SIGEION Promontory near Troy, commanding the mouth of the Hellespont. *33*

SIMONIDES Greek elegiac poet of the seventh century BCE. The uncle of Bakchylides, he is famous for his heroic epigrams. *xix, xxi, xxiii, xxiv, xxvii, 96, 118, 119, 121, 123, 125, 126, 133, 138, 140, 142, 147, 277*

SIRENS Fabulous creatures of the sea that drove men to destruction by their song. Often represented as birds with the heads and torsos of women. *28*

SIRIOS The Dog Star in the constellation of the Great Dog. *27*

SIRIS A river in southern Italy. *6*

SISYPHOS A mortal who persuaded Hades to release him from Hell for a time. When he failed to return, he was forcibly retrieved by Hermes. He was punished by being forced to roll a stone up a hill, only to find it ever rolling back again into the valley. *41*

SKAMANDRONYMOS Father of Sappho. *42, 253, 272–74*

SKAPTE HYLE A town of Thrace. *147*

SKOPELINOS Flute teacher of Pindar. *126*

SKYLLA A fearful monster with

twelve feet and six heads. Once the lover of Poseidon, Skylla was turned into a monster by her rival Amphitrite. *183*

SKYTHIA Region of southern Russia. *27, 121*

SMYRNA City on the Ionian coast. *17, 89, 92, 104*

SMYMEID A long poem on the history of Smyrna. *See* Smyrna.

SOKRATES The most famous of Greek philosophers. Left no writings and is chiefly known through the works of Plato and Xenophon. *96, 155, 157, 159–61*

SOLON Athenian poet and statesman (ca. 640–559 BCE). He was one of the "Seven Wise Men." *xix, xxiii, xxviii, 84, 85, 87, 93, 276*

SOPHOKLES Athenian tragic poet of the fifth century BCE. *140*

SPARTA The capital of Lakonia and the most important city of the Peloponnesos in historical times. *xix, xxi, 18, 23–25, 36, 96, 101, 120, 121, 130, 137, 149, 158*

SPERCHEIOS A river in the southern part of Thessaly, named after the river god Spercheios. *121*

SPORADES A group of scattered islands in the Aigaian Sea, off the island of Kriti and on the west coast of Asia Minor. *20*

STATHMI Town of Lakonia. *30*

STEPHANAS OF MELEAGROS The wreath or anthology of poems of Meleagros, forming part of the Palatine Anthology.

STESICHOROS His name means literally "setter or arranger of the chorus." Contemporary with Sappho, Stesichoros was one of the "nine great Greek lyric poets." *xxi, 96, 97, 147*

STOBAIOS Compiler of a small anthology or excerpts from Greek writers. His work preserved many valuable fragments. *301, 311*

STRABON Geographer of first century CE. *253*

SUDA LEXICON A Greek lexicon (ca. 970 CE) of unknown authorship, formerly attributed to Suidas. It is valuable for its quotations, explanations of words, and biographical information. *18, 20, 23, 99, 127, 135, 157, 272, 273*

SUSA The winter residence of the Persian kings, in the province of Susi and of the Persian Empire. *162*

SYRACUSE A city in Sicily. *102, 118, 140, 163, 171, 180, 254, 273, 277*

SYRIA A general name for the country north of Palestine. *vi, 157, 185, 207, 234, 249, 257, 278, 309*

TANAGRA A town in Boiotia famous for its statuettes. *135, 136, 253*

TANAIS The Don River. *121*

TANTALOS Father of Pelops and Niobe. For the sin of serving his son's flesh to the gods as a test, Tantalos was punished in Hades by being set thirsty in a pool of water that always receded when he tried to drink. *7, 31, 238, 281*

TARENTUM An important city and harbor on the southeast coast of Calabria. *112, 174, 175*

TARSOS The chief city of Cilicia. Birthplace of the apostle Paul. *242*

TARTAROS A place of torment in the underworld. *138*

TARTESSOS Ancient town in Spain settled by the Phoenicians; river near town. *97*

TATIAN Christian writer (fl. 160 CE). *154, 257*

TAYGETA A nymph sacred to Artemis. *146*

TEGEA An ancient city of Arkadia and capital of the district of Tegeatis. *119*

TELEPHOS Father of Philetas. *16*

TELESIKLES Father of Archilochos. *3*

TEOS An Ionian city on the coast of Asia Minor. The birthplace of Anakreon. *107, 231, 279, 281*

TEREUS The son of Ares and king of the Thracians. Husband of the sisters Prokne and Philomela. He deprived Philomela of her tongue. *233, 286*

THASOS A rocky island off the coast of Thrace. *3, 6*

THEBES (THIBAI) Principal city of Boiotia. Birthplace of Pindar and Korinna. *xxiii, 135, 142, 308*

THEMISTOKLES A celebrated Athenian statesman and archon in 493 BCE. Important for his role in the second Persian War. *118*

THEOGNIS Elegiac poet (fl. second half of sixth century BCE). He is the best preserved of the Greek elegists. *xix, xxiv, 33, 93, 127–28, 131*

THERMOPYLAI A narrow pass between the spurs of Mount Oita and the sea, the gate of eastern Greece, where the Spartans delayed the Persians in a famous battle in 486 BCE. *119*

THERON Tyrant of Akragas, victor in the Olympian Games. *See* dedication of Pindar's "Olympian Ode III." *140, 145, 146*

THESEUS Attic hero who went to Kriti to slay the Minotaur. In Bakchylides he is represented as a son of Poseidon. *150–53*

THESSALY The largest division of Greece. The mythological home of the Centaurs and also a country of magicians. *29, 107, 118, 253*

THETIS A Nereid, daughter of Nereus and Doris. The mother of Achilles. *36, 37*

THIBAI (THEBE) A city of Mysia, in the northwest of Asia Minor. *53*

THRACE The northern part of the Greek peninsula. *100, 147, 268*

THUCYDIDES Greek historian who started a history of the Peloponnesian War. *147*

THYONI Semele, mother of Dionysos, was raised to the sky, deified as a star, and known as Thyoni.

TIMAS One of Sappho's companions. *83, 306*

TIMOKRITOS Celebrated Greek lyric poet of Rhodes (fl. fifth century BCE). *112*

TITANS Monstrous children of the primeval couple of Uranus and Ge. *115*

TITHONOS Lover of Eos (Dawn), who left him each morning. Through the prayers of Eos he became immortal but he did not retain his youth and so became synonymous with decrepitude. *82, 192, 303*

TROIZEN District in the Peloponnesos; southeast of Argolis, where Theseus was born. *151*

TROJAN WAR A war between the Achaians and the people of Troy

in the first quarter of the twelfth century BCE; the subject of Homer's *Iliad. 20, 224*

TROY/TROJAN Ancient city near the Skamandros River on the Asian shore of the Hellespont. *33, 42, 46, 53, 59, 96, 97, 234*

TYNDAREOS King of Sparta, husband of Leda, father of Helen, Klytemnestra, and the Dioskouri (Kastor and Polydeukes). *98*

TYROS (TYRE) A famous city of the ancient world on the coast of Phoenicia. *182, 185*

TYRRHENIANS The Tyrrhenians (Etruscans) were defeated by Hiero in a great sea battle off Naples in 474 BCE. *121*

TYRTAIOS Athenian elegiac poet of the seventh century BCE. *xix, xxi, xxviii, 16, 18, 293*

VERGIL Roman poet of the first century BCE. Author of the Aeneid, the story of the founding of the Roman Empire. *171, 174, 191*

XANTHIPPE Wife of Sokrates and said to have been a shrew. *160, 314*

XANTHIPPOS Father of Perikles. *107*

XANTHOS A river of Troy. *28*

XENOPHON Historian, author of the Anabasis; lived in the fifth century BCE. *147*

ZENOBIOS Rhetorician of the second century CE. *317*

ZENONIS Proper name. *200*

ZENOPHILA Girlfriend of Meleagros. *18, 184*

ZEPHYR/ZEPHYROS The West Wind. *148*

ZEUS The ruler of the gods, wielder of the thunderbolt, and seducer of many goddesses and women. *3, 8, 14, 17, 21, 23, 32, 34, 35, 37, 39, 43, 46, 48, 53, 73, 91, 96, 108, 122, 123, 135, 142, 145, 146, 149–52, 161, 177, 197, 198, 202, 242, 270, 298, 301, 304, 311, 312*

Bibliography

TEXTS IN GREEK

Andrados, Francisco R. *Líricos griegos: elegiascos y yambógrafos arcaicos.* Madrid: Alma Mater, 1990.

Bowra, C. M. *Pindaricarmina.* Oxford: Oxford University Press, 1947.

Diehl, Ernst. *Anthologia Lyrica Graeca.* vol. 1. Leipzig: B.G. Teubner, 1949. 1949–84.

Dover, Kenneth James. *Greek Homosexuality.* Cambridge, Mass.: Harvard University Press, 1989.

———. *Sex and Difference in Ancient Greece and Rome,* ed. Mark Golden and Peter Toohey. Edinburgh: Edinburgh University Press, 2003.

DuBois, Page. *Sappho Is Burning.* Chicago: University of Chicago Press, 1995.

Garzya, A. *Alcamane, I Frammenti.* Naples: S. Viti, 1954.

Gentili, B. *Ancreon.* Rome: In Aedibus Athenaei, 1958.

Gow, A. S. f. *Bucolici Graeci.* Oxford: Oxford University Press, 1952.

Heitsch, Ernst. *Die grieschischen Dichterfragmente der Römischen Kaiserzeit.* Göttingen: Vandenhaek & Ruprent, 1961–64.

Lobel, Edgar, and Denys Page. *Poetarum Lesbiorum Fragmenta.* Oxford: Oxford University Press, 1955.

Masson, Olivier. *Les fragments du poète Hipponax.* Paris: C. Klincksieck, 1962.

Moore, J. A. *Selections from the Greek Elegiac, Iambic, and Lyric Poets.* Cambridge, Mass.: Harvard University Press, 1947.

Murray, Gilbert, et al. *The Oxford Book of Greek Verse.* Oxford: Oxford University Press, 1930.

Page, Denys. *Alcman: The Partheneion.* Oxford: Clarendon Press, 1951.

———. *Corinna.* London: Society for the Promotion of Hellenic Studies, 1953.

———. *Epigrammata Graeca.* Oxford: Oxford University Press, 1974.

———. *Poetaie Melici Graeci.* Oxford: Oxford University Press, 1962.

———. *Supplementum Lyricis Graecis.* Oxford: Oxford University Press, 1974.

Powell, John U. *Collectanea Alexandrina.* Oxford: Oxford University Press, 1925.

Prato, Carlo. *Tyrtaeus.* Rome: In Aedibu Athenaei, 1968.

Smyth, Herbert Weir. *Greek Melic Poets* (with commentary). London and New York: Biblo and Tannen; reprint 1963.

Snell, Bruno, and H. Maehler. *Bacchylidis carmina cum fragmentis.* Leipzig: B.G. Teubner, 1998.

———. *Pindari carmina cum fragmentis.* Leipzig: B.G. Teubner, 1980.

Tardidi, I. *Archilochus.* Rome: In Aedibus Athenaei, 1968.

Turyn, A. *Pindari carmina.* Oxford: Oxford University Press, 1947.

Voigt, Eva-Maria, ed. *Sappho et Alcaeus: Fragmenta.* Amsterdam: Athenaeum, 1971.

West, Martin L. *Iambi et Elegi Graeci.* 2 vols. Oxford: Oxford University Press, 1971–72.

Young, Douglas, and Ernst Diehl. *Theognis.* Leipzig: Teubner, 1971.

TEXTS IN GREEK WITH TRANSLATIONS

Barnstone, Willis. *Sappho: Lyrics in the Original Greek with Translations.* Foreword by Andrew R. Burn. New York: Doubleday Anchor, 1965.

Campbell, David A. *Greek Lyric.* 5 vols. Cambridge, Mass.: Harvard University Press; London: W. Heinemann, 1982.

Edmonds, J. M. *Elegy and Iambus: Anacreontea.* 2 vols. London:

W. Heinemann; New York: G. P. Putnam's Sons, 1931.

——. *The Greek Bucolic Poets.* Rev. ed. London: W. Heinemann; Cambridge, Mass.: Harvard University Press, 1928.

——, ed. and trans. *Lyra Graeca.* vol. 1, 2nd pr. London: William Heinemann, 1928; Cambridge, Mass.: Harvard University Press, 1940.

Farnell, L. R., trans. *The Works of Pindar.* 3 vols. London: Macmillan, 1930–32.

Gerber, Douglas. E. *Euterpe. An Anthology of Early Greek Lyric, Elegiac and Iambic Poetry.* Amsterdam: Hakkert, 1970.

Gow, A. S. F. *Theocritus.* 2 vols. Cambridge: Cambridge University Press, 1952.

Jebb, R. C. *Bacchylides: The Poems and Fragments* (with English commentary). Cambridge: Cambridge University Press, 1905.

Mackail, J. W. *Select Epigrams from the Greek Anthology.* 3rd ed. London: Longmans, Green, 1911.

Page, Denys. *Epigrammata Graeca.* Oxford: Oxford University Press, 1975.

——. *Poetae Melici Graeci.* Oxford: Oxford University Press, 1962.

——. *Sappho and Alcaeus.* Oxford: Oxford University Press, 1959.

——. *Sappho and Alcaeus: An Introduction to the Study of Ancient Lesbian Poetry.* Oxford: Clarendon Press, 1979.

Paton, W. R., ed. 5 *Greek Anthology.* 5 vols. Cambridge, Mass.: Harvard University Press, 1916–1918.

Wilamowitz-Moellendorff, Ulrich von. *Sappho und Simonides.* Berlin: Weidmann, 1913.

TRANSLATIONS WITHOUT GREEK TEXT

Barnard, Mary, trans. *Sappho.* Berkeley: University of California Press, 1958.

Barnstone, Aliki. *The Collected Poems of C. P. Cavafy.* New York: W.W. Norton, 2006.

Barnstone, Willis. *Sappho: Lyrics in the Original Greek with Translations.* Preface A. R. Burn.

New York: New York University Press, 1965; Doubleday Anchor Books, 1965.

——. *Sappho, Poems: A New Translation.* Los Angeles: Green Integer Press, 1999.

——. *Sappho and the Greek Lyric Poets.* trans. and annotated; introduction by William E. McCulloh. New York: Schocken Books, 1987.

Carson, Anne, trans. *If Not, Winter: Fragments of Sappho.* New York: Vintage Books, 2002.

Chandler, Robert, ed. and trans. *Sappho.* Introduction by Richard Jenkyns. London: J. M. Dent, 1998.

Davenport, Guy. *Carmina Archilochi.* Berkeley: University of California Press, 1964.

——. *Sappho: Poems and Fragments.* Ann Arbor: University of Michigan Press, 1965.

——. *7 Greeks.* Translations. New York: New Directions, 1995.

Fagles, Robert. *Bacchylides: Complete Poems.* Intro. and notes by A. M. Parry. New Haven, Conn.: Yale University Press, 1961.

Fitts, Dudley. *Poems from the Greek Anthology.* New York: New Directions, 1938.

Groden, S. Q. *The Poems of Sappho.* Indianapolis: Bobbs-Merrill, 1966.

Higham, T. F., and C. M. Bowra. *The Oxford Book of Greek Verse in Translation.* Oxford: Oxford University Press, 1938.

Jay, Peter, and Caroline Lewis, eds. *Sappho Through English Poetry.* London: Anvil Press Poetry, 1996.

Lombardo, Stanley. *Sappho: Poems and Fragments,* ed. Susan Warden; introduction by Pamela Gordon. Indianapolis: Hackett, 2002.

Longinus. *Longinus on Sublimity.* Trans. D. A. Russell. Oxford: Oxford University Press, 1966.

——. *On the Sublime.* Ed., intro., and notes D. A. Russell. Oxford: Oxford University Press, 1964.

Marx, Olga, and Ernst Morwitz, trans. *Poems of Alcman, Sappho, Ibycus.* New York: Alfred A. Knopf, 1945.

Mills, Bariss. *The Idylls of Theokritos.* West Lafayette, Ind.: Purdue University Press, 1963.

Nims, John Frederick. *Sappho to Valéry: Poems in Translation.* New

Brunswick, N.J.: Rutgers University Press, 1971.

Powell, Jim, trans. *Sappho, A Garland. The Poems and Fragments.* New York: Farrar, Straus, Giroux, 1993.

Quasimodo, Salvatore. *Lirici greci.* Tradotti, con un saggio di Luciano Anceschi. Milano: A. Mondadori, 1960

Rayor, Diane J., trans. *Sappho Poems.* With illustrations by Janet Steinmetz. Colorado Springs: Press at Colorado College, 1980.

Roche, Paul, trans. *The Love Songs of Sappho.* Introduction by Page Dubois. New York: Signet Classic, 1991.

Santos, Sherod. *Greek Lyric Poetry: A New Translation.* New York: W.W. Norton, 2006.

Wilhelm, James J. *Gay and Lesbian Poetry: An Anthology from Sappho to Michelangelo.* New York: Garland, 1995.

STUDIES IN ENGLISH

Abbott, Sidney, and Barbara Love. *Sappho Was a Right-On Woman: A Liberated View of Lesbianism.* New York: Stein and Day, 1972, 1986.

Barnstone, Willis. *The Poetics of Ecstasy: From Sappho to Borges.* New York: Holmes and Meier, 1983.

———. *The Poetics of Translation: History, Theory, Practice.* New Haven, Conn.: Yale University Press, 1993.

Bergk, T. *Poetae Lyrici Graeci.* 3 vols. Leipzig: Apud Reichenbachios, 1882.

Boardman, John, and E. La Rocca. *Eros in Greece.* London: Phaidon, 1978.

Bowie, A. M. *The Poetic Dialect of Sappho and Alcaeus.* New York: Arno Press, 1981.

Bowra, C. M. *Early Greek Elegists.* Cambridge, Mass.: Harvard University Press, 1938.

———. *Greek Lyric Poetry.* 2nd ed. Oxford: Oxford University Press, 1961.

———. *Pindar.* Oxford: Oxford University Press, 1964.

Bremmer, Jan, ed. *From Sappho to De Sade: Moments in the History of Sexuality.* London, New York: Routledge, 1989.

Burn, Andrew R. *The Lyric Age of*

Greece. London: Edward Arnold, 1978; New York: St. Martin's Press, 1960.

Burnett, Anne Pippin. *Three Archaic Poets: Archilochus, Alcaeus, Sappho.* London and Cambridge, Mass.: Harvard University Press, 1983.

Burton, R. W. B. *Pindar's Pythian Odes.* Oxford: Oxford University Press, 1962.

Bury, J. B. *The Isthmian Odes of Pindar.* London: Macmillan, 1892; rpt. 1965.

———. *The Nemean Odes of Pindar.* London: Macmillan, 1890; rpt. 1965.

Campbell, David A. *The Golden Lyre: The Themes of the Greek Lyric Poets.* London: Duckworth, 1983.

———, ed. and trans. *Greek Lyric.* vol. 1, *Sappho and Alcaeus.* Cambridge, Mass.: Harvard University Press (Loeb Library Series), 1988.

———, ed., intro., and notes. *Greek Lyric Poetry.* London: Macmillan, 1967; rpt. 1976.

Carson, Anne. *Eros the Bittersweet.* Princeton, N.J.: Princeton University Press, 1986.

Davison, J. A. *From Archilochus to Pindar.* London: Macmillan, 1968.

Farnell, L. R. *Critical Commentary to the Works of Pindar.* Amsterdam: A.M. Hakkert, 1932; rpt. 1961.

Frankel, H. *Early Greek Poetry and Philosophy,* trans. Moses Hadas and James Willis. Oxford: Oxford University Press, 1975.

Freedman, Nancy Mars. *Sappho: The Tenth Muse.* New York: St. Martin's, 1998.

Gentili, Bruno. *Poetry and Its Public in Ancient Greece.* Trans. A. Thomas Cole. Baltimore, Md.: Johns Hopkins University Press, 1988.

Gerber, Douglas. *A Companion to the Greek Lyric Poets.* Amsterdam: Brill, 1997.

Gildersleeve, Basil L. *Pindar: The Olympian and Pythian Odes.* New York: American Book Co., 1890; rpt. 1970.

Grahn, Judy. *The Highest Apple: Sappho and the Lesbian Poetic Tradition.* San Francisco: Spinsters Ink, 1985.

Green, Ellen, ed. *Reading Sappho: Reception and Transmission.*

Berkeley: University of California Press, 1996.

———, ed. *Re-Reading Sappho: Reception and Transmission.* Berkeley: University of California Press, 1996.

Green, Peter. *The Laughter of Aprhodite: A Novel about Sappho of Lesbos.* Berkeley: University of California Press, 1993.

H. D. (Hilda Doolittle). *Notes on Thought and Vision; and, The Wise Sappho.* London: Peter Owen, 1988.

———. *Trilogy.* Introduction and edited by Aliki Barnstone. New York: New Directions, 1998.

Hutchinson, G. O. *Greek Lyric Poetry: A Commentary on Selected Larger Pieces: Alcman, Stesichorus, Sappho, Alceaus, Ibycus, Anacreon, Simonides, Bacchylides, Pindar, Sophocles, Euripides.* Oxford, New York: Oxford University Press, 2001.

Jenkyns, R. *Three Classical Poets: Sappho, Catullus, Juvenal.* Cambridge, Mass., and London: Harvard University Press, 1982.

Kirkwood, Gordon M. *Early Greek Monody.* Cornell Studies in Classical Philology 37. Ithaca, N.Y.: Cornell University Press, 1974.

Körte, Alfred. *Hellenistic Poetry,* trans. Hammer and Hadas. New York: Columbia University Press, 1929.

Ledwidge, Bernard. *Sappho: La première voix d'une femme.* Paris: Mercure de France, 1987.

Lefkowitz, Mary R. *Heroines and Hysterics.* London: Duckworth, 1981.

———, trans. and ed. *The Victory Ode: An Introduction.* Park Ridge, N.J.: Noyes Press, 1976.

Lloyd-Jones, Hugh. *Females of the Species: Semonides on Women.* Park Ridge, N.J.: Noyes Press, 1975.

Mackail, J. W. *Lectures on Greek Poetry.* London and New York: Longmans, Green and Co., 1926.

Martin, Hubert. *Alcaeus.* New York: Twayne, 1972.

Norwood, Gilbert. *Pindar.* Berkeley: University of California Press, 1945.

Pomeroy, Sarah. *Goddesses, Whores, Wives and Slaves: Women in Classical Antiquity.* New York: Schocken Books, 1975.

Prins, Yopie. *Victorian Sappho.* Princeton, N.J.: Princeton University Press, 1999.

Rabinowitz, Nancy Sorkin. *Among Women: From the Homosocial to the Homoerotic in the Ancient World.* Austin: University of Texas Press, 2002.

Rankin, H. D. *Archilochus of Paros.* Park Ridge, N.J.: Noyes Press, 1977.

Reynolds, Margaret. *History of Sappho.* New York: Vintage Books, 1999.

———. *The Sappho History.* New York: Palgrave Macmillan, 2003.

Rissman, Leah. *Love as War: Homeric Allusion in the Poetry of Sappho.* Königstein/Ts.: Hain, 1983.

Robinson, David M.[David Moore]. *Sappho and Her Influence.* New York: Cooper Square Publishers, 1963.

Rosenmeyer, Thomas G., James W. Halporn, and Martin Ostwald. *The Meters of Greek and Latin Poetry.* New York: Bobbs-Merrill, 1963.

Segal, Charles. *Aglaia: The Poetry of Alcman, Sappho, Pindar, Bacchylides, and Corinna.* Lanham, Md.: Rowman & Littlefield, 1998.

Snyder, Jane McIntosh. *Lesbian Desire in the Lyrics of Sappho.* New York: Columbia University Press, 1997.

Snell, B. *The Discovery of the Mind,* trans. T. G. Rosenmeyer. Cambridge, Mass.: Harvard University Press, 1953.

Webster, T. B. L. *Greek Art and Literature, 700–400 B.C.* Oxford: Clarendon Press, 1939.

West, Martin L. *Greek Lyric Poetry.* Oxford: Clarendon Press, 1993.

———. *Greek Metre.* Oxford: Clarendon Press, 1982.

———. *Studies in Greek Elegy and Iambus.* Berlin; New York: de Gruyter, 1974.

Wilson, Lyn Hatherly. *Sappho's Sweetbitter Songs: Configurations of Female and Male in Ancient Greek Lyric.* New York: Routledge, 1996.

WILLIS BARNSTONE is Distinguished Professor Emeritus of Comparative Literature and Spanish and Portuguese at Indiana University. He has published more than sixty books of poetry, scholarship, translation, and memoir, including *Sweetbitter Love: Poems of Sappho; The Gnostic Bible* (with Marvin Meyer); *The Restored New Testament: A New Translation with Commentary, including the Gnostic Gospels of Thomas, Mary, and Judas; The Other Bible: Jewish Pseudepigrapha, Christian Apocrypha, Gnostic Scriptures, Kabbalah, Dead Sea Scrolls; Algebra of Night: New & Selected Poems, 1948–1998; The Secret Reader: 501 Sonnets; We Jews and Blacks: Memoir with Poems* (Indiana University Press, 2004); *With Borges on an Ordinary Evening in Buenos Aires: A Memoir;* and *The Poetics of Translation: History, Theory, Practice.*